Morality and medicine are deeply intertwined in rural Haiti, and both are shaped by the competition between different religious traditions: Catholicism, Vodoun, and fundamentalist Protestantism. When people fall ill, they seek treatment from not only Western biomedicine, but also herbalists, midwives, and religious healers. Moreover, sickness can raise troubling questions about a person's innocence or guilt. Caught in a web of accusation and moral danger, the sick struggle to portray themselves as upright ethical actors. Dr. Brodwin examines the local cultural logic that guides people as they negotiate between different healers and conflicting ethical systems. He shows how, in the crisis of illness, people rework religious identities and creatively address the fundamental contradictions of rural Haitian society.

Medicine and morality in Haiti

Cambridge Studies in Medical Anthropology 3

Editors
Ronald Frankenberg, *Medical Anthropology Programme, Brunel University*
Byron Good, *Department of Social Medicine, Harvard Medical School*
Alan Harwood, *Department of Anthropology, University of Massachusetts, Boston*
Gilbert Lewis, *Department of Social Anthropology, University of Cambridge*
Roland Littlewood, *Department of Anthropology, University College London*
Margaret Lock, *Department of Social Studies of Medicine, McGill University*
Nancy Scheper-Hughes, *Department of Anthropology, University of California, Berkeley*

Medical anthropology is the fastest growing specialist area within anthropology, both in North America and in Europe. Beginning as an applied field serving public health specialists, it now provides a significant forum for many of the most urgent debates in anthropology and the humanities. Medical anthropology includes the study of medical institutions and health care in a variety of rich and poor societies, the investigation of the cultural construction of illness, and the analysis of ideas about the body, birth, maturation, ageing, and death.

This series includes theoretically innovative monographs, state-of-the-art collections of essays on current issues, and short books introducing the main themes in the subdiscipline.

Other books in the series:
1 Lynn M. Morgan, *Community participation in health: the politics of primary care in Costa Rica*
2 Thomas J. Csordas, *Embodiment and experience: the existential ground of culture and self*

Medicine and morality in Haiti

The contest for healing power

Paul Brodwin

University of Wisconsin – Milwaukee

Published by the Press Syndicate of the University of Cambridge
The Pitt Building, Trumpington Street, Cambridge CB2 1RP
40 West 20th Street, New York, NY 10011-4211, USA
10 Stamford Road, Oakleigh, Melbourne 3166, Australia

First published 1996

Printed in Great Britain at the University Press, Cambridge

A catalogue record for this book is available from the British Library

Library of Congress cataloguing in publication data
Brodwin, Paul.
Medicine and morality in Haiti: the contest for healing power /
Paul Brodwin.
p.   cm. – (Cambridge studies in medical anthropology 3)
Includes bibliographical references.
ISBN 0 521 57029 8
1. Social medicine – Haiti. 2. Medicine – Haiti – Religious aspects.
3. Medicine – Haiti – Moral and ethical aspects. 4. Medical
anthropology – Haiti. I. Title. II. Series.
RA418.3.H35B76 1996
306.4'61'097924 – dc20   96–6843 CIP

ISBN 0 521 57029 8 (hardback)
ISBN 0 521 57543 5 (paperback)

WD

To my family,
for their gifts of curiosity
and critical intelligence

Contents

Illustrations

Tables

Acknowledgments

Professors Arthur Kleinman, Byron Good, and Robert Levine opened the doors for me to medical and psychological anthropology, and their high standards and scholarly encouragement have been invaluable in the writing of this book. Professors Sally Falk Moore, Stanley Tambiah, and Orlando Patterson also contributed to my intellectual growth, as have Terry O'Nell, Richard Grinker, Norbert Peabody, and Jay Levi. The influence on my work of Professors Steven Piker and Donald Swearer is indirect but profound.

I have benefited from the encouragement of my colleagues in the Department of Anthropology at University of Wisconsin–Milwaukee (UWM), in particular Lynne Goldstein, Sidney Greenfield, and Bill Washabaugh. Part of this book was written during a fellowship year (1992–93) at the UWM Center for Twentieth Century Studies, and I thank the Center's director, Professor Kathleen Woodward. I am also grateful to the UWM Center for Latin America and the Dean of the Faculty of Letters and Science for their on-going support, and to the staff of the American Geographic Society Collection and UWM Cartographic Services Laboratory (especially Dan Weber and Sona Andrews) for their research assistance.

Field research in Haiti was made possible by a fellowship from the Fulbright Foundation and a Doctoral Student Award from the Health Services Improvement Fund (HSIF) of New York City. I gratefully acknowledge their generous support. Shelagh O'Rourke provided not only invaluable material support but also her friendship and a rare wisdom about Haitian affairs. I also benefited from the advice of Professors Max Paul and Waltraud Grohs-Paul, then of the Bureau National d'Ethnologie in Port-au-Prince, Dr. Ira Lowenthal, Dr. Jacques Bartholi, Ms. Sherry Walters, and Mr. Peter Buys. The support of Monica Yriart, Pam Varley, and Leonard Glass was also crucial during the planning, research, and writing stages.

For my friends in the village of Jeanty, what counts is not these acknowledgments but my skills in conveying their stories to *moun lòt bò*, the capacious Creole category of "the people on the other side" who will read my academic work. If this book helps correct the ignorant misrepresentations of Haiti in the American popular and scholarly consciousness, it would help repay my debt to François Lormier, Père Joseph, Jerline Liron, Janine Dutoit, and innumerable others whose friendship sustained me and whose voices make up this work.

Note on transliteration

Haitian Creole is chiefly a spoken language, and until recently it did not have a standard orthography or rules for transliteration (see Dejean 1980; Hoffman 1990). From the several alternative systems now available for written Creole, the one chosen here conforms to the widely accepted guidelines of the Institut Pédagogique National in Port-au-Prince (see Institut Pédagogique National 1979). The spelling of common words follows the dictionary published by the Centre de la Linguistique Appliquée, Université d'Etat d'Haiti (Vernet and Freeman 1988).

In citing scholarly and historical documents, however, I preserve the spelling of Creole words as they originally appeared. Moreover, for ease of reading I slightly alter the plural and possessive forms. The plural in Haitian Creole is formed by adding the suffix "yo." I omit this suffix in most instances. However, I add an "s" and apostrophe to indicate the possessive noun. Thus "the *divinò* [plural] call up their titular spirits," but "the *divinò*'s [plural possessive] spirits are not familiar to all clients."

Consonants have roughly the same value as in English, with the following exceptions: "g" is always hard, "j" represents the soft [zh] sound as in the English "vision", and "ng" represents a nasalized, almost guttural [g]. There are four nasalized vowels. "An," "on," and "oun" have approximately the same value as in French, while "en" is pronounced as the French "in." For the other vowels, English speakers may use the following pronunciation guideline.

Creole	English Equivalent
a	[ä] as in father
e	[ā] as in ace
è	[e] as in bet
i	[ē] as in easy
o	[ō] as in go
ò	[ò] as in saw
ou	[ü] as in loot

Glossary

This glossary lists words and expressions in Haitian Creole which appear more than once in the text and are not translated each time. These definitions reflect the usage in Jeanty, which may differ from other parts of Haiti.

maladi manj gadyen	Guardian angel; a person's moral conscience, sometimes personified as a beneficent titular spirit.
anj kondiktè	Conducting angel; see *anj gadyen*.
blan	"White" or European-descended person; by extension, any non-Haitian foreigner.
bon nanm	The "good soul"; the principle of virtuous and effective action in the world.
divinò (male) *divinèz* (female)	Religious specialist in serving the spirits whose practice centers on divination, diagnosis, and healing.
dlo majik	"Magical waters": water- and oil-based remedies effective for cases of *maladi satan*.
doktè fèy	"Leaf doctor" or herbalist.
eklampsi	Eclampsia, a severe and sometimes fatal toxemia of pregnancy.
ekspedisyon	The sending of pathogenic spirits by an *houngan* on behalf of a client who wishes to cause the victim to sicken or die. Also, the resulting illness.
fèy	Herbal remedies.
foli	Madness, marked by florid, uncontrollable, and transgressive behavior.
gwo nanm (*move nanm*)	The "bad soul"; the principle of immoral and chaotic behavior.
houngan (male) *mambo* (female)	Religious specialist in serving the spirits whose practice includes healing, services for ancestors, and yearly ceremonies for the *lwa*.

indispose	Suffering from *indisposition* (see below).
indisposition	A disorder or condition marked by weakness, loss of consciousness, and mental confusion.
kiltivatè	Peasant or small land-holder.
kriz	Seizure or convulsive spasm.
kriz de ner (*maladi ner*)	A disorder marked by seizures, dissociation, or other alterations in consciousness.
lakou	Compound of houses belonging to members of the same bilateral kin group and their families.
lwa	Spirits in popular Haitian religion, often derived from West African prototypes and corresponding to Catholic saints.
maladi bondye	An "illness of god," due to natural causes.
maladi majik	A "magical illness"; see *maladi satan.*
maladi mò	An illness caused by the spirit of a dead person sent upon the victim.
maladi mò ti moun	An illness caused by the spirit of a dead child sent upon the victim.
maladi moun	A "humanly caused illness"; see *maladi satan.*
maladi satan	An "illness of satan," typically sent upon the victim by her/his human enemies out of jealousy or the desire for revenge.
malkadi	A seizure disorder with symptoms resembling epilepsy.
mò	The spirit of a dead person, used as the vehicle to send an illness upon someone.
poud majik	"Magical powders": dry powders, comprised of chemicals, ash, or other substances, effective for cases of *maladi satan.*
séwom	Any intravenous medication
sezisman	The combined psychological and physical reaction to shock, especially in the face of great personal loss.
ti bon anj	"Little good angel"; see *anj gadyen.*
tibèkiloz	Tuberculosis.

Introduction

This book explores the cultural conversation about illness, healing, and morality in the Haitian countryside. When people fall ill, their search for effective treatment opens up a realm of complicated moral concerns. Certain kinds of illness, and the decision to seek out certain kinds of therapy, can raise disturbing questions about personal innocence and guilt. People must then reassert their moral worth, and they do this in specifically religious terms. They ally themselves with a morally upright source of healing power – connected to one or another spiritual being – and ardently denounce the competing religious options. The contest for healing power thus takes place in the shifting and plural realm of Haitian religion. Conversely, people stake a claim to a particular religious identity largely through participating in a given set of healing rituals. Finally, these religious idioms of suffering and healing mediate between the local world of isolated rural communities and the national and global forces that are transforming Haitian society.

The two strands in this conversation – competing religious identities and the moral dimensions of sickness and healing – came together gradually in the course of my research in the rural community of Jeanty, near the southern port city of Les Cayes. I heard the first strand loud and clear on one of my first trips out to Jeanty. The second strand remained submerged much longer in the details of illness episodes and the practical talk about remedies.

Every day scores of public buses leave Port-au-Prince bound for the provincial towns of southern Haiti. Conversation is impossible for the first hour as the bus crawls through the impossibly congested neighborhood of Kafou, on the expanding western fringe of the city. Tin shacks, half-built cinderblock houses, and the unending crowds compete for space from the gouged hilltops right to the water's edge. The heat, the exhaust fumes, and the sudden swerves around potholes or squads of uniformed schoolchildren reduce most passengers to a mute stupor. Finally breaking free of the urban sprawl, the bus picks up speed in the verdant agricultural plain near Léogane, still planted in sugar after 300 years. The landscape changes yet again during the long climb up the mountainous spine of the southern peninsula, stretching away from the city into the Caribbean Sea. Cooled by the fresh mountain air, this is when people – total strangers when they boarded the bus – start to talk.

I have taken this ride often, and it is where I first learned about the passionate debates surrounding religious identity. The first exchange I remember went something like this. A woman sighs loudly and thanks Jesus, but someone else breaks in with a pointed joke, "It wasn't Jesus, it was our driver who saved us." "But we are all children of God," responds the woman amid scattered laughter. Then an aggressive voice pushes the debate further: "Are you a child of God? Then why do you say that we Catholics worship the devil?" A murmur – of approval? embarrassment? – stirs the passengers; that question was a little too direct. The first speaker protests, "No, it's not all Catholics. But there *are* those who deal with 'other things'" (*Se pa tout katolik, non? Men, gen moun ki konn sèvi ak lòt bagay*). The conversation then explodes into a free-for-all about the sincerity of converts to Protestantism (like the original speaker) and about Catholics who are morally upright as opposed to those who need "other things." Meanwhile we pass other buses heading back to Port-au-Prince, and I try to guess the religious affiliation of their owner from the colorful exterior paint job. Are the buses adorned with lines of scripture (Protestant), crucifixes (Catholic), or stylized images of snakes and water-sprites (devotees of the *lwa*, or African-derived spirits)?

It took much longer to connect the lively debate about religion to the realm of bodily suffering and healing. I entered this conversation slowly and at the most practical level when I actually began living in Jeanty. In ordinary discussions and formal interviews, I traced the steps people took when they fell ill: which healers they consulted, what treatments they accepted, and how they interpreted their suffering. I also sought out the healers themselves and asked how they learned their art and carried out specific treatments. I thus spent many months immersed in the practical details of illness episodes: how people noticed their symptoms, chose healers, and evaluated the treatments they received.

That was the easy part. Before long, I had collected long lists of herbal remedies and hours of taped conversations about how people reacted to crises such as an infant son's high fever or an aging mother's muscle pains and fatigue. Local midwives and herbalists allowed me to watch them prepare tea infusions and herbal compresses for my friends and neighbors. In rural Haiti, the practical knowledge of illness and healing is not a hidden cultural domain and it is not guarded by high-status professionals. To the contrary, even a child will easily list the medicinal uses of thirty or forty wild plants. People will recite to any interested listener all the expenses and troubles caused by their current sickness. Healers need little prompting to boast about their diagnostic skills or to explain why they offer more effective treatments than their competitor in the next village.

In the midst of these straightforward conversations, however, people occasionally dropped a comment or proverb which disrupted the aura of common sense. The conversation veered away from the practical questions at hand to linger for a moment in an entirely different realm. One evening, for example, I sat with a young mother as she patiently explained which local leaves and roots she used for a range of common childhood sicknesses. What would happen, I wondered out loud, if neither these domestic remedies nor the dispensary medicines improved the child's health? "That means it's another kind of sickness altogether," she said curtly and glanced away. With that comment she ended the discussion. During another conversation a few weeks later with her neighbor, the topic turned to illnesses that are sent upon you out of jealousy or spite by an enemy. I asked what treatment is possible, and received the cryptic response, "You know what they say about the saw." Much later I figured out the full reference. The Creole proverb states that the block of wood cannot cut the saw; only a saw can cut another saw. Only by resorting to pathogenic magic can you cure an illness caused in the same way.

Fieldwork setting and method

This cultural conversation about medicine and morality and the dense meanings of innocence and guilt, God and the spirits, furnished the conceptual framework for my research in Jeanty. (The names of the village and all of its residents are pseudonyms.) I lived there for a total of seventeen months: one year in 1987–88 and five months during 1990 and 1992. The village (and parish) of Jeanty is tucked into the foothills at the edge of the Cayes plain, one of the wealthiest sugar-growing areas in colonial St. Domingue. The Acul River, which forms one boundary of the parish, appears on a colonial map published in 1731 (Vilaire *et al.* 1981), and directly across the river, hidden in weeds, lie the ruins of French-built irrigation works and the skeleton of a plantation "great house." The land of Jeanty, however, is hilly and rocky, and was probably first populated by freed slaves escaping plantation labor in the first few years after Haitian independence (officially declared in 1804). For most of the nineteenth century, it remained a small hamlet under the administrative control of Port-Salut, a wealthier coastal town. However,

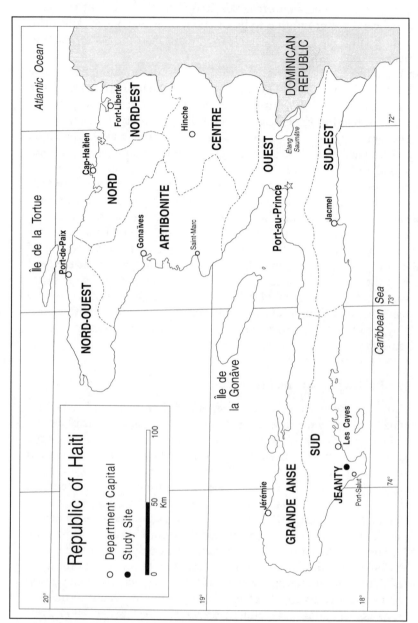

1 Map of Haiti

its autonomy increased as its population grew; it became a *quartier* of Port-Salut in 1934 and a commune in its own right in 1978. The official population of the commune was 11,820 in 1986, but only about 3000 people actually resided in the central "village" of Jeanty (Thomas 1988) (see map, Fig. 1).

The village itself is little more than a collection of small tin-roofed houses, clustered along a grid of unpaved streets which dwindle into footpaths as they climb the hills (see Figs. 2–4). Nonetheless, it is a magnet for people who live in scattered hamlets throughout the parish. They come to sell their produce at the twice weekly market, to have their babies immunized at the dispensary, to attend mass at the central Catholic church, or to get a few years of secondary education. The market, in turn, is one of three rural markets held in neighboring parishes on alternate days. The dispensary is the lowest rung in the national health services, and regularly refers patients to the public hospital in Les Cayes. Students wishing to finish high school must also move to Les Cayes. This regional system is itself dependent on, and penetrated by, centers of economic and administrative power in Port-au-Prince. Finally, in even the smallest hamlet far from the village center, most people know someone who lives *lòt bò* ("on the other side") in the United States, and who sends monthly cash remittances to offset the worsening poverty of rural life.

In the fall of 1987, I arrived in Jeanty through these same connections which link the village to regional, national, and international centers of power. I came with a letter of introduction from the CARE office in Les Cayes (CARE, a relief agency, had installed a potable water system in Jeanty with American funding). A week later I began living in the guest quarters of Père Joseph, the French Catholic priest who had been posted to Jeanty. My first friends were folks who had relatives in Boston, the city I had just left. However, the Catholic connection determined my public identity for most people, and it thereby fundamentally affected my research. Most people assumed I was Catholic (even more, that I was a relative of Père Joseph). So in our discussions about religious healing, they adopted the formal Catholic position and vehemently denounced the realm of the *lwa*. Jeanty residents have nothing to do with "those dirty things," I was told, and if I wanted to learn about them I should go to Port-au-Prince. Moreover, they made scathing indictments of Protestant converts as hypocrites who continued to worship the spirits in hiding and who just wanted to get a salaried job, and maybe a green card, from their North American missionary sponsors (see chapters 5 and 6).

I took their denunciations seriously, not as an accurate map of social and religious divisions, but as a legitimate strategy to consolidate their

2 Low hills surround Jeanty on three sides. The village center is barely
visible through the trees.

3 In small hamlets throughout the parish, people usually live in small wattle-and-daub houses with thatched roofs.

4 The village center is filled early in the morning with children walking to school and adults going to sell produce in the market or to work their land.

own identity. I thus began to explore the interstices between religious groups, not their stable centers. My goal was to examine how people construct the boundaries between distinct forms of religious affiliation and religious experience, as well as how they enforce (and breach) these boundaries. My methods were the standard ones for participant-observer ethnography: semi-structured interviews, attendance at religious and healing rituals, and collection of life histories and illness narratives. As an anthropologist/outsider, I do not take on the dubious project of representing anyone's authentic experience as a devotee of the *lwa*, the Trinity, or the Holy Spirit. On both epistemological and ethical grounds, such a project would quickly founder in its own contradictions. I remain much more interested in how people view each other's doctrinal and moral position, and how their rhetorical construction of religious difference animates the overall system of religious and medical pluralism.

Besides these theoretical concerns, the texture of daily life in Jeanty and the larger political convulsions affecting Haitian society also shaped my actual research activities. Because I was a novelty in the village, it was not hard to find people willing to talk to me. Only a handful of outsiders had ever lived there for more than a few weeks at a time, and these folks were either missionaries or development workers who had clearly defined tasks to accomplish. Moreover, it took me only a short time to become fairly proficient in Creole, since I had studied the language before leaving the USA and again at the Haitian-American Institute in Port-au-Prince. Finally, I was eager to speak at length with all parties in the religious debates which circulated through the village, which made me a willing audience for declarations of faith, conversion stories, and strident denunciations of opposing views.

For the first few months, I conducted every interview with the help of François Lormier, a young man who began as my paid research assistant and soon became my friend and confidant. François was part of an amorphous group of village men – aged from their late teens to mid-thirties – who are perpetually underemployed. Unwilling to follow their fathers' generation and become simple *kiltivatè* (peasants), these men would occasionally go to Port-au-Prince or Les Cayes to seek salaried jobs, and just as likely return empty-handed after a few months. For many of them, the ultimate goal was migration to the USA, and perhaps they befriended me because I was connected with their idealized picture of North American life.

François is a mono-lingual Creole speaker, but he provided help by rephrasing my questions in the correct idioms and repeating or clarifying people's answers. Our trips to interview far-flung healers often attracted other young men, who were probably bored with the slow pace of life in Jeanty and welcomed the diversion. Although they were all raised in the village, many of these men had spent a few years living in Port-au-Prince. Because of their skeptical and somewhat aloof attitude towards rural society, they made the perfect conversation partners as I was learning about local religious and medical systems. Like me, they straddled the perspectives of cultural insider and outsider, but they obviously had a vastly greater fund of personal experience and very different stakes in the religious debates animating Haitian society. Their imprint is felt throughout these pages.

This research was conducted during an especially violent period in Haiti's recent history. During my residence in Jeanty from September 1987 to September 1988, three distinct governments ruled the country, and one week after I left there was another *coup d'état*. The election-day massacre of November 29, 1987 dashed the hopes held by the progressive political sectors for a democratic regime. Leslie Manigat's ineffectual and unpopular rule lasted from the rigged election of January 17, 1988 until June 1988, when General Henri Namphy ejected Manigat and formally installed himself as President. Namphy himself was overthrown on September 17, one week after he sponsored a horrific attack on parishioners in the church of St. Jean-Bosco as Mass was being celebrated by Père Jean Bertrand Aristide (see Wilentz 1989).

Despite the brutal political violence played out on the national stage, rural communities like Jeanty remained mostly placid during this period. I witnessed little evidence of direct state repression and no overt violence. The reign of the *Volontiers de Sécurité National*, the network of informers who penetrated every rural community under the 29-year Duvalier regime, ended with Jean-Claude Duvalier's own departure in February 1986. The harsh repression inaugurated by General Raoul Cédras's overthrow of Aristide in September 1991 had not yet begun. Nonetheless, this political turbulence affected my research in more subtle ways. Many village families were sheltering relatives who had escaped the violence in Port-au-Prince, and these included many of the young men described above. Moreover, I never directly broached political topics with the people I did not already know very well. The contest for healing power is intimately tied to strategies of rule, the oppression and political constraints of rural life, and micropolitics of resistance. By necessity, I examined these issues in the broadest possible context, without overt reference to the ever-changing and highly sensitive political events of the time. (Because the situation remains volatile, I use pseudonyms for all village residents and do not identify the people in photographs.)

Goals and limitations

In exploring the network of religious and medical pluralism, this book diverges from the approach of several recent excellent studies of illness, healing and Haitian religion. Unlike Desmangles (1992), I do not provide an exhaustive theological account of any single Haitian religion. I develop a heteroglossic model of religious pluralism, not a stratigraphic model in which Catholicism is a superficial veil for more authentic neo-African doctrines and practices (1992:77). Unlike Brown (1991, 1989), I focus on the collective practices of religious affiliation, not the psychological or spiritual significance of devotion to the *lwa*. My rural ethnography does not, of course, address the innovations within Vodoun made by transnational Haitians (Brown 1991). Although I share her interest in the religious response to social fragmentation, I pursue it through the study of Protestant conversion and its harsh condemnation of Vodoun.

This book complements Farmer's writings on AIDS in Haiti (especially 1988, 1990, and 1992) in two respects. I explore the signs and practices available to frame all afflictions, not just the ways people marshall them in response to HIV disease. Secondly, I examine the implicit, not explicit, connections which people draw between disorder in the body/self and the body politic. Because AIDS appeared in the midst of radical political upheaval in Haiti, and so unjustly stigmatized Haitian people, the Haitian discourse on AIDS explicitly encompasses personal experience, local moral worlds, and Haiti's place in the West Atlantic system (see Farmer 1992:254ff). In Haiti (as elsewhere), AIDS has the ability to bring to the surface deep inequalities of race, class, nation, and gender. This awareness, however, is not unique to AIDS. It also emerges – albeit in more mediated, more embodied, and more "practical" forms – in the contests for healing power, religious affiliation, and moral authority, and these contests are the topic of my book.

However, no single study can encompass the enormous range of healers and medical practices in rural Haiti. For example, many people in Jeanty, especially older women, possess an incredibly detailed empirical knowledge of herbal remedies (see Weniger 1985; Weniger *et al.* 1986). This knowledge largely makes up the realm of domestic medicine (Hess 1983), and it cuts across individual religious affiliation. Moreover, the common explanation for many diseases and everyday aches and pains grows from another widely shared frame of reference: the humoral theory which connects symbolically hot and cold types of food and environmental exposure to subsequent illness (Wiese 1971, 1976; cf. Foster 1994). Precisely because these notions about the body, illness, and healing are so pervasive, they do not differentiate between the various positions people take in the debates about morality and religious identity, and therefore they do not receive center stage here.

Finally, my interest in the complicated search for healing power which takes place during long-term episodes of illness necessarily limited the number of cases I could document. The descriptions of routine inter-actions between herbalists and their clients are drawn from over fifty such consultations which I personally observed. Descriptions of the healing and divination practices of *houngan* (specialists in serving the spirit) or Protestant pastors come from a much smaller statistical universe (perhaps a total of twenty each).

1   The dialectics of healing power

Overview of book

People who fall ill must choose between multiple and competing systems of healing: this is true both in the small-scale communities where anthropologists usually work and in the urban centers of post-industrial society. There are very few settings which offer only one way to conceive of the body and its suffering, or where people have recourse to only one brand of treatment. In the pragmatic quest for therapy, people routinely combine elements from diverse or even contradictory medical traditions. Moreover, the practice of healers – both their actual therapies and their authoritative conceptions of health and disease – typically contains hybrid elements, borrowed from other traditions and grafted onto their own. This book examines these contests for healing power across the history of Haiti and in people's lives from a single rural community in the late 1980s.

The book explores the struggles for healing power in the context of religious and medical pluralism in Haiti. The seemingly stable array of religions and medical traditions in rural Haiti is deceptive. There is, in fact, a continual struggle over the effectiveness, political potential, and moral meanings of healing power. This struggle both reproduces and destabilizes the conventional categories of healing practices and religious identities. Part I traces the history and ethnography of metropolitan medicine (contemporary Euro-American biomedicine and its eighteenth- and nineteenth-century precursors). Control of Euro-American medicine has always articulated with strategies of political rule. Nonetheless, the relatively powerless have often appropriated the resources and prestige associated with official medical services as a form of oblique resistance. Metropolitan medicine therefore mediates some of the fundamental political and ideological conflicts in Haitian society, and along the way it has diffused throughout the plural medical system of rural Haiti. It has not, however, erased other non-biomedical therapies and alternate readings of the body and disease.

Part II examines the competing moral and religious discourses which people use to frame affliction and negotiate among various healers. Medical pluralism is embedded in Haitian religious pluralism, in particular the overlapping signs and practice of formal Catholicism, fundamentalist Protestantism, and the worship of African-derived spirits (Vodoun). By taking up a position within this plural religious system, healers authorize their own therapeutic knowledge and challenge the moral legitimacy of other options. Faced with the emergent crisis of sickness, people deploy different religious rhetorics to interpret affliction, and each one poses different threats to the personal virtue of the sufferer. In negotiating among multiple therapies, therefore, people seek both to cure the illness and to present themselves as upstanding ethical actors who have made the right choice among competing moral worlds. Finally, through these religious contests for healing power, people creatively respond to the ongoing fragmentation of rural Haitian society in supremely practical ways. They pitch their response not at the level of overt political debate, but rather the reformation of bodily practices and the elaboration of new rhetorics of identity.

Medical pluralism and anthropological theory

Medical pluralism refers first of all to the social organization of healing practitioners, who often occupy different religious, ideological, "ethnic," or class positions in their communities. It also refers to the cultural organization of their practice: the coexisting and competing discourses of affliction and healing with which they legitimate their therapeutic power. The study of medical pluralism further addresses how people choose between competing therapies. Anthropologists have classically portrayed these as "health-seeking behaviors" – defining a symptom, seeking out a healer, evaluating treatment – and explored the underlying logic which guides people's choice (see Chrisman 1977; Young 1981). Finally, in the widest context, medical pluralism alludes to the way that competing medical discourses mediate between bodily experience, the local moral order, and supra-local institutions and ideologies.

By the early 1980s, the analysis of plural healing systems had become a routine part of medical anthropology (see Leslie 1978, 1980 and Rubel 1979). Although most highly developed for Asian societies (owing to the several literate medical traditions of India and China), research from around the world explored the complex operation of plural healing systems, their internal variations, and their historical articulation with colonialism and capitalism.[1] The relation between biomedicine ("Western" or "scientific" medicine) and other therapeutic systems was the explicit theme for much of this literature. It analyzed the inter-penetration of biomedicine with other formal schools of medicine (e.g., homeopathy or Ayurveda), as well as non-literate, regionally bounded systems, such as herbalism or religious healing. This research analyzed the superimposed and contradictory elements within plural medical systems either to solve problems in applied health policy (Foster 1982) or to advance larger debates in social theory about language, subjectivity, and power (Good 1977; Lock 1987).

Before long, however, the study of medical pluralism had reached a theoretical impasse. There was never a single unified approach to the field: controversy raged on such fundamental issues as the definition of medical systems, their internal divisions, the boundary separating medical from other cultural activities, and the coherence of any single group of healers. Attempts to categorize plural medical systems often produced rigid functionalist typologies or broke down in a welter of non-comparable terms (Kunstadter 1978). Without a common vocabulary, the field could not produce a core set of questions for future work (see Dunn and Good 1978). Medical pluralism was thus eclipsed by newer theoretical concerns. Academic interest shifted to the body as a site of coercion and resistance, the political economy of health and health services, the hegemonic power of biomedicine, and the hermeneutic construction of clinical realities (see Johnson and Sargent 1990; Lindenbaum and Lock 1993). Medical pluralism dropped out as a central topic in its own right.

Research in medical pluralism during the 1970s and early 1980s became caught in the theoretical antinomies between symbolic vs. materialist studies and between structure vs. history which plagued anthropology as a whole (Ortner 1984). Ecological research into the adaptive value of plural medical systems largely omitted social relations and cultural meanings (Singer 1989). The subordination of indigenous healing by capitalist biomedicine was a core narrative in the political economy approach, but it minimized other forms of power, resistance, and defiance in plural societies (Csordas 1988; Morsy 1990). Symbolic and structuralist studies de-emphasized the clinical interactions between patients and healers as well as the dynamic, fragmentary nature of cultural meaning (Comaroff 1983).

A few voices in these debates called for a new approach to medical pluralism: an alternative to reifying medical systems in terms of their core symbols and institutional forms. Anthropologists should instead show how seemingly stable notions of illness and healing are instead embedded in the informal logic of everyday life, animated through specific healing activities, and articulated with overarching material and ideological forces (see Comaroff 1985). We should focus not on the continuity of medical traditions, but on their conceptual interruptions and breaks; not on consensus, but on contestation between different forms of medical knowledge (cf. Zimmerman 1978). This new approach would be at once more synthetic – connecting phenomenology, history, and praxis – and more closely calibrated to the dual construction of local worlds by both individual intentions and constraining structures and ideologies (see Giddens 1984; Bourdieu 1977 and 1990).

In the same vein, this book portrays medical pluralism in rural Haiti entirely as a social process and embodied practice. In this setting, the contest for healing power is both a product of past political struggles and a crucible for emerging forms of identity and collective action. People's short-term maneuvers in the face of illness thus reproduce and destabilize what appear as durable structures of healing power. From the actors' perspective – that is, from the standpoint of people seeking treatment or becoming a healer themselves – competing forms of healing propose genuinely different accounts of the body and of personal identity and morality. However, healing practices also mediate – in palpable and immediately persuasive ways – between disorders in the body/self and the body politic (from the family to the village, nation, and global system).

By negotiating among competing medical discourses and practices, people creatively respond to the immediate crisis of sickness, to specific contradictions in their family and community, and to the overall fragmentation of traditional rural society. Moreover, they couch their responses in an idiom that is at once moral, religious, and therapeutic. These are the dialectics of healing power in rural Haiti represented in the following chapters. The chapters therefore argue against a static view of health-seeking in rural Haiti and a determinist account of the history of Haitian medical systems. They do not provide formal models of treatment choice, based on a utilitarian or symbolic calculus.[2] Nor do they portray the erasure of local symbolic worlds by an encroaching biomedical hegemony.

The book instead describes how the multiple healing practices in rural Haiti are interwoven with other domains of social life, in particular, the local forms of religious worship and affiliation. The plural medical system is not a fixed background against which people act in pursuit of various ends (physical health, social mobility, or an existential response to suffering). It is rather a "continuously negotiated compromise structure" (Leslie 1980), built up by individual acts of consultation and containing several principles whose very legitimacy is affirmed or challenged through each healing encounter. People do pursue these ends, but in a constantly shifting and contradictory cultural landscape.

Medical and religious pluralism in Haiti

The discourse and practice of healing is a perennial theme for students of Afro-Haitian religion. A staple feature of ethnographies from the 1940s to the 1990s (see Métraux 1972; Brown 1991), it underlies the entire spectrum of competing and overlapping religions which coexist in rural Haiti. These three religions include the official state-sponsored Catholic church, numerous Protestant denominations (usually founded by North American missionaries), and that syncretic amalgam of West African religions and French Catholicism which non-Haitians know as Vodoun. Of course, this third religious complex (known in the village of Jeanty by such expressions as "to serve the spirits" or "to serve the mysteries") attracts the greatest interest, too often lurid, romanticist, or racist.[3] However, both classic ethnographies as well as more recent studies by theologians and historians of religion have thoroughly explored the history of Vodoun, its syncretic cosmology, and the actual ways individuals serve the spirits: building domestic shrines, attending quasi-public ceremonies, and invoking the spirits to possess their devotees, or, in Creole, "to mount their horse."[4]

It is difficult even to fix the boundaries between these three syncretic religious groups. Taken together, they do not constitute a rigid, unchanging structure of beliefs and practices, since different religions cross-reference each other and even share key symbols and forms of worship. In the village of Jeanty, people repeatedly choose which rituals to attend, which saints and/or spirits to venerate, and which claims to power and moral authority they will accept. They make these choices, however, not through careful deliberation, but rather from the immediate need to shore up their moral worth and to defend themselves from the jealousy or moral condemnation of others.

The conflicts which animate this religious system are most dramatically visible in the ways people interpret and heal sickness (Clerismé 1979; Coreil 1979; Conway 1978). People have recourse to a number of conventional readings of sickness even within the same nominal faith. For example, consultations for healing with an *houngan* (a specialist in serving the spirits, or *lwa*) abound with explicit references to Catholic saints and the use of prayer books from French mission societies, despite the formal Catholic opposition to such traffic with African-derived spirits. Healing during a Pentecostalist service simultaneously rejects and affirms aspects of the Vodoun complex: in particular, its construction of the danger implicit in social relations, of the individual's body, and the body's vulnerability to other invisible entities (Conway 1978).

This book thus embeds the competing notions of affliction and healing power in Haiti within the shifting structure of religious pluralism. The contests between different religious codes endanger people's moral status, and these moral risks motivate the way they negotiate between competing forms of healing. The book emphasizes the rhetorics of accusation and self-defense which circulate throughout the religious system of Jeanty. Devotees of each religion advance a moral commentary upon the other options, which they usually cast in terms of the innocence or guilt of the sufferer or the healing specialist. Through their responses to illness, people simultaneously proclaim their moral worth and defend themselves against other people's moral condemnations.

The approach to Haitian religions taken here is explicitly processual, rather than categorical. The goal is to examine first and foremost how people take up a position among these competing religions, not the structure of religious pluralism *per se*. Religious pluralism in Jeanty arises from people's moves towards and away from certain kinds of healing power. Religious affiliation, therefore, is neither given at birth nor established through cognitive acceptance of a singular world-view. It is worked and reworked over the life course, and the crisis points are illness episodes and the ensuing struggles for physical health and moral worth. Religious affiliation emerges from people's response to bodily and social affliction, not their cognitive acceptance of a set of cosmic principles or abstract propositions about good and evil.

People's religious identity is thus the outcome of practical negotiations rather than solely theological reflection. This book therefore does not try to capture the theological or experiential essence of any single religion (Vodoun, Catholicism, or fundamentalism). It instead illuminates the spaces between religions – the multiple meanings of icons or practices which cut across religious boundaries, and the ambivalent experience of people as they move from one professed faith to another. Most students of Haitian religions, especially Vodoun, regard them as syncretic: the reconciliation or coalescence of historically separate traditions. But they are also heteroglossic: orders of signs and practices which intersect each other in many different ways, but which cannot all be juxtaposed on a single plane (Bakhtin 1981:291; Bastide 1978). Moreover, this structure of religious pluralism, like medical pluralism, is not a stable and unchanging background. It shifts – usually subtly, sometimes dramatically – in accordance with people's practical moves within it.

Outline of chapters

Medical pluralism in the village of Jeanty provides a set of discourses and practices through which people negotiate their identity, religious status, and possible futures (this also holds true for rural Haiti in general and much of post-colonial Latin America; see Crandon-Malamud 1991). These themes are examined here first through the history and ethnography of Euro-American medicine, and secondly through the shifting structure of religious healing, as illustrated by illness narratives and the practice of particular healers.

Chapter 2 examines who brought metropolitan (French and American) medicine to Haiti, how it articulated with other strategies of political rule, and how it was controlled and transformed once it arrived.

Chapter 3 examines how biomedicine in Jeanty was shaped by the gradual insertion of this peripheral area into regional, national, and international systems of power. It documents the local fate of a major internationally funded program of rural primary care.

Chapter 4 presents extended case-studies of illness and the quest for therapy. These cases introduce the range of non-biomedical healers and discourses on affliction, especially the crucial etiologic and moral distinction between an "illness of God" and an "illness of Satan," which indexes the pathogenic danger of social relations.

Chapters 5 and 6 embed the contest for healing power within the fundamental moral oppositions which animate Haitian religion. Profiles of herbalists, midwives, and specialists in serving the spirits illustrate the various positions which villagers take towards the *lwa* and those who serve them, from outright moral condemnation to actual invitations to the *lwa* to enter one's body.

Chapter 7 documents the "Satanic illness" of Jerline Liron, a young woman from Jeanty. This case sets into motion the models of therapeutic and religious pluralism introduced so far. It illustrates the three mutually dependent religious codes of rural Haiti as well as the strategies people deploy to portray themselves as upright ethical human beings who have made the right choice among competing moral worlds.

Chapter 8 theorizes "healing power" as a central issue for medical anthropology. The search for religious healing turns on a form of embodied knowledge which people deploy in order to link personal suffering to wide-scale social change and dislocation. This perspective addresses recurring anthropological debates about the local and global contexts of research as well as phenomenology and symbolic analysis.

Part I

History and ethnography of biomedicine

2 Metropolitan medicine and strategies of rule

Roots of present-day medical pluralism

Biomedicine is diffused throughout the plural health care system of Jeanty. Outside the dispensary walls and away from the control of its professional nursing staff, elements of Euro-American biomedicine have entered virtually the entire range of local therapies: from everyday domestic practices to the specialized treatments offered by herbalists, midwives, Protestant pastors, and servitors of the *lwa*. It is impossible to locate biomedicine in a single physical, social, or ideological space.

Biomedicine thus exerts a broad effect on people's response to illness, and it enters the practice of other healers in complicated, unpredictable ways. For example, the village's sole official site of biomedical treatments is the state-run dispensary – a squat, five-room cinderblock building in the center of town. However, the influence of biomedicine extends into the most isolated hamlets through weekly visits by health care workers. Moving in the opposite direction, local midwives travel to the dispensary for monthly meetings where they receive medical supplies. Among the most faithful attendees are several women who routinely become possessed by their *lwa* during difficult deliveries (see chapter 3).

The flow of biomedical pharmaceuticals also illustrates the inter-penetration of biomedicine, other local institutions, and categorically distinct healing systems. People purchase pharmaceuticals not only at the dispensary, but also at the twice-weekly village market, from the store-room of the French Catholic priest, and out of the bulging valises of itinerant vendors. They usually consume these medicines not under the watchful eye of medical professionals, but at home and in private, or even during healing rituals of the *houngan*, the specialist in serving the spirits (see chapters 4 and 6).

Finally, biomedicine is deeply embedded in local notions of morality. A biomedical cure for an illness usually means that it was caused by unremarkable natural processes (an "illness of God," in Creole). But when biomedicine fails, people classify the illness as "Satanic," that is, caused by other humans. This diagnosis endangers the moral status of the ill individual and inaugurates the search for healing from Catholic, Protestant, and Vodoun practitioners (see chapters 5, 6, and 7).

These vignettes immediately complicate any conventional analysis of medical pluralism in Jeanty. Biomedicine is not a stable and bounded "sector" of a more elaborate health care system, internally differentiated into discrete, if overlapping, zones: folk, popular, and professional (Kleinman 1980) or local, regional, and cosmopolitan (Dunn 1976). This book, therefore, cannot analyze biomedicine without remainder in a single chapter, and it cannot represent villagers' action in the face of illness as the movement through parallel but essentially separate health care sectors (biomedical, herbal, religious, etc.).

Fragments of biomedical ideology and techniques appear in settings far removed from the superficially Europeanized or Americanized spaces of rural Haitian society, and in signs and practices usually associated with "non-biomedical" healing forms. The entire range of healing specialists employs biomedical substances in their treatments, and they freely appropriate certain biomedical representations of affliction and the body. Moreover, the failure of biomedical treatment sets into motion profound transformations in one's religious affiliation and personal identity. Although biomedicine has not subverted other healing forms, it does set the terms for public debates about their efficacy and morality. Mapping the diffusion of biomedicine throughout the plural healing arrangements of Jeanty is the first task for this book. This will illuminate how "medicalization" occurs in Jeanty: the ways that biomedicine transforms bodily practices and discourses on affliction, and the local response to biomedicine's symbolic and institutional power.

We must begin this task by placing everyday medical activities in historical perspective. At whatever level villagers engage biomedicine, their actions are already structured, in part, by the histories of particular institutions. Think of a routine activity such as buying a capsule of tetracycline in the marketplace from an itinerant drug vendor, or the more difficult decision to spend a year's income for in-patient surgery at a Baptist mission hospital. In each case, the social field where villagers seek out biomedical services is historically produced; the marketplace and hospital have emerged over many years in response to shifting local, national, and international forces. The histories of these settings influence how people make medical decisions, whatever other short-term calculus guides their action. In other words, utilitarian motives, such as the pill vendor's search for profit or the patient's calculation of the cost and benefit of various treatments, do not alone explain how people use biomedicine. People's therapeutic strategies – especially the ways they resist and appropriate biomedical categories and treatments – have grown out of specific historical conditions: imperialism, dependency, and the competition between multiple ideologies which cannot easily be labelled indigenous or foreign.

Biomedicine has diffused throughout Jeanty as part of almost two centuries of exchanges between this rural area and the world outside. Biomedicine, in this sense, is metropolitan medicine: it originates in societies with greater global reach (and vastly greater resources) than the one occupied by local practitioners and their clientele. (For most of Haiti's colonial and post-colonial history, the metropolitan power was France. The United States has largely played this role since the first American occupation from 1915 to 1934). To call the forms of bio-medicine in Jeanty "metropolitan" emphasizes the flow of persons, technologies, institutions, and ideologies from the world outside to this particular village, from the capitalist center to the dependent periphery, and from former colonial metropolis to present-day neo-colony.[1] The anthropological analysis of metropolitan medicine in present-day Jeanty thus demands a historical account of who brought it to Haiti, and how it was received, controlled, and transformed once it arrived.

This chapter examines the articulation of metropolitan medicine with the strategies of European and American rule in Haiti as they have unfolded over time. The account follows the standard periodization of Haitian social history, from French colonization and imperial control (1697–1804), to the emergence of competing national elites (1804–20), the consolidation of the peasantry and urban bourgeoisie as two distinct groups (1820–1915), the American Marine occupation (1915–34), and the current politics of dependency between Haitian institutions and international aid agencies. In each period, the dominant class deter-mined what forms of metropolitan medicine would be introduced (with varying degrees of resistance from below), who would have access to medical services, and how competing healing specialists would be treated.

Illness, healing, and colonial power

The social history of metropolitan medicine in rural Haiti begins in the late seventeenth century, as imperial France strengthened its *de facto* control over the western one-third of the island of Hispaniola, then legally claimed by Spain. For 200 years after the arrival of Columbus, the sheer difficulty of maintaining an adequate population – for both productive labor and defense against rival European states – was the overriding problem faced by Spanish and French agents of colonization on the island. European medicine was introduced to colonial St. Domingue as part of France's efforts to solidify its control over the territory wrested from Spain and repopulate it with French settlers. Spain retained its legal claim to Hispaniola throughout the sixteenth and seventeenth centuries. However, the first wave of Spanish settlers deserted the island in the 1520s and 1530s for more lucrative opportunities in the gold and silver fields of New Spain (present-day Mexico) and Peru. Western Hispaniola soon became a likely target for French imperialism. French colonists first arrived on the nearby northern island of La Tortue in 1629, and by mid-century the entire northwest coast of Hispaniola became a staging ground for French *flibustiers* (pirates) as they harassed Spanish fleets (Cauna 1987:11ff).

Spain evacuated the entire west and north coasts of Hispaniola in 1603, and the architects of the fledgling French Antillean empire quickly capitalized on this opportunity. The early colonial society of French St. Domingue arose from deliberate imperial strategies to consolidate a scattered and even stateless population on territory which Spain had abandoned, and to repopulate it with new arrivals from France. By 1697, when France formally took control of the area by the Treaty of Ryswick, the heterogeneous population comprised military personnel, colonial administrators, export/import merchants, petty bourgeois, artisans, peasants, *engagé* laborers, and African slaves, free blacks and mulattoes (see James 1963; Hall 1972; Bellegarde 1953).

The first European medical institutions were established in this fragmented and rapidly changing society. They bore the marks of their dual origin in both the sharp social divisions of St. Domingue and the structure of medical care in pre-Revolutionary France. The King's Ordinances of 1670–71 accorded part of the wealth produced by the Indies to the construction of hospitals, and as early as 1694 the Sisters of Charity received royal funds to operate hospitals in the two largest colonial towns: Léogane and the capital of Cap François. Housed provisionally in the Magasin du Roy – the governor's official residence – the hospital at Cap François received the poorest French residents, new arrivals from France, and soldiers and sailors from the royal militia (Moreau de St.-Méry 1958:550ff).

The history of the Cap François hospital exemplifies how the medical system of the *ancien régime* was reconfigured in colonial St. Domingue. In seventeenth- and eighteenth-century France, the word *hôpital* referred to several types of institutions. The *hôpital* established by a church for parish residents would take in not only the sick, but also abandoned children, invalids, and the elderly, and it also distributed food and clothing to the poor. The *hôtel Dieu*, the type of *hôpital* staffed by surgeons, provided strictly medical care, and generally served several parishes.[2] Finally, the *hôpital général*, founded originally in Paris to house beggars, gradually broadened into a place of confinement for the insane, the homeless, and other marginalized groups perceived as a threat by the rising urban bourgeoisie (Joerger 1980; see also Ramsey 1988 and Foucault 1973).

The *hôpital* founded in Cap François combined elements from each of these institutions. It originally served both the indigent and the sick, and both civilian and military colonists, from the entire northern plain. The Sisters of Charity provided most medical care, but they also supervised surgeons and African slaves who worked as aides, and the Sisters were in turn supervised by the king's physician and surgeon who resided in the capital (Moreau de St.-Méry 1958). Whereas most parish-based *hôpitaux* in France derived their income from church revenue, landed endowments, taxes, and other sources (Vess 1975), the Cap François *hôpital* depended entirely on yearly support from the king. From its founding, therefore, this colonial *hôpital* diverged from the structure of medical institutions in the metropolis, but these differences were at first no more than improvised reactions to local circumstances: e.g., the shortage of medical personnel, the meager resources of a newly established parish, and the importance of royal subventions for any public services in the colony.

Over the course of the eighteenth century, the changing political economy and strategies of rule in St. Domingue transformed the French medical system in more fundamental ways. When it was founded, the Cap François *hôpital* (along with the only other urban *hôpital* in Léogane) treated both civilians and soldiers who were transported from garrisons throughout the colony. In 1732, the Intendant – the highest-ranking civilian administrator – ordered the construction of military medical hospitals in several other coastal towns, and in 1763, a royal ordinance directed the *hôpital* at Cap François to accept only officers and other members of the French militia (Moreau de St.-Méry 1958:553–54). Founded at the beginning of French rule as an *hôpital général* for the marginal ranks of white colonial society, in sixty years this institution had come under the exclusive control of the military. The crown did not establish any other institution to take its place. Indeed, the Hôpital La Providence, founded in Cap François in 1741 for poor children, the elderly, the infirm, and beggars, also became a strictly medical *hôpital militaire* forty years later (Bordes 1979:7). In general, the network of military hospitals in St. Domingue expanded throughout the eighteenth century, while the earlier institutions modelled after the *hôpitaux généraux* of the *ancien régime* virtually disappeared. By the 1780s, the military had constructed or appropriated for its own uses five medical institutions (in the towns of Cap, Port-au-Prince, Léogane, Port-à-Piment, and Les Cayes). The hospital at Cap was the largest (825 patients), followed by the one in Port-au-Prince (150 patients) (Bordes 1979).

The emergence in St. Domingue of several competing groups with conflicting interests, different sources of power, and vastly different stakes in the legitimate social order explains the transformation of the French hospital system. One conflict, pitting local landowners against metropolitan administrators and militiamen, led to the decline of the *hôpital général*. The other conflict, between white planters and African slaves, underlies the next stage in the history of metropolitan medicine in Haiti: the creation of the plantation infirmary as an entirely novel medical institution, the production of a complicated discourse on slaves' illness, and the suppression of African healing practices.

Army officials, along with state bureaucrats and merchants, knew their stay in St. Domingue was temporary and that their own economic fortunes lay with France (Curtin 1990:161). The landowners and locally born colonists, in turn, hated the imperial bureaucracy, which they criticized as bloated and inefficient. They particularly resented the mercantilist policies of the French crown, which systematically favored metropolitan over colonial interests through tariffs and trade restrictions (James 1963:34–35). Their resentment occasionally erupted into violent revolt against the Crown's representatives: in 1722, for example, colonists arrested and imprisoned the Governor in protest against the monopolistic Company of the Indies (Girod 1972:27). The military thus supported the merchant elite and colonial administrators against the active opposition of local planters. Indeed, this was arguably the primary purpose of the French military in St. Domingue in years before the massive slave uprising of 1791.[3] Maintaining military regiments – which required extensive medical facilities in this unfamiliar tropical climate – became an important ingredient of French imperial rule and the pursuit of profit in a global mercantilist system. The fault line which divided white residents of St. Domingue into two groups (the locally born Creoles vs. the military and state functionaries) largely explains why military hospitals dominated metropolitan medicine in the early colony.

However, the non-military *hôpital général* declined not simply by default, but rather because of the rise of sugar plantations during the eighteenth century, and the accompanying demographic and social upheavals. The combination of large-scale sugar production and African slave labor – the so-called "plantation complex" – was introduced from Brazil to Martinique and Barbados in the 1640s, and from there to

French and British possessions in the Greater Antilles a few decades later (Curtin 1990). In the following eighty years, the plantation complex completely transformed the political economy and types of social control in St. Domingue.[4]

The creole society that rapidly emerged during these years had no need for medical institutions derived from the contemporary French *hôpital général*. Under the *ancien régime*, urbanization, rising unemployment, and changing moral views on labor and idleness led to the interment of marginal groups in urban welfare institutions such as the *Hôpital Général* of Paris (Foucault 1973). The *hôpitaux* of eighteenth-century France were therefore concentrated in cities, not the countryside. After all, the move to confine the poor and disinherited came from the urban elite, who regarded them as carriers of epidemics and sources of political and moral disorder (Joerger 1980:111). Poor white residents of the small, makeshift cities of St. Domingue – the shopkeepers, artisans, or clerks who constituted the class of *petits blancs* – were a small and politically marginal minority in colonial society. They never posed a real or perceived threat to the local urban elite, and there was consequently no move to intern them in urban *hôpitaux*.[5] The major threat to the colonial social order came rather from the overwhelming majority of agricultural slaves, and rural plantations thus became the site of new medicalized forms of coercion and social control.

The large-scale Caribbean sugar plantation of the seventeenth and eighteenth centuries was a historically novel form of agroindustrial organization, and it dehumanized slaves in an especially brutal fashion (Mintz 1974:72). The tasks of sugar manufacture (planting, harvesting, grinding, boiling, etc.) demanded speed and coordination among a large and tightly controlled labor force. Although colonists first imported indentured Europeans, the African slave trade was a cheaper and more abundant source of labor (Williams 1984:102; Mintz 1985). Planters controlled slaves through extreme bodily sanctions (whipping, confinement, and other corporal punishments), juridical enforcement of the slaves' status, and a complex ideology of racial, religious, and moral inferiority (see Tomich 1990:128; Patterson 1967). Metropolitan medicine was a pragmatic and ideological support for this exploitative labor system. Planters gradually created a distinctive form of colonial medicine out of the economic, legal, and customary structures of slavery, the image of the slave as recorded in colonial correspondence, and the social conditions of daily life on large-scale sugar plantations. In this process, they selectively preserved and transformed the medical institutions and ideas about illness from contemporary France.

Owners attempted to transform slaves into socially dead persons by refusing to recognize the social relations of slaves and by alienating them from their labor and even their own bodies (Patterson 1982). Nonetheless, slaves remained valuable because the profitability of the entire system depended on their labor, and because they represented a substantial economic investment for the planter. Attending to their health protected this investment, and the master's sheer economic interest underlies many of the contacts slaves had with European medicine.

The first encounter of African slaves with European medicine could well occur long before they were sold to a particular plantation. In the latter half of the eighteenth century, some slaves received a crude vaccination against smallpox while they were held in the *barracons* on the Guinea coast or on the very ships which transported them to the New World (Girod 1972:149; Klein 1986:142). The inhuman conditions of the Middle Passage killed off many of the captives and left the survivors ill, weak, and malnourished. Because traders tried to hide these effects (e.g., by providing extra food during the last few days of the voyage or rubbing slaves' bodies with oil before the sale), wealthy planters of St. Domingue planning to buy new arrivals would first pay a local surgeon to assess their health (Wimpffen 1797:225ff; see also Cauna 1988:214). Three coastal cities (Cap François, Petite Anse, and St. Marc) had small private infirmaries which took in ill slaves directly from the ships (Bordes 1979:7–8), and certain plantations had small hospices where the few survivors from smallpox-infected ships were kept in quarantine for weeks or months (Debien 1941:95).

Large plantations on St. Domingue typically had an *hôpital* for slaves, and virtually all of their contacts with European medicine took place within its walls. The size and layout of these institutions varied on different plantations, although they could generally house between ten and thirty slaves at a time. On the Boucassin estate near l'Arcahaye, the *hôpital* was made of brick with a tile roof and had three separate rooms for men, women, and slaves disabled by yaws. Slaves interned there had wooden beds with mattresses and sheets, which one historian claims were better accommodations than in their own huts (Debien 1945:26).[6] The smaller and cruder *hôpital* on the Thomas plantation near Fort Dauphin was constructed of wattle and daub under a thatch roof and had five small rooms. The Sauvage plantation featured a larger *hôpital* with five rooms, some of which had been subdivided to create thirteen cubicles for individual slaves (Girod 1972:148–49). The manager for Fleuriau's plantation at Bellevue on the Cul-de-Sac plain constructed separate buildings for slaves with smallpox and for pregnant women (Cauna 1988:219).

A female slave generally served as *hospitalière* in these institutions, with day-to-day responsibility for dressing slaves' wounds, administering medications, and following the course of their illnesses and fevers. In some cases, the *hospitalière* was joined by younger female aides (also slaves) and a midwife (either slave or free) (Bordes 1979). In addition, the plantation owner or manager often retained a local white surgeon on a yearly contract to oversee the *hôpital*, prescribe treatments, and compile annual accounts of the number of slaves interned and their ages and illnesses. At Boucassin, the surgeon received a base salary plus additional payments for medications, especially long treatments, and delicate operations (Debien 1945:27). Bordes (1979), citing a contemporary account, describes one surgeon who visited each infirmary in his circuit twice a week (more often by special request) and received as payment 10 *livres* per slave and 150 *livres* for each treatment of yaws.

However, this arrangement did not always satisfy plantation owners and managers who were zealously concerned with protecting their investment. The surgeons retained under contract had limited experience and little dedication to their job. They generally arrived in the colony quite young (some less than twenty years old) and, like most French *émigrés*, quickly set about earning money in order to purchase a small plantation and enter the colonial bourgeoisie themselves (Cauna 1988:219; Debien 1956:11). By the 1780s, when valuable slaves came down with illnesses that exceeded the local surgeon's skill, planters could send them to recently opened clinics in Cap and Port-au-Prince which specialized in the treatment of slaves (Debien 1945:27; Girod 1972:95). Surgeons were not uncommonly fired for gross incompetence, as on the *Habitation Du Fort* in 1758. Faced by a smallpox epidemic among the slaves, the manager of this estate quarantined seventy slaves in an isolated building and let the surgeon treat them. But when thirty had died, he fired the surgeon and took over medical care for the survivors (with, he claimed, better results) (Debien 1941:93).

The treatment of slaves thus took place on the bottom rung of European medicine in St. Domingue. By the mid-eighteenth century, the trained professional medical corps – approximately twenty physicians, sixty surgeons, and fifteen pharmacists – served primarily in military hospitals and the homes of wealthy civilian colonists (plantation owners, higher civil servants, and the merchant elite) (Bordes 1979:10). A large cadre of untrained surgeons and other "empirics" similar to those practicing in contemporary France (midwives, bonesetters, herbalists, oculists, etc.) served the *petits blancs* (Hess 1983).[7] Slaves were confined in the plantation *hôpital*, overseen by another slave acting as *hospitalière*, and occasionally visited by a surgeon. In this transformed version of French medicine, the structure of specialists conformed to the social hierarchy in the colony.

Nonetheless, these specialists all drew from the same repertoire of therapies and diagnostic notions. Under the *ancien régime*, learned and popular medicine interpenetrated each other. (Goubert [1980] analyzes the overlapping therapeutic practices of physicians, surgeons, and empirics in eighteenth-century France.) Empirics and surgeons who treated the *petits blancs* and slaves practiced a version of the same humoral-based therapy as the wealthier physicians called to the bedside of plantation owners. Indeed, plantation owners residing in France explicitly recommended contemporary medical treatments for slaves in letters to the managers of their St. Domingue plantations (Girod 1972:56). Therefore, the treatments which slaves received in the crude plantation *hôpital* derived conceptually from the same European medical system relied on by the white colonial elite. The visiting surgeon, obviously, transmitted prevailing therapeutic ideas to the *hospitalières*. Slaves who had served as aides in military hospitals may also have communicated the logic and practices of European medicine to the wider slave community (Moreau de St.-Méry 1958:559). The specific remedies administered to slaves came directly from the contemporary French pharmacopeia (Debien 1945:26).[8] Scattered references to other treatments for slaves recall contemporary French medical practice, such as bloodletting, enemas, purges, and special diets. At times, the owner or manager of the plantation prepared and administered these treatments, drawing on the popular medical textbooks which colonists enthusiastically ordered from France and which were common in the libraries of large plantations (Debien 1941:70; Bougerol 1985:139; Fouchard 1988:81)

Medicine and the contradictions of slave society

Metropolitan medicine in St. Domingue thus showed clear continuities with contemporary French practices. But it also became part of the ideological and practical apparatus of plantation slavery, and thus developed in several new directions. White colonists transformed metropolitan medicine in accordance with their contradictory image of slaves as both commodities *and* persons, both chattels *and* human subjects capable of resistance and revenge. This contradiction – which recalls the basic contradiction of all Caribbean slave systems (Mintz and Price 1992) – created the distinctive character which French medicine assumed in St. Domingue by the end of colonial rule. It lies at the core of both colonial medical discourse and the medical veneer given to forms of punishment and social control on the plantation.

In the dominant colonial ideology, African slaves were units of production, expensive investments in an agroindustrial system that generated huge individual profits, as well as two-thirds of France's colonial revenues by 1789 (Bellegarde-Smith 1990:35). Galbaud du Fort – proprietor of one of the oldest sugar estates in St. Domingue – invokes this image of the slave as wealth-generating commodity in letters written in 1765:

I strongly wish, my dear wife, to think of my return to France, but how can I do it? We shouldn't fool ourselves, there are many expenses to take care of. We need at least another 40 negroes and 20 mules. Since I have been here, I count 23 negroes who have died . . .
The remittances I will send you this year will not be as high as usual. I'm desperate, but I can't do any better. We've lost negroes and I have had to buy 16 new ones, which cost 22,600 *livres*. (Debien 1941:70)

Du Fort's litany of complaints and the image of the slave he invokes have countless parallels in the voluminous correspondence from St. Domingue (Debien 1959:14). The sickness of slaves was a constant theme in the letters between planters and their families or business associates in France. For example, the manager of the Fleuriau plantation routinely informed its owner about current sicknesses among slaves and the operation of the plantation *hôpital* (Cauna 1988:214). The expense accounts from Fleuriau track the purchase of medicines from France and the ongoing costs of the *hôpital*, and its annual slave census lists the disabled and infirm along with reports of slaves stricken by the smallpox epidemics which periodically swept the colony.

In general, colonists complained about the illness of slaves in the same tone used to describe floods, droughts, and other daily risks to the smooth operation of the plantation. The health of slaves corresponded directly to their productivity, and ultimately to the planters' own profits. Planters invested in slaves' health in the hope of financial return, and they regarded building an *hôpital*, paying the surgeon's fees, and purchasing medicines from France as capital investments just like any other.

Planters thus introduced metropolitan medicine to their estates in accordance with the organizing fiction of Caribbean slave societies: that masters hold property rights in their slaves, and that slaves are not persons, but rather commodities whose lives and labor belongs entirely to their owner (Mintz 1974). However, this fiction was constantly undercut by the undeniable humanity of slaves. Commodities, after all, cannot learn a new language or fashion the skills needed to survive in a foreign culture, and they cannot revolt against their own servitude (Mintz and Price 1992). Despite the legal fiction of ownership and the delegitimation of slaves' family and community ties, slavery in St. Domingue (and throughout the Caribbean) was actually maintained through complex social relationships: the infinite daily interactions between slaves and the white owner, manager, craftsman, surgeon, etc. Each of these relationships – e.g., between a slave caretaker and the owners' family, a black overseer and the plantation manager, or a slave *hospitalière* and the white surgeon – was by definition coercive and rested on a baseline of legally sanctioned violence. But each relationship also presupposed the slaves' basic human capabilities: to socialize children, carry out a work plan, or learn the rudiments of French medicine. The relationship between master and slave on Caribbean sugar plantations was hideously unequal, but it never conformed completely to the planters' ideology of the slave as pure commodity. (This ideology was explicitly articulated, for example, by pro-slavery publicists such as Edward Long [Lewis 1983:109ff] as well as in planters' correspondence on the Code Noir [Williams 1970:183ff]).

The contradiction between the legal definition of the slave and the necessities of daily life on a plantation lay at the core of colonial medical discourse. Slavery is a process of social transformation: not a fixed or unitary status. Individuals who become enslaved pass through the sequential stages of commodification (when they are stripped of their previous identity redefined as a non-person) and resocialization into a new setting with a new status (Kopytoff 1986:65). The cultural biography of most slaves in St. Domingue, therefore, followed a uniform sequence of phases from individual (in Africa) to commodity (during capture and sale) to resocialized individual (on the plantation). However, the potential for resale and the masters' near total power meant that slaves occupied both statuses at once: they were at the same time potential commodities *and* individuals with distinct social identities. This doubleness characterized the image of the slave held by planters and managers in St. Domingue. The dual construction of the slave as both chattels and subjective agents influenced how slave-holders transformed metropolitan medicine in the late eighteenth century.

Colonists deployed contemporary French medicine not only to wrest more labor from slaves, but also to code slaves' subjective response to their condition, to control slaves' resistance, and finally to protect themselves from the real and imagined revenge which slaves took against their masters. The shape of metropolitan medicine on the colonial sugar plantation thus arose not only from the planters' actual exploitative practices or the ideology of the slave as a commodity. It also arose from the complicated reality of social control: the dialectic between the planters' domination and the slaves' overt and covert resistance.[9]

On many plantations the *hôpital* itself became a place of confinement; for example, most slaves in Fleuriau *hôpital* were routinely kept in stocks or chains (Cauna 1988:219). According to the plantation manager, confining ill slaves had two goals: to minimize contagion (and avoid further lost productivity) *and* to discourage "fraud" among healthy slaves wanting to avoid work. This single medical institution thereby served both the profit motive and the need for coercive social control. It exemplifies the double image of sick slaves at the core of colonial medical thought: not only as simple economic debits, but also as human beings engaged in malingering, a highly conscious act of dissembling and passive resistance.

The discourse on the illness of slaves also implicitly recognized their humanity, but in a defensive, moralizing tone which continually circled back to the masters' power and social prerogative. Planters invoked a heterogeneous collection of disease terms to describe sick slaves, which they drew from the multiple traditions of eighteenth-century French medicine. Many of the illnesses they mention are familiar to us, such as tuberculosis, pleurisy, dysentery, or smallpox. But others have a more archaic ring, and these express the planters' speculation on the emotional and imaginative life of slaves. For example, several plantations reported an illness variously called "heart trouble," "stomach trouble," or "languor." This condition afflicted chiefly African-born slaves, and it was often fatal, especially for newly arrived slaves.[10] Although its symptoms – pallor, bloating, weakness, and fatigue – strongly suggest malnutrition, the St. Domingue colonists assigned it an emotional etiology. Such slaves, they wrote, died of nostalgia and moral despondency (*abbatement moral*) over their lost homeland. They simply "wasted away" because of their dislocation (*marasme* was another term used in medical reports) (Cauna 1988:215).

This discourse exposes some of the ironies of colonial medical ideology. Planters openly recognized the slaves' subjective and embodied response to their own enslavement. As inscribed in planters' correspondence, the sufferers of "languor" were not chattels or commodities, but human beings who had been captured and forcibly transported to harsh, alien surroundings, and who then responded to their lot in recognizably human ways. The speculation about morbid nostalgia and despondency, however, neatly elided the complicity of the other set of human beings in this process: the European slave traders who created the inhuman and pathogenic conditions of the Middle Passage, and the French planters who depended on the trade. In this discourse on "languor," colonial medicine constructed the subjectivity of slaves through a sentimental trope of pathogenic homesickness, which hid the power and interests of the planter class.

The irony deepens in the speculation surrounding another well-known affliction of slaves: *mal de mâchoire* (jaw sickness). The symptoms of *mal de mâchoire* largely correspond to the current biomedical diagnosis of infantile tetanus. The disease afflicted newborns in their first ten days of life, beginning with paralysis of the jaw and nearly always leading to death. Because deaths far outnumbered births on the typical plantation, combatting *mal de mâchoire* became an important strategy to maintain the slave work force (along with improving the conditions of childbirth and encouraging mothers to have large families; see Cauna 1987:98ff). The opinions of both slaves and planters about the causes of this disease are recorded in contemporary accounts from the Fleuriau plantation. Writing in 1786 to its owner in La Rochelle, the plantation manager Arnaudeau adds this note to a report on newborn slaves:

three boys and two girls . . . perished from the sickness called *mâchoire,* this sickness that is not quite real, but rather born from the mothers' malice and libertinage, and which has always especially touched me. There is nothing I haven't tried to prevent it . . . There is only one inflexible response which could suppress it: the punishments which I have carried out, but I don't have enough resolve to push them to the extreme. (Cauna 1987:102).[11]

Mal de mâchoire is caused by mothers killing their children to keep them from slavery: such was the conventional wisdom among white colonists which Arnaudeau faithfully repeats in this passage. This interpretation of *mal de mâchoire* acknowledges the general humanity and emotional life of slaves. However, it goes further than the sentimental speculation about "languor," which accorded slaves only a passive and self-negating response to enslavement. The discourse about *mal de mâchoire* actually considers the disease as a form of covert resistance. From a twentieth-century biomedical perspective, the colonists probably misread the symptoms of infantile tetanus as infanticide, but the mis-reading betrays their experience with slaves' suicide and self-mutilation, the other well-known forms of protest which usurped the masters' control over their bodies (James 1963). Colonists who write about the motives for *mal de mâchoire*, therefore, not only acknowledge the slaves' subjectivity as such. They accurately (though implicitly) note the oppression experienced by slaves and the sometimes desperate forms their protest took.

However, the recognition of slaves' resistance is quickly followed by Arnaudeau's ruthless response. He suggests that killing the mother (the "extreme punishment" mentioned in the passage) is the only effective deterrent to *mal de mâchoire*. It is a contradictory and paranoid logic that recommends killing mothers who diminish the work force by murdering their own children. Nonetheless, the contradiction passes by unnoticed in the rest of Arnaudeau's correspondence, though he wrote at length about the disease. He eventually revised his opinions about the causes of *mal de mâchoire* – he decided that midwives, not mothers, were the guilty party – although he still argued that the cause is malice, rather than simple ignorance or unhygienic conditions. Taken as a whole, Arnaudeau's writings suggest the multiple constructions of *mal de mâchoire* within colonial medical discourse: as a disease rooted in slaves' subjectivity (hence, like malingering, "not quite real," or not purely physical), as covert resistance against their own enslavement, and as a blow to the reproduction of the labor force (hence, a malicious attack on the manager himself).

Arnaudeau's peculiar logic derives from deeper contradictions in the agro-capitalist society of late eighteenth-century St. Domingue, and thereby illustrates the formative conditions of colonial medical discourse on the island. The increased world demand for sugar during these years led planters to import more slaves, to work them harder, and to ignore even the flimsy safeguards for slaves' welfare provided by the Code Noir of 1685 (Curtin 1990:161; James 1963:55). The overwork and under-nourishment produced extraordinarily high mortality rates: so high, in fact, that the slave force could not reproduce itself. The colony met its labor needs by ever greater importations of enslaved Africans, and by 1789, two-thirds of the half million slaves had been born in Africa. Planters applied the severest discipline to these newly arrived slaves, and such slaves were also the most likely to escape captivity and become maroons (see Debien 1973; Debbasch 1973; Price 1973).

As a result, French colonial society became preoccupied by fears of slave revenge and rebellion. The threats posed by maroons to white settlements and the brutal and sadistic discipline on plantations where the ratio of slaves to free whites could approach 200 to 1 led one planter to write in 1783 that "a slave colony is like a city under siege; you walk there [as though] on a powderkeg" (Girod 1972:189). The owners suspected that only sheer terror and the threat of lethal violence could keep the slaves from killing them off (Fick 1990:34). They needed occasionally to exercise this brute force – to kill individual slaves with impunity – in order to maintain their repressive control over the rest of the slave population. As the value of slave labor rose, therefore, so did the need for more repressive control of slaves' bodies, both as workers and potential assailants.

Killing slaves was the ultimate display of this control, which, para-
doxically, both destroyed their labor value and strengthened the overall
form of rule by terror. This paradox may also explain the brutality in the
way slaves were executed (e.g., live burial or slow death by fire) as well
as the gratuitous reasons why they were killed (e.g., minor infractions of
plantation discipline or the mere suspicion of sabotage). The "excessive"
killing of slaves – excessive in both the manner of and reasons for
execution – lent crucial support to this regime of terror. To kill slaves on
the whim of the master (in the absence of any customary or judicial
regulation), and to torture slaves who had committed no crime was the
most convincing performative display of the masters' power, which they
deployed in hopes of attaining the total submission of slaves.[12]
Arnaudeau's way to combat *mal de mâchoire* thus contains a calculated
logic, at least in this social system based on terror. It illustrates C. L. R.
James' comment about "the unusual spectacle of property-owners
apparently careless of preserving their property: they had first to ensure
their own safety" (James 1963:12).

As the objects of this regime of terror, however, the slaves on the
Fleuriau plantation had a different response to *mal de mâchoire*. They
flatly rejected the notion that women were killing their children. The
slaves had a blunt and highly personal rebuttal to Arnaudeau's interpretation of the disease, which the manager of Goureaud (a neighboring
plantation) recorded in Creole:

That manager is just too much of a liar. When he sees a pregnant [slave] woman,
he swears like the devil, when the children come into the world, right away he
wants the mother to go to work, he never gives anything to the wet-nurse. When
the mother mentions the children at Gouraud, he says that the manager there
spoils the blacks . . . (Malenfant 1814:206, in Cauna 1987:77–78)[13]

These slaves rejected the dominant discourse on *mal de mâchoire*; they
traced the disease instead to Arnaudeau's callous disregard for the health
of newborn babies and their caretakers. The attitude of the slaves is not
surprising. After all, they were the best observers of their own families,
and they surely had a more accurate knowledge of child survival than
Arnaudeau. Even if the death of infants was sometimes due to infanticide, they would certainly have denied any such motives of resistance or
malice while talking to a white French colonist such as Malenfant. The
puzzling question is not what the slaves meant in their critique of
colonial medical discourse, but rather why Malenfant took the trouble to
record it. This is one of the rare moments when colonial correspondents
recorded the voice of slaves. Why did these slaves offer their critique
so readily, when the risks of open protest were so great? And why

did Malenfant – a member of the same insecure and repressive white minority as Arnaudeau – record it directly in Creole and seemingly without censorship?

The dispute over *mal de mâchoire* held high stakes for both Arnaudeau and the slaves who spoke to Malenfant. These individuals deployed and criticized colonial medical discourse within a local social field and in pursuit of their own short-term interests. Arnaudeau was a distant relative of the Fleuriau family, raised in French rural peasant surroundings, who had worked on its plantation since 1775. He had gradually risen through the ranks from bookkeeper to general manager, and he continually presented himself as an honest, hardworking, and competent employee in his monthly letters to Aimé-Benjamin Fleuriau, living in France. The conventional discourse on *mal de mâchoire* provided an excellent opportunity for him both to proclaim his personal commitment to the profitability of the plantation (the disease "has always especially affected me") and to escape blame for real financial losses (the frequent deaths of newborn slaves).

The slaves also had several strategic reasons to contest Arnaudeau's interpretation. Immediately after rejecting his view of *mal de mâchoire*, they made another potentially more damaging critique:

We didn't know that the job of manager made him into our master. He has an *habitation* in the hills; it's the Fleuriau blacks who plant the coffee, who do all the work there. He has 15 to 20 blacks of his own. Every week he sends to his own *habitation* 30 to 40 of the Fleuriau blacks. Isn't he a rascal, that white?[14] We know we don't have to work on the *habitation* of our manager. (Malenfant 1814:206, in Cauna 1987:77–78)[15]

Indeed, Arnaudeau was not as honest or loyal as he presented himself in letters to Fleuriau. Like many managers in St. Domingue, he was slowly acquiring his own land and stealing the labor of his employer's slaves to cultivate it. When speaking to Malenfant, these slaves exploited the social distance and suspicion between absentee plantation owners and the local *petit blanc* class (which included managers) in order to avoid the extra labor Arnaudeau was demanding. Malenfant recorded these complaints and sent them on to Fleuriau as part of the general policing of plantations by colonial neighbors for their owners in France.[16] Read in this light, the slaves' rejection of the conventional discourse on *mal de mâchoire* illustrates the most common sort of resistance on St. Domingue plantations: *ad hoc*, aimed at more room to maneuver at the margins of the owners' power, and conducted with a canny understanding of the customs and tensions within white colonial society.

The dispute over *mal de mâchoire* provides a case-study of the transformation of metropolitan medicine in St. Domingue. First of all, it illustrates how the image of the slave as a human agent, not just a wealth-producing commodity, structured the categories and practices of colonial medicine. However, Arnaudeau and Malenfant were not simply mouth-pieces for a generic colonial medical discourse. They invoked it while pursuing particular short-term strategies, which in turn contributed to the reproduction of the political economic arrangements in the colony at this time. Similarly, the slaves' challenge to Arnaudeau's views on *mal de mâchoire* came not from a principled opposition to colonial medical discourse *per se*. They disputed this interpretation of illness to support a specific complaint about a subordinate colonizer who did not recognize the legitimate hierarchy of the plantation, and thus exploited their labor in a way considered improper even at that time.

The same contradictory images of slaves as both chattels and subjective human agents capable of resistance motivated colonists' reaction towards slaves' healing practices. A vast assortment of medicinal herbs, empirical therapies, and religious responses to affliction constituted "slave medicine" in colonial St. Domingue (Laguerre 1987). This was not an indigenous medical system, but rather a reinvented and syncretic one which drew from African, Amerindian, and European sources. Slaves relied on this loose collection of treatments as their primary form of healing. Indeed, it was probably more effective than the French medicine practiced in the plantation *hôpital*, and white planters occasionally sought out its remedies themselves.[17] However, the figure of the slave healer was gradually replaced by that of the slave poisoner in the colonial imagination of the late eighteenth century. Fears of slave rebellion and revenge fueled a panic about poisoning which spread throughout the French Antilles during these years, and this panic led directly to the suppression of slave medicine in St. Domingue.

Most plantations in the colony included slaves from diverse African ethnic and linguistic groups: a result of both deliberate imperial policy to prevent organized rebellion as well as the natural randomization of capture, transport, and sale (Klein 1986). Newly arrived Africans were forced to rely on their own memory or the expertise of healing specialists from different ethnic groups to respond to the bodily crises of birth, illness, and death (Laguerre 1987). Slaves therefore devised medical treatments through a process of reinvention and *ad hoc* improvisation. The system of "slave medicine" which emerged from this process undoubtedly included specific African healing forms, but they were refigured in new ecological zones and within the daily constraints of plantation life.[18] This system also encompassed medical knowledge originally acquired from the indigenous Arawaks, who had worked alongside slaves in the early years of the plantation complex.[19] Finally, the slaves' repertoire of treatments probably included elements from European medicine, learned by those who worked in a plantation or military *hôpital* and in the master's house.

The medical practices of slaves arose out of their struggle to create new social forms and cultural expressions in the shadow of the masters' power (a process which recalls the general model of the origin of Afro-Caribbean societies outlined by Mintz and Price [1992]). Like the Creole language (a complicated hybrid of French lexical elements and West African syntax) and the slaves' religion (which interwove Catholicism and African spirit cults), this eclectic medical system combined elements from diverse sources to answer the basic expressive and practical needs of the slave community. Slaves' medicine, like their language and religion, actually helped create their community as a coherent and self-reproducing social group, and in this sense its very existence challenged the dominant legal definition of slaves as chattels (Mintz and Price 1992).

However, the white colonists of St. Domingue did not immediately take up the challenge. To the contrary, they occasionally sought out black healers for themselves (Trouillot 1969) and their slaves (Cauna 1988:219). Until the mid-eighteenth century, colonists tolerated the healing practices of slaves for two pragmatic reasons. First of all, the therapies of contemporary metropolitan medicine were no more effective in keeping slaves healthy and productive. More importantly, planters preferred to have slaves attend to their basic survival needs in their own time and at their own expense. By consulting healers in the slave community, they were ultimately less of a drain on the owners' resources.

Allowing slaves' medicine to flourish in St. Domingue in the early eighteenth century thus made sense within the planters' calculus of cost and earnings. This calculus represented the slave as an economic variable in the plantation's profits, so the planter welcomed whatever kept them alive and productive, all the better if it came at no cost. The planter's calculus of fear later drove planters to suppress this medical system, and their sometimes brutal efforts to combat it were animated by the counter-image of the vengeful, rebellious slave. Beginning around 1740, colonists routinely attributed the deaths of both whites and slaves to poisoning (see Girod 1972:186–87). The fear reached new heights in 1758 with the discovery of a general conspiracy, led by the charismatic slave Mackandal, to poison the water in every colonist's house in Cap François as the first step in a general massacre (James 1963:21). Although Mackandal was captured and burnt alive, the colonists did not lose their fear of poisoning in subsequent years. In correspondence from the Cottineau plantation in the 1760s and 70s, for example, owners and managers readily claim that torture is needed to root out and punish poisoners. These were not idle words: one reputed slave poisoner from Cottineau was condemned to die slowly in a "cachot effrayant" – a crude box without air or light – after which his body was burnt (Girod 1972:188).

A planter's letter from 1782 provides a case study of the colonial panic about poisoning:

It is inconceivably difficult to constrain the negroes of this plantation and it is only by the most fortuitous chance that . . . my family and I escaped from the frightful plot which they had devised to destroy us. A washerwoman was surprised in my water reserve on the verge of poisoning our jars. She fled and threw into the air a powder which she held in her hand; however, she was caught and questioned in the drying oven (where she tried to hang herself to avoid disclosing her secret).

She avowed to me that the first commander, her uncle, had given her this powder to put in the vases . . . to inspire my indulgence for a mulatress of his family whom I had wanted to put in the garden for having wrongly had an abortion. This commander and the mulatress conscientiously denied having any part in this hideous crime of the washer-woman and only the law [i.e., torture] was able to discover the truth . . . I also took the precaution of putting in chains these three monsters. (Debien 1974:408, in Bougerol 1985:129–30)

Unfortunately (but typically), this letter does not include the voice of slaves, so it does not allow the same insight into possible forms of resistance as the writings about *mal de mâchoire*. Nevertheless, it shows continuities with the general colonial image of the slave as rebelliously plotting to kill the owner and maliciously damaging the owner's property (i.e., other slaves). In this instance, the sign of rebellion was abortion, which owners regarded in the same light as infanticide: an attempt to decimate the work force, and hence the owner's profits. To punish an abortion was therefore not uncommon, and fear of revenge for this punishment was also predictable, given the extreme tension at the heart of colonial society at this time (Bougerol 1985:132). No matter if the fear was unfounded; schemes for revenge would be "confirmed" by torture and, in turn, punished by confinement.

In general, colonists rarely doubted that poisoning caused the many unexplained deaths on plantations.[20] Their only questions concerned how slaves managed to carry out their crimes and how colonists could prevent them. Had slaves brought the formulae for poisons from Africa? Did they steal arsenic or other toxins from the plantation *hôpital*? Such questions occur throughout colonial correspondence, newspapers, and letters from travellers (Girod 1972). They suggest that slaves' skills as healers and poisoners were linked in the colonial imagination. Colonists concluded that the best way to protect themselves from slave poisoning was to prohibit related practices, especially slave medicine. This policy led both to precautions taken by individual planters and to region-wide colonial legislation. For example, Stanislaus Foache, a St. Domingue planter, instructed his managers to choose a slave attendant for the *hôpital* who was firm enough to prevent the relatives of patients from bringing their own remedies (Girod 1972:150). On a regional level, colonial policy throughout the French Antilles outlawed slave healers entirely (Bougerol 1983, 1985). For example, an ordinance enacted in 1767 in Guadeloupe forbade slaves to practice surgery and pharmacy, forbade teaching slaves any knowledge of roots and plants, and prohibited whites from consulting slave healers for any illness whatsoever (Bougerol 1985:134).

The suppression of slave healers on St. Domingue thus grew out of the whites' fear of slave poisoning. The intensity of their fear, in turn, grew from the distorted social conditions already mentioned: the massive imbalance between slaves and free citizens, the racist ideology which maintained a strict separation between black and white (no matter how often this divide was breached in daily life), the depredations of the maroons, and the insecurity of whites who planned to reside there only long enough to make their fortune, return to France, and buy a noble title (Lewis 1983:123ff). The colonists' fear of poisoning took on a life of its own, fed by these chronic conflicts as well as an older concern with poisoning under the *ancien régime*. Colonists attributed all varieties of death to poison: rapid deaths, lingering deaths, even deaths due to other known diseases, such as *languor* or malignant fevers (Girod 1972:189). They blamed slave poisoners for the death of whites, plantation livestock, and also other slaves. Colonists even extended their discourse on poisoning to include slaves' suicide: for example, they suspected that the reason certain slaves ate small amounts of earth each day was in order gradually to kill themselves and thereby spite their owners (*ibid.*)

The suppression of slave healers and the confinement of slaves in the plantation *hôpital* were the major ways that French colonists imposed metropolitan medicine on the majority African-American population of St. Domingue. These practices elaborated the same themes as colonial views on slaves' infanticide and suicide (expressed through the speculation about *mal de mâchoire* and *languor*). At its core, colonial medicine on St. Domingue plantations rested on a contradictory image of slaves as both commodities and willful agents capable of resistance.[21] These images fundamentally structured the planters' efforts to control slaves' bodies, combat displays of their resistance, and suppress their medical system.

Nation-building and medical control

The transformation of French medicine in St. Domingue thus took place through the militarization of the urban *hôpital* system and the emergence of a medical discourse on slaves' subjectivity and medicalized social controls on plantations. This first chapter in the history of metropolitan medicine in Haiti ended with the thirteen-year armed struggle against the French (1791–1804). The forced departure of all ranks of French colonial society – the militia, administrators, planters, and *petits blancs* – created a power vacuum which new black and mulatto elites rushed to fill. The contests for state power within this elite class, and between the elite and the mass of newly freed slaves, influenced the development of metropolitan medicine throughout the nineteenth century.

Two years after Haiti won its independence from France, the country split into two warring sovereign states: a southern republic led by a Alexander Pétion, a wealthy mulatto, and a northern kingdom ruled by Henri Christophe, a black war hero. The fourteen-year civil war between these two states was essentially a contest between two self-seeking elites for control of the new nation's political and commercial institutions. Neither ruler was especially interested in the interests of the majority of freed slaves (Nicholls 1979). Christophe sought to re-create the profits generated during the colonial period by binding the ex-slaves to particular plantations, strictly regulating their work, and severely punishing any attempt to escape (Leyburn 1966:45ff). He established an authoritarian and paternalistic labor system, where both the harsh discipline and medical care of workers conformed to pre-revolutionary patterns.

Each plantation had its own *hôpital* staffed by a nurse and midwife, and some also had another isolated *hôpital* for contagious illnesses. Laws passed by Christophe mandated that the staff be supervised by a visiting *officier de santé*, and that plantation owners pay for the medical treatment of workers (Madiou 1988:75, 515). Christophe also maintained the links between medicine in Europe and in Haiti which existed in colonial St. Domingue. Christophe's statecraft was pro-British: he cultivated commercial ties and military alliances with England in order to protect against the threat of a French reconquest (Nicholls 1979:52). Moreover, he invited English visitors into his kingdom to expand public instruction and the professions. As part of this policy, Christophe founded a school of medicine at Cap Haïtien in 1816, and named an English Protestant,

Dr. Stewart, as its director (Madiou 1988:348). Metropolitan medicine in Christophe's kingdom was thus remarkably similar to its colonial precursor, despite the end of slavery and the absence of the old French medical corps.

Outside the refurbished plantations, the militarization of medicine also showed clear continuities with French St. Domingue. Both Christophe and Pétion inherited the network of military *hôpitaux* from the colonial period, and the chronic warfare between north and south gave them no reason to dismantle it. In 1816, Christophe assimilated all doctors and surgeons to the militia: his medical staff became *maréchaux de camp*, ordinary doctors became colonels, and surgeons became lieutenant colonels. Each specialist wore the decoration appropriate to his rank (Madiou 1988:337). To submerge the entire medical hierarchy within the military command fit with Christophe's despotic strategy of rule (Leyburn 1966:49). However, Pétion administered metropolitan medicine in much the same way, even though the military played a much smaller role in his Republic. Pétion established a national *service de santé*, but its inspector general, head pharmacist, and health officers were all connected to the military (Madiou 1988:479). Pétion's Senate also refused to establish an *hôpital* for the aged and infirm in each department, deciding instead simply to send them out of the towns and back to their plantations and villages (Bordes 1979).

The militarization of metropolitan medicine thus continued into the early nineteenth century because of the ongoing armed confrontation between Christophe and Pétion, as well as the lingering threat of French reconquest. Throughout this period, therefore, most of the country's organized health services treated chiefly the armed forces. However, even these state-financed military hospitals gradually fell into disrepair. An 1871 governmental report states that the military hospitals in Port-au-Prince and the provincial capitals were ill-equipped and did not function regularly. By 1890, according to another official report, there existed at Jérémie only the debris of a hospital, and the hospital at Cayes was a failure. Finally, in 1891, a Port-au-Prince journalist described the Cayes hospital as a shed with neither furniture nor a pharmacy; another observer maintained simply that it was in ruins (Bordes 1979).

The degradation of military medicine reflects the shifts in state power over the nineteenth century. The military emerged as the strongest national institution after independence, and Christophe's northern kingdom represented the apogee of military rule. For a short time, he had turned the ex-slaves into serfs and created a black aristocracy of wealthy planters. However, Christophe's profitable but strictly regimented plantations disappeared soon after the king died in 1820. With the demise of Christophe's kingdom and the reunification of the country in 1820, Pétion's policies became the template for the entire nation. Pétion had democratized land tenure by reducing the minimum acreage for sales, and Haitians who could not afford to buy squatted on inferior land in the hills. Under Pétion's rule, ex-slaves thus became peasants, not serfs, and the mulatto elite of the south essentially surrendered land in order to win the loyalty of the masses and gain control of the state (Trouillot 1990a:48).

After reunification, planters in both the north and the south turned their backs on agriculture and entered politics as a quicker route towards wealth and social advancement. The military was thus no longer needed for the discipline of plantation workers. Moreover, after French diplomatic recognition in 1825, the military was not needed to defend against possible reconquest. Although the military remained one of the only routes of upward mobility for poor blacks, military medicine in general underwent a sharp decline.

The peasant majority of Haiti had negligible exposure to metropolitan medicine throughout most of the nineteenth century. With the end of large-scale plantation agriculture, control of the state became the major source of wealth for the elite. Haitian society thus bifurcated into two geographically distinct and culturally distant groups: an urban elite which controlled state revenues and a reconstituted rural peasantry farming small, independently owned plots of land. Members of the elite rarely confronted the peasant producers whose labor they continually (though silently) exploited. As long as they could siphon off peasants' profits through tariffs and taxation, they were patently uninterested in the welfare of rural areas (see Trouillot 1990a). The scarcity of medical services provided for rural dwellers attests to the elite's disinterest.

Although Pétion directed charitable hospitals to be built in the capital of each department for the care of the "invalid poor and the infirm" of all ages, only one such building was constructed in Port-au-Prince, and before long it fell into disuse (Bordes 1979:47–48). A few charitable hospices staffed by Catholic healing orders did operate in cities, such as the Sœurs Bleues de St. Rose de Lima, a medical order comprising both white Europeans and Haitians that was founded after independence (Parsons 1930:41). A handful of foreign-born doctors drew on their own funds and appealed to wealthy townspeople to establish public clinics, for example in Jérémie (the American Dr. Lowell, in 1833) and Cap Haïtien (the American Dr. Wilson, in 1852) (Mathurin 1972). However, these few clinics and hospitals reached only a small percentage of rural dwellers.

In the near absence of formally trained personnel, numerous

individuals with no recognized education or authorization began to practice as healers throughout the country. In 1819, an unusual institution, the Jury Medical, was formed to regulate these unorthodox practitioners. Composed of the Inspector-in-Chief of the (military) health service and a small council of physicians, the Jury was charged with examining and licensing all individuals claiming to practice medicine and surgery or selling medications. However, its chief concern was the suppression of unqualified practitioners, or, as an official document of 1861 phrased it, *sauvegarder la société contre les charlatans* ("to protect society from charlatans") (Bordes 1979).

The identity and actual therapies of such "charlatans" remains unclear. The term probably referred to healers who used African religious or herbal tradition or archaic European medical practices.[22] The formation of the Jury Medical thus represents the second time in Haitian history that agents of metropolitan medicine attempted to suppress other forms of healing. Like earlier attempts under slavery, the drive to root out "charlatanry" exposes some central preoccupations among the ruling class. The ideology of educated Haitians in the nineteenth century was an ambivalent mixture of (black) nationalism and disdain for Africa. In their pamphlets, political tracts, and multivolume histories, contemporary Haitian writers heralded the defeat of Napoleon's forces and the construction of a wholly new society as markers of black dignity and power in the face of racist Europe. They argued that Haiti's success disproved reigning theories of Africans' racial inferiority, and that the Creole mixing of Indian and African origins would produce a new and vigorous civilization (Lewis 1983:252ff). Nevertheless, these well-educated writers often assumed that Africa was a barbaric and backward continent (albeit for socio-historical, not biological reasons). Scholars such as Madiou and St.-Rémy thus argued against white racism, but in favor of European cultural superiority and assimilation to Western norms (Bellegarde-Smith 1990:56).

The goals of the Jury Medical conformed to the elite's equivocal nationalism. The continued circulation of African (or archaic European) healing forms among peasants was no doubt embarrassing to professional physicians, who were uniformly from the elite class. Rooting out such practices supported their self-image as the modernizing and pro-European vanguard of Haiti. However, this vanguard provided peasants with virtually no alternatives to the so-called "charlatans." In its nationalism, as in its social and economic affairs, this cosmopolitan class oriented itself towards Port-au-Prince (or France) and neglected the rural regions of Haiti (see Janvier 1979; Plummer 1988:xii). The ruling class constructed precious few public medical facilities, even after metropolitan medicine became fully institutionalized in Port-au-Prince in the late 1800s. The national medical school began granting degrees in 1870.[23] In the following years, several French-trained physicians returned to Haiti to begin private practices in surgery and obstetrics for wealthy patients. In 1891, a medical society was organized in Port-au-Prince, and by 1905 Dr. Leon Audain (the leader of many of these new medical activities) had drawn on his own funds to establish a research laboratory in parasitology and bacteriology (Bordes 1979).

Throughout this expansion of metropolitan scientific medicine, the state played only a minor role in providing medical benefits to the general public. In the 1890s, a movement began among the elite to establish almshouses and charitable hospitals in major cities. This goal was reached entirely through the efforts of private citizens and representatives of the Catholic church. Typically, an individual would start by donating his land and then raising money for the actual construction of the building through subscriptions from other wealthy townspeople. One of the medical orders of the church would then assume responsibility for direct patient care. If these individuals or the church requested state aid, it was only after the hospital had already begun operation (Bordes 1979).

This pattern most likely accounts for the opening, in 1890, of the Hospice du Bon Pasteur in Les Cayes, near the village of Jeanty. The hospice soon passed into the hands of the Sœurs de la Sagesse and became the Hospice de l'Immaculée Conception. Only in 1917, under the American occupation, did it fall under state control. It is now the main hospital in Les Cayes, and is still operated by a Catholic order, although it depends on public funding and administration. The combination of private initiative and funds, clinical staffing by religious orders (often sponsored by European and American missions), and state administration still characterizes many medical institutions in Haiti, and it reflects the influence of the American occupation in development of metropolitan medicine after 1900.

Progressive imperialism? Biomedicine under American rule

The American occupation (1915–34) radically transformed medical institutions and practices in Haiti.[24] The Americans' authoritarian, paternalist strategy of rule and their technocratic goals for the occupation have influenced metropolitan medicine until today. The occupation of Haiti was among the most systemic intrusions into the internal workings of any Caribbean country during this period of American imperialism (Langley 1980:68). Ruling through a combination of direct martial law and a Haitian client government, Americans quickly took over most major national institutions. The Haitian treasury was indirectly controlled by American financial interests. American naval officers supervised customs offices, and hence controlled the chief source of government revenues. American officers reorganized and commanded the *Gendarmerie d'Haïti*, which became the main instrument of American authority throughout the country. Finally, Americans took charge of public works and sanitation agencies, which gave them direct control over much of the nation's medical services.

The wholesale takeover of major institutions and professions, including medicine, was justified by a condescending belief that Haitians had an inherent inability to govern themselves. American diplomats involved with the occupation were explicit on this point. William Phillips (Assistant Secretary of State) defended American rule by pointing to "the failure of an inferior people to maintain the degree of civilization left them by the French, or to develop the capacity for self-government entitling them to international respect and confidence" (in Schmidt 1971:63). Robert Lansing (State Dept. counselor) offered a more openly racist version of the same ideology: the African race, he wrote, was "devoid of any capacity for political organization and lack[ing] genius for government. Unquestionably there is in them an inherent tendency to revert to savagery and to cast aside the shackles of civilization" (*ibid.*). According to the evolutionist brand of scientific racism popular in early twentieth-century America, Haitians (assimilated to the biological category of Africans) had not yet reached the level of responsible self-government and therefore required paternalistic American control.[25]

Whereas popular racist ideas helped to justify intervention, the ideology of Progressivism suggested what Americans should actually accomplish during their rule. The occupiers made few attempts to implant democratic institutions (Schmidt 1971). They followed instead the reformist Progressive-era credo that organizational efficiency and technocratic competence are the best guarantors of good government. The occupation was heralded as "an experiment in pragmatism," in which an "elaborate process of building" would precede any democratic reforms (Weatherly 1926, in Schmidt 1971:157). Under the American regime in Haiti, the "civilizing mission" of contemporary European colonialism was transformed into a drive for efficient technocratic management. Indeed, the American occupation force excelled in building things – roads, bridges, government buildings, and hospitals – and in subordinating Haitian workers to the American technical experts who ran governmental agencies. In the rhetoric of American administrators, economic development and material progress were the chief goals of the occupation, which would bring in their wake other forms of cultural and political progress.

Guided by this reformist ideology, Americans began to reorganize Haitian medicine within a month of the Marine landing. In August, 1915, American navy doctors began work among poor Port-au-Prince residents, and by the following January the American Red Cross contributed a small fund to continue these medical services (Schmidt 1971:69). In 1916, a commission of Haitian physicians presented the Americans with a plan to organize a new public health service. Their ideas, however, were largely ignored by Dr. N. T. McLean, the US Navy Regimental Surgeon officially designated as responsible for public health and hygiene. McLean instead founded his own *Service National d'Hygiène et d'Assistance Publique* (National Hygiene and Public Welfare Service). Controlled by American administrators, this agency had sole authority over the teaching and practice of medicine, the administration of hospitals, and the distribution of pharmaceutical products (Bellegarde 1953:264).

The American Navy medical corps, operating through the *Service d'Hygiène*, gradually took charge of virtually the entire structure of metropolitan medicine in Haiti. In 1919, it divided the country into nine regions (a tenth was added in 1924), each with a public health headquarters and a new district hospital built to American specifications. Americans staffed this bureaucracy for the duration of the occupation, from the Director General of the *Service d'Hygiène* down to district health officers (Parsons 1930). By 1925, the *Service d'Hygiène* had constructed eleven hospitals, a hospital training school, and sixteen rural dispensaries. It had also established a system of 102 rural clinics, which were run by a priest or Haitian women trained as practical nurses, and visited once a month by physicians (Balch 1972:87–88). The *Service d'Hygiène* also inoculated schoolchildren, drained and filled swamps, distributed quinine, sanitized water supplies, etc. (Millspaugh 1931:140).

To carry out these reforms, the *Service d'Hygiène* depended on the financial support and technical expertise of the Rockefeller Foundation. The Foundation underwrote a national medical survey of Haiti in 1924–25, and in 1926 provided funds to purchase new equipment at the national medical school and to send its graduates to the US for advanced training (Millspaugh 1931). The *Service d'Hygiène* took full control of the medical school in 1927, over the objections of leading Haitian physicians. By 1930, the bureaucratic reach of the *Service d'Hygiène* was so complete that only a few Catholic hospitals and approximately 200 private Haitian physicians escaped the Americans' control (Balch 1972).

Apologists for the occupation celebrated the *Service d'Hygiène* with the Progressive rhetoric commonly used to justify American intervention. "The energy and earning power of the people are naturally materially increased by improving their health," wrote its director, Capt. Smedley Butler (Millspaugh 1931:138). Moreover, the peasant "was getting a valuable and novel political idea . . . that a government can be one of popular service," according to the 1929 Report of the American High Commissioner (1931:140). However, the most significant short-term accomplishment of the *Service d'Hygiène* – the expansion of medical services to rural areas – was only partly motivated by the drive for efficient governmental services. It was also the outcome of a power struggle between Americans and the Haitian elite.

The Americans who controlled governmental agencies resented the sophisticated mulatto elite of the capital city, and generally preferred dealing with poor peasants. The occupiers' attitudes towards both groups reflected the dominant North American images of blacks; transplanted to Haiti, these images cast the elite as "uppity" and the peasants as dependent and childlike (see Schmidt 1971:135ff). The Francophilic elite, in turn, despised the Americans as crass and materialist. These racial and cultural animosities reflected the fundamental power struggle between the Haitian political class and the Americans who had usurped their traditional leadership position. Consequently, Americans designed their development programs – including medical services – to favor the peasants and thereby further undermine the elite's privileges (Schmidt 1971:148). They built hospitals in provincial capitals and rural areas in order to undercut the centralized power of the national upper class (Schmidt 1971; Trouillot 1990a).

The mass uprisings and strikes of 1929 sped up Washington's plans to end the occupation, and control over metropolitan medicine was gradually transferred to Haitians over the next few years (Langley 1980:119). In late 1931, the government of Haiti assumed full leadership of the *Service d'Hygiène*. The immediate evaluation of American medical reforms was mixed, even by members of the occupation force. Parsons' unabashedly triumphalist *History of Haitian Medicine* (1930) is belied by the High Commissioner's admission that the *Service d'Hygiène* had accomplished "only the first phase in the necessary program, final success in which [could] only be reached after many years" (Millspaugh 1931:182). The verdict of later historians is equally divided. Heinl and Heinl, who generally defend the occupation, acknowledge that because Marines implanted no democratic institutions in Haiti, the *Service d'Hygiène* was vulnerable to corruption soon after American control ended (Heinl and Heinl 1978:513). Dantès Bellegarde praised the occupation medical services as "one of most useful institutions organized in the country by the Americans" (Bellegarde 1953:265), while Nicholls criticizes medical reforms as "largely guided by the need to make Haiti an attractive country for foreign investment" (1979:148).

The development of metropolitan medicine after the Marines left justifies Suzy Castor's claim that the American occupation of Haiti provided the veneer of modernization with no true development (Castor 1988:215ff). The actual buildings and the national health bureaucracy are the chief legacies for biomedicine from the occupation period. They have lasted since the departure of the American forces in 1934 until today, in contrast to both the network of rural clinics and the specific medical activities undertaken by the *Service d'Hygiène*.[26] The Americans provided neither the training nor a consistent source of capital to sustain their public health activities. However, the bureaucracy they founded continues to flourish to this day. The Americans organized medical services according to a modern, rationalized scheme which divided the country into discrete departments, regions, and districts. This administrative hierarchy was soon consolidated in Port-au-Prince, contrary to the intentions of its American founders (but consistent with the centralization of most other state services during occupation). Under the renamed *Département de la Santé Publique* (Department of Public Health), public biomedical services after 1934 were confined to curative care in Port-au-Prince and the district capitals. The state furnished virtually no operating budget to these hospitals, which perforce often relied on religious orders for the actual delivery of services (Rohde 1986:119). Nonetheless, the state health care bureaucracy has continued to grow and to solidify its control of biomedical institutions.

Medicine, empire, and social control

Metropolitan medicine in Haiti has undergone radical transformations since the beginning of French colonization in the late seventeenth century. The military hospitals and rude plantation infirmaries for slaves during the colonial period continued for a brief period after independence, but soon gave way to a handful of private and religious institutions, the first laboratories and clinics patterned after European medicine of the late nineteenth century, the network of rural dispensaries and regional hospitals built by the Americans during the Marine occupation, and the health facilities operated by the state, foreign missionaries, and international aid agencies since World War II (examined through a detailed case-study in the next chapter). The conceptual foundations of metropolitan medicine have obviously changed along with these institutions: from the Hippocratic-based, "bedside medicine" of eighteenth-century France to twentieth-century biomedicine and the successive post-war trends of international health.

The strategies of dominant groups to consolidate their hold on material and symbolic power have shaped metropolitan medicine throughout this entire period. Since the late seventeenth century, metropolitan medicine has been introduced by members of the topmost group in a highly stratified society: from French planters to Haitian generals, professional elites of Port-au-Prince, and medical officers of the American Marine occupying force. Successive dominant groups have deployed metropolitan medicine in different ways to advance their interests, because each historical period posed unique problems of rule. Over the years, their strategies (and the resistant counter-strategies of less powerful groups) have pushed metropolitan medicine in contradictory directions. Colonial slavery deployed contemporary medical services as a form of social control; they later became merely a source of income for state bureaucrats. Biomedicine in the early twentieth century was restricted to the elite; the Ministry of Public Health now diffuses it throughout rural areas.

This 300-year history thus adds to the burgeoning literature on medicine, empire, and social control. However, it complicates some of the reigning perspectives on how metropolitan medicine operates in peripheral areas, and how it has furthered imperial or neocolonial rule. Anthropologists and historians typically invoke two processes to explain this: the reformation of consciousness and the medicalized control of bodies and populations. At the risk of reducing a complex reality to simple formulae, I begin by summarizing the conventional wisdom about each process.

The narrow physical emphasis of Western medicine, it is claimed, has a powerful effect on individual subjectivity (see Gordon 1988). By locating pathology in the individual, and treatment in private settings divorced from everyday life, biomedicine weakens alternate accounts of the social sources of suffering and health. Biomedical knowledge desocializes disease, and thereby authorizes the particular "truth" that diseases are biological events, arising through impersonal, natural laws, rather than social ties and interests. Biomedicine thus helps construct the individual as an autonomous subject – a center of cognition and feeling – who exists against a background of facts and material objects (Comaroff 1982). This form of subjectivity – in fact, produced by both biomedicine and Christian conversion – advances colonial rule. It subverts pre-colonial forms of consciousness, instills habits of self-reliance, efficiency, and work discipline, and hence paves the way for wage labor and other forms of colonial capitalism (e.g., Ranger 1992).

In a related process, biomedicine advances the state regulation of bodies and populations. Public health campaigns supported by colonial states offer a good example. While these campaigns are overtly aimed at poor hygiene or nutrition, they also accomplish other bureaucratic and political ends. They create lists of dispersed populations, they establish new modes of surveillance, they justify large-scale relocations which strengthen centralized political control. In many regimes, the workplace (the copper mine or sugar plantation) has been the chief point of contact with biomedicine. In these cases, the medical care of workers' bodies merges directly with the state's overall economic plans (see Vaughan 1991).

However, neither of these accounts explains the key turning points in the history of metropolitan medicine in Haiti. Metropolitan medicine in Haiti has rarely been used to reform individual subjectivity, despite its deep association with imperialist interests. In colonial St. Domingue, the French constructions of slave subjectivity circulated only among the colonists themselves. The speculations about slaves' emotional life found in colonial medical discourse were not impressed upon the slaves (unlike the models for slave subjectivity in the British Caribbean, such as the racist "Sambo" image in Jamaica; see Patterson 1967). These images did not contribute to the hegemonic and ideological policing of slaves, and even confinement in plantation *hôpitaux* was only a minor part of the direct repressive apparatus. Under the subsequent rule of neocolonial elites, metropolitan medicine was barely accessible to most people. The American occupying force used medical reforms to convince Haitians of the efficiency and technological superiority of the United States. However, the Marines never deployed biomedicine to enforce a policy of "internal colonialism," unlike other twentieth-century colonialists (e.g., the French in Algeria, whose use of biomedicine is criticized in Fanon 1965). Biomedicine – the current incarnation of metropolitan medicine – therefore does not carry the connotations of a "tool of empire" (Arnold 1988) or vanguard of modernization for most residents of rural Haiti.

Neither the Foucauldian account of Western medicine's "capillary power" to create a self-policing subject, nor the more straightforward critique of biomedicine as an agent of direct colonial domination fits the Haitian case very well. These accounts are best suited to a single historical period: roughly 1870 to 1920. This was the classic era of European empire-building, especially in Africa. During these same years, scientific medicine became consolidated as an internally consistent and professionally sovereign set of signs and practices. Because these two processes occurred at the same time, they have structured scholarly paradigms for the study of medicine, empire, and social control. A certain kind of empire was at its peak then, which encompassed vast regions without a single "national elite," because they had not yet been organized as nation states. These regimes deployed a certain kind of medicine: newly consolidated along the still recent doctrines of specific etiology and localized pathology. It was a potent combination, which allowed (or demanded) an unprecedented degree of direct bodily control and oblique, diffused persuasion.

In St. Domingue, however, power was still coercive and repressive; this was a "pre-modern" colony, where "pre-modern" European medicine was implanted. Consequently, the technologies of control involved brute coercion and confinement, not oblique ideological persuasion (Vaughan [1991] makes a similar argument for nineteenth-century African colonialism). Although colonial medical discourse was centrally concerned with the subjectivity of the subordinate group, it deployed its tropes of identity and difference for repressive, not productive ends. Secondly, the entrance of American power in the Caribbean, begun in 1898, aimed at a different type of political control than practiced in contemporary European colonies, and it used different techniques to control bodies and populations (see Anderson 1992). The next chapter surveys the most recent forms of American-derived medical power in Haiti.

3 Biomedicine in Jeanty

The paradox of biomedicine

Although metropolitan medicine has always served as a tool of empire in Haiti (cf. Arnold 1988), it does not have this meaning for residents of Jeanty. For most people, attending a clinic and accepting a biomedical diagnosis are routinized parts of everyday life. Most villagers do not single out biomedical therapies as foreign or contrast them to a separate category of "indigenous healing." People do not oppose biomedicine on moral or political grounds. Nor do they seek out biomedicine as a way to show that they are "modernizing" or to identify with the national elite in Haitian society. Villagers easily intermix biomedicine with other types of healing, without invoking the historical association of metropolitan medicine with foreign or neo-colonial domination.

This is the paradox of biomedicine in Jeanty. On the one hand, it is undeniably a metropolitan import, and it arrives with the full weight of foreign power and cultural cachet. On the other hand, it does not threaten to replace the work of midwives, herbalists, and religious healers with its own set of reductionist and culturally foreign interventions. Despite its origins, biomedicine does not exist as a bounded "health care sector" in isolation from other forms of therapy, and it has not subverted the local healing system. This chapter examines the roots of this paradox and its effects on the structure of medical pluralism in Jeanty.

The local history and ethnography of metropolitan medicine demonstrate one way (out of many) that this Caribbean micro-community is permeable to the intrusion of global forces (see Trouillot 1990b). Particular institutions – centered in Port-au-Prince, the United States, or France – have directed enormous resources into this village which local residents have struggled to control. From the start of the twentieth century up to the late 1980s, people working in these institutions have (wittingly or not) transferred the resources, symbols, and authority of biomedicine to Jeanty. Most of the time, they appropriated biomedical power for their own short-term goals. Over the years, however, their struggles to control biomedicine have reproduced and transformed local patterns of help-seeking and healing. Biomedicine has thus diffused across the plural healing system, without losing its mark as a Euro-American import, but also without subordinating other forms of healing to its hegemonic control.

Local history of medical services

Before the local dispensary opened in 1976, Jeanty had no single organized and consistent source for biomedical services. Nonetheless, Jeanty residents have had access to various types of biomedicine through-out this century, even if they were unavailable in the village itself. One wealthy villager born in 1908 recalls being treated exclusively with herbal remedies during his childhood. However, people who needed (and could afford) biomedical care would take the day-long journey to private doctors in Les Cayes, the nearby provincial capital, via mule or horse-drawn wagon. They could also obtain more elaborate and expensive treatments at hospitals in Port-au-Prince, although this required a three-day bus ride over decrepit roads.

Until the late 1940s, the resident priest was virtually the sole local source of proprietary drugs. This began to change, however, with the improved fortunes of Jeanty during the general post-war upturn in the national economy. International shipping resumed in 1946, and peasants began to earn larger profits from the sale of their coffee and sisal to satisfy the pent-up world demand (Paquin 1983:103). Because Les Cayes had an active port at that time, the economic activity of the entire region increased. In the late 1940s, a leading Jeanty resident arranged for the state to construct a permanent road link to Les Cayes. By 1950 Jeanty had its own weekly market where individual farmers could sell their produce without needing to travel to Les Cayes and deal with its agricultural brokers and speculators. This significantly decreased the economic dependence of Jeanty upon its provincial capital.

Merchants and vendors came to the weekly market in Jeanty to sell all manner of mass commodities produced abroad, including European- and American-made pharmaceuticals. Moreover, a number of small shops were established near the marketplace which sold simple medications along with other general merchandise. To this day, both the general market and the few stores clustered nearby remain important local sources for proprietary drugs such as analgesics, anti-helminth powders, tetracycline, and other antibiotics which people usually purchase for self-treatment. However, Catholic priests probably provided the only direct biomedical treatments in Jeanty and the surrounding rural region until the 1960s, when the present network of dispensaries was built. Père Joseph (the current priest in Jeanty) as well as older French, American, and Dutch clergy from neighboring parishes recall many villager requests for simple medical procedures during these years. The priests responded by drawing on their personal knowledge of first aid and relying on medications purchased in larger Haitian cities or received as donations from their home countries.

Most villagers associate the physical building housing the dispensary with Père Joseph. People list the dispensary along with the many other buildings and services which Père Joseph has provided to the parish over the years, such as a parish hall, primary and secondary schools, a trade school, a mill, numerous chapels throughout the parish, food and cash aid after natural disasters, and electrification. Joseph purchased the land for the dispensary and paid for its construction with money from various Catholic and secular sources in North America and Europe (including a donation from the French government). Soon after it was built, however, he decided not to continue as the owner and director of the dispensary, and he gave it instead to the state. Joseph did not want the added administrative responsibility of managing a nursing staff from, e.g., the Sisters of Charity, in addition to the secondary school he built and kept under church control. Moreover, he hoped to deflect criticisms voiced by villagers that his building projects simply bolstered his own power and prestige. Relinquishing control of the dispensary, he now claims, demonstrates his wish to have Haitians take up leadership positions in the various organizations established by the church.

Villagers no longer associate the actual operation of the dispensary with the Catholic church. Both Catholics and Protestants say their religious membership does not affect the quality of treatment they receive. However, the level of care offered to all patients at the Jeanty dispensary is probably lower as a result of Père Joseph's decision to hand it over to the state. If they can afford the higher fees and transportation costs, villagers prefer to attend the clinics operated by the Sisters of Charity in nearby towns. They point out that these other settings offer laboratory examinations of blood, urine, and stool that are unavailable in Jeanty. When comparing medical facilities in the region, most people give first rank to the large Baptist medical complex north of Les Cayes. But they also complain that religious affiliation does make a difference at the Baptist hospital; Baptist patients reportedly receive favored treatment, and medical care is often delivered along with intense and unwelcome proselytization.

The profile of biomedical services in the Jeanty region is typical for the

5 A family readies corn to be sold at the Jeanty market.

entire country. In larger Haitian towns with both governmental and church-related medical facilities, the latter are consistently better staffed and have a better supply of medications. In general, governmental health services throughout Haiti are run down, poorly utilized, and lacking supplies, whereas facilities operated by private voluntary organizations, especially churches, attract substantial outside funding and supplies and are often flooded with patients (Rohde 1986).

The arrival and development of organized biomedical services in Jeanty repeats some familiar themes from the longer history of metropolitan medicine in Haiti. Rural residents generally have not benefited from the biomedical services implanted in Haiti during this century (Bordes 1979). Biomedical resources are concentrated in the capital, where they remain inaccessible to most peasants because of sheer physical distance and economic barriers. However, as the American occupying force and successive governments built roads which integrated the national space and hastened the emergence of new circuits of exchange, Western pharmaceutics travelled these circuits to enter isolated villages such as Jeanty.

In Jeanty, a single priest significantly enlarged and improved the bio-medical services available in the town at a time of national economic decline and increasing rural poverty. He did so by staying as far outside of governmental structures as possible, and relying instead on the Church and other foreign funds. His accomplishment reflects the general role of the Church as the main institutional provider of medical, education, and other welfare services for most of the countryside. More-over, throughout this century private single citizens and church leaders have historically played a far greater role than the state in the spread of biomedicine.

Planning for health: the rural health delivery system

By the 1970s, however, the expansion of biomedicine in rural Haiti was no longer a matter of private initiative. It had become intimately linked to the work of international development agencies – secular, church-related, multilateral, bilateral, governmental, and non-governmental. Medical personnel participated at the very start of international develop-ment work in Haiti: the 1949 UNESCO project in the Marbial Valley, near Jacmel (which was one of the earliest experiments in post-colonial planned development). Foreign aid for health development projects increased in the 1950s and 1960s from international sources (the World Health Organization) as well as American or American-dominated agencies (especially the United States Agency for International Develop-ment [USAID]). Various embassies began to sponsor their own health projects, and the increasing number of missionaries also built hospitals and clinics throughout the country. Haiti is now a "country of projects" (Graham Greene's phrase) where virtually every scheme for rural development and public health proposed by international experts in the past thirty years has been implanted, monitored, and evaluated (Maguire 1984; see also Plummer 1992 and Trouillot 1990).

Jeanty was the site for one such project, the Rural Health Delivery System (RHDS) – an internationally funded rural primary health program – which took control of the dispensary and reconstituted its personnel, its clinical services, and its overall value in the community. Throughout this century, the practice of biomedicine has been shaped by the gradual inclusion of Jeanty into regional, national, and international systems of power, and the blueprints for the RHDS project certainly fit this trend. However, the ultimate shape of biomedical services illustrates something quite different from the relentless expansion of medical authority or increased dependency on foreign capital. The following case-study instead shows how particular individuals became (witting or unwitting) agents of metropolitan biomedicine, and how they resisted, circumvented, or appropriated the material and symbolic resources which flowed through the dispensary into this rural community.

The Rural Health Delivery System was a nationwide project, lasting officially from 1980 until 1985, which involved virtually the entire Haitian *Département de la Santé Publique et Population* (Department of Public Health and Population, or DSPP). The project depended on the technical and financial resources of the United States Agency for International Development, and it was an ambitious example of planned development in a liberal and post-imperialist vein (cf. Robertson 1984). It explicitly advanced preventive care in rural areas and involved Americans not as an occupying army but as a cadre of economic and managerial advisors.

When Jean-Claude Duvalier succeeded to the presidency of Haiti in 1971, he temporarily relaxed the repressive state apparatus erected during his father's regime. The younger Duvalier's administration also actively sought foreign aid, and it tolerated calls for modernization and infrastructural development (Nicholls 1979:240). These changes were soon felt in the health field. In a 1975 study, the Pan American Health Organization (PAHO) recommended decentralizing the DSPP bureaucracy, and in the same year, the DSPP began a long period of close collaboration with American donor agencies. For the following decade, the United States would supply approximately one-third of Haiti's development budget in health; the Rural Health Delivery System was the centerpiece of this multilateral health development effort (Rohde 1986).[1]

In the words of its American director, the RHDS project was a classic example of infrastructure development, in which project personnel (USAID staff and consultants, and Haitian technocrats and physicians) introduced North American administrative and management tools to the weak and "underdeveloped" DSPP bureaucracy (Rohde 1986:149). However, these individuals transferred more than money and managerial techniques. They also communicated emergent trends in international health to the state health care bureaucracy, and then supervised the translation of health policy into particular programs. For example, the project envisioned a network of rural dispensaries staffed by trained health workers and specializing in preventive services. This plan embodied the preference for accessible and affordable primary health care outlined at the WHO conference at Alma Ata (World Health Organization 1978). Known as comprehensive primary health care

(CPHC), this became one of the dominant paradigms for public health projects in the 1980s.

A 1982 planning document targeted three specific child health problems (diarrheal disease, infectious diseases, and malnutrition) (Département de la Santé Publique et Population n.d.). These were also the focus of many other contemporary international health development schemes, and they reflect the concurrent development of several effective low-cost interventions (i.e., oral rehydration solution and easily administered immunizations) (see Halstead et al. 1985). They also issue from the major strategy in international health which competed with CPHC for monies and professional favor: selective primary health care (or SPCH), in which scarce resources are dedicated to control the specific diseases causing the highest morbidity and mortality (Walsh and Warren 1979).

Finally, the RHDS project implicitly advocated a new role for the state health bureaucracy. The DSPP had long been a source of political patronage for well-connected residents of the capital city. (Many stories circulate of DSPP workers with extremely few actual responsibilities and of imaginary names added to the payrolls of state-funded hospitals whose salaries are pocketed by DSPP bureaucrats.) Urban-based curative services had much higher cachet than preventive care in rural areas, both in the pronouncements of the Ministry of Health and in its actual spending priorities (Rohde 1986). The RHDS project advocated just the opposite approach: building rural clinics and extending the administrative and technical reach of the DSPP into villages. In keeping with the liberal reformism of contemporary international development and the specific policies of comprehensive and selective primary health care, the RHDS rhetoric emphasized the equitable distribution of resources and more cost-effective preventive interventions.

Deference, authority, and biomedicine

The RHDS project linked activities in the Jeanty dispensary to decisions made by health planners in both Port-au-Prince and Washington DC. This linkage, however, means different things for the architects of the project and the intended "recipients" of aid. According to the planners who conceived of it, the project transferred managerial and medical resources from the developed world to isolated rural communities. It accomplished this by placing the village dispensary under the administrative control of the national health bureaucracy, and, in turn, American-based aid agencies. In narrating the history of the project, residents of Jeanty rarely criticize these relations of dependency which weakened the village *vis-à-vis* the state. More often, they describe the way a few local villagers gained control of the new RHDS-introduced resources and thereby advanced their own prestige or material well-being. Moreover, daily social life in the dispensary was produced not by formal plans from above but rather by the practices of deference to authority characteristic of other dominant village institutions. Only by interweaving these interpretations can we explain how the RHDS program reconstructed biomedical services in Jeanty.

The project was yet another step in the historical insertion of Jeanty into systems of regional or global control. The process began in 1912 with the appointment to Jeanty of the first resident parish priest from France who obtained medications through the Catholic church and distributed them to villagers. It continued with the post-war inclusion of Jeanty into the regional system of agricultural markets, which brought vendors of pharmaceutical products directly into the village. The RHDS project represents the most recent stage in this process, although it is historically novel in several respects. First of all, it linked Jeanty and larger urban centers as part of a formal bureaucratic plan encompassing the entire nation. The Jeanty dispensary was inserted into the hierarchy as a bureaucratically defined unit equal to all others at the same level; the project officially fixed it in one of three *districts sanitaires* comprising the southern *région sanitaire*, one of four such regions in Haiti (Bisaillon 1988).

Operating in a rationalized and featureless national space, the DSPP could not calibrate its programs to unique local needs or conditions, and it could not maintain firm control over the resources it introduced. Moreover, the supra-local system which controls the Jeanty dispensary is a state bureaucracy, and rural Haitians have absolutely no expectation of benefits or services from the state (cf. Nicholls 1984). Incorporating the Jeanty "health district" into a national hierarchy, therefore, did not guarantee more biomedical services to its residents. To the contrary, it actually opened the way for well-positioned and ambitious villagers to appropriate the symbolic and material resources which flowed into the village through the state-owned dispensary.

This is the context for the formal guidelines for dispensary services mandated by the national DSPP hierarchy. The RHDS project determined the make-up of the medical staff (a resident nurse, two nurse auxiliaries, a visiting physician, and four community health workers). The clinical schedule also conforms to the priorities laid out in RHDS documents. Pediatric and pre-natal clinics are each offered once a week, and walk-in clinics for first aid and referrals are held on the other three days.[2] The pervasive bureaucratic organization of clinical work is largely the result of RHDS reforms. The dispensary staff follows a standard set of administrative procedures for every villager who requests care. For example, each woman attending the pediatric clinics is processed through the same routine: retrieving her child's growth chart/immunization record, writing the required immunization on the mother's appointment card, weighing and immunizing the child, and entering the new injections on the chart.

All of the printed forms used in these routines are provided by the DSPP, and they clearly define the necessary and sufficient steps in patient care. The dispensary staff actually relies on this paperwork in order to process a large number of anonymous patients through the mandated clinical procedures. By furnishing minimal criteria, the forms facilitate clinical work, given insufficient personnel and scant material resources. The forms also enforce the social control of the centralized DSPP bureaucracy over this peripheral clinic, since the staff's salary depends on the timely submission of monthly reports to the regional DSPP office. Moreover, reliance on these forms significantly shapes the social interaction between villagers and the nurse and auxiliaries. The most sustained contact between them (and often the only contact) occurs when members of the dispensary staff ask for information required by DSPP forms. However, most patients are largely illiterate, and they rarely understand either the meaning of or the need for the forms. Owing to these omnipresent bureaucratic procedures, actual medical transactions at the dispensary remain opaque to most villagers.

However, dispensary life in Jeanty has not been wholly medicalized. Undoubtedly, the RHDS project laid down a template for biomedical services which satisfies the administrative needs of the DSPP in Port-au-Prince, but which seems entirely foreign to the texture of local social life. Both patients and nurses seem to acquiesce to the same authoritarian and impersonal relations between provider and patient that accompany biomedicine most places in the world. Nonetheless, dispensary personnel and patients have assimilated interactions in the clinic to the specific codes of behavior appropriate to other arenas of village life. "Code" here means neither a formal symbolic structure nor a reified script, but rather the mutual expectations and taken-for-granted rules which pattern unfolding activities in a predictable way. In particular, the local code of deference which tacitly guides acceptable behavior in several other public settings structures social life in the Jeanty dispensary as much as the bureaucratic procedures imposed from above.

Villagers do not expect dispensary personnel to treat them as equals. They conform to the endless bureaucratic procedures with only rare complaint. They routinely defer to the staff's medical judgments, and they offer little resistance to the embarrassing public criticism which staff employ to instruct other villagers in hygiene and nutrition. But their deference is not produced by a foreign code which has replaced local rules of behavior. To the contrary, people have assimilated the dispensary, as a bounded social arena, to several other hierarchical institutions in Jeanty, in particular the schools and the civil court, where villagers petition representatives of dominant national institutions for needed services.[3]

The nurse and auxiliaries depend on this code of deference to make their work flow more smoothly. These women exert nearly exclusive control over their rate of work. Unless they have come simply to purchase medications, patients usually sit on the benches waiting for one of the dispensary staff to notice them. Most people do not come prepared with a story of their illness to tell to the dispensary staff, but instead expect the staff to take the initiative and give them a physical exam and prescription for medication.

The nursing staff sometimes relentlessly criticize patients in the waiting room, and their tactics best exemplify the code of deference. This public teasing and shaming is silently borne by the patient who is used as instructional example for the others. During the pediatric clinic, for example, one of the auxiliaries approached a sickly girl sitting with her mother. When she lifted up the child's straw hat to reveal her hair, red and thinning from malnutrition, she exclaimed, "Look at that, she's malnourished! You don't have to give her medicine, just give her good food, food that nourishes her body: vegetables, juice, carrots." Both auxiliaries then delivered a vehement and even angry explanation about the importance of good nutrition that lasted at least ten minutes. The woman was acutely uncomfortable and weakly offered a few inaudible words in her defense as the rest of the waiting room looked on.

Another striking instance of public shaming took place in the waiting room during the pre-natal clinic. An auxiliary was filling out the Pre-natal Chart for a young woman wearing a new fashionable pink dress with matching hat. The nurse walked out of her office and immediately began to tease her in front of the other expectant mothers: "Oh, you're looking pretty stylish today. This isn't how a pregnant woman should dress, with such a tight belt; your baby can't even breathe!" The woman smiled in embarrassment and the nurse turned to a younger woman wearing a tight turquoise dress. She continued her lesson: "Why are *you* wearing this dress? You don't want people to think you're pregnant? How old are you, anyway? Fifteen years?" The young woman gazed downward and muttered, "I'm seventeen." The nurse turned on her heels to face the two auxiliaries and said in a loud voice, "Oh, look at the child who's already having children of her own!"

Why do people accept this teasing with at most an embarrassed glance at other patients? The aggressive verbal give and take of the marketplace is absent here in the waiting room. These women are following a well-known code of deference already enforced by the other institutions where villagers interact with the local representatives of supra-local bureaucracies. For example, in both schools and the dispensary, villagers do not contest the superior knowledge of those who instruct them. The pedagogy employed in the local elementary and secondary schools – whether affiliated with churches or the state – treats students as passive recipients of knowledge. Most subjects are taught by rote, and until the early 1980s, the schools utilized French as the language of instruction, although no child raised in Jeanty can speak or understand French very well. They therefore spend hours after school repeating their lessons out loud, as they attempt to memorize them with little comprehension. In the dispensary, of course, everybody speaks Creole. But patients pay the same unquestioning respect to the dispensary staff as they do to teachers, and they rarely challenge even the harshest criticisms about their appearance, their children's health, the foods they eat, etc.

Social relations in the dispensary also replicate the deference and respect for hierarchy typical of the Jeanty Tribunal (civil court). In both settings, villagers appear as petitioners who address their request to experts whose cultural authority and social power remain largely unquestioned. The Tribunal, staffed by a Justice of the Peace and his assistant (both high-status villagers), features a large public waiting room where most individual cases are heard. As in the dispensary, villagers wait patiently until the judge calls their name and hears their complaint or request. Dispositions are usually rendered on the spot and in public: like the majority of medical interventions, the settlement of legal disputes is afforded little privacy. The final decisions rendered by the judge, like the moralizing public health lessons delivered by the nurses, are not open for debate, and in both cases the authorized experts retain uncontested control over the pace of work.

This perduring code of deference shows how little the RHDS project reshaped the social context for formal biomedical services in Jeanty. Bio-medicine did not arrive here like a juggernaut, imposing an essentially foreign code of patient–practitioner interactions on those who seek care. People have constructed the social relations in the dispensary according to the same codes of behavior appropriate to the schools and in civil court. Undoubtedly, the pervasive bureaucratic procedures, the particular range of clinical services, and the medicines for sale originate from beyond the village (in Port-au-Prince, North America, and Europe). Yet despite its origins, clinic-based biomedicine has not remained a foreign presence; it is no more hegemonic or intimidating to villagers than their own schools and courts. It is probably no *less* hegemonic or intimidating, but that is precisely the point: people regard the dispensary as yet another site where local representatives of powerful outside forces provide valued resources and techniques for ordering life.

In the dispensary, as in school classrooms and the civil court, residents of Jeanty enter at the bottom of a national hierarchy whose rewards and legitimacy come from far outside the village itself. To gain the rewards offered in these settings (such as certification to advance to a secondary or trade school in Les Cayes), villagers must defer to codes of behavior they enforce (such as accepting the teachers' authority and speaking only French). Patients submit to the interminable bureaucratized procedures and public shaming with similar motivations and expectations. They thus reproduce the social relations typically found in the interface between formal national institutions and members of the rural or urban poor in Haiti: social relations that are formal, authoritarian, and partially inscrutable to the petitioners from below.

However, people have done more than reconstruct dispensary life according to wider codes of behavior governing the interface between local residents and hierarchical institutions. Particular villagers have actively incorporated the resources of the dispensary into their ongoing strategies for prestige or personal profit. Their maneuvers explain the major failure of the RHDS project: the demise of the dispensary-based "community pharmacy."

The community pharmacy was specified in RHDS plans as a locally owned low-cost source of medicines for dispensary patients. However, both residents of Jeanty and development workers knowledgeable with the project claim that the pharmacy has failed. Particular individuals gradually took control of it for their personal profit, and assimilated it to the circuits of exchange which have diffused biomedicines in rural Haiti since the 1940s. The community pharmacy now operates as just another commercial source of medical commodities controlled by local entrepreneurs; it has met neither the RHDS goals nor the needs of Jeanty residents. But its failure is instructive, for it offers a fine-grained study of the diffusion of biomedicine in Jeanty, in particular the way people's short-term strategies for wealth and prestige transformed the formal plans for health development.

The history of the community pharmacy begins soon after the dispensary was built in the mid-1970s (ten years before the arrival of the RHDS project). A number of wealthy and politically prominent villagers had become active members of the *Groupement Communautaire* ("Community Group"), a local improvement association begun by the Catholic church. Alarmed by the lack of medications at the newly built dispensary, they formed a "cooperative pharmacy," an organization of about fifty members, each of whom contributed 5 dollars towards the purchase of medications in bulk at Port-au-Prince. With this initial investment, they created a stock of inexpensive and widely used drugs at the dispensary, which they hoped would be continually replenished through sales to patients.

According to the *Groupement*'s former president, the "cooperative pharmacy" was quickly well stocked with aspirin and other analgesics, anti-helminth drugs, vitamins, oral rehydration solution, and various cough and cold medications. He claims that this selection of drugs, while not as wide as at a large city pharmacy, was perfectly adequate for Jeanty. Moreover, Père Joseph occasionally donated gifts of medications received from France for free distribution: usually included a random assortment of medications (most past their expiration date) and supplies such as syringes, gauze, and intravenous equipment. The cooperative pharmacy sold drugs according to individuals' ability to pay; not by actually reducing the price, but by allowing individuals to purchase smaller amounts, such as 40 cents worth of a bottle of medication costing three dollars, instead of the entire prescribed regime. The cooperative pharmacy (like many other aspects of biomedicine throughout the history of Jeanty) thus had several diffuse ties to the Catholic church. It was begun by the *Groupement Communautaire*, a Church-related organization, operated out of the dispensary, built with Catholic funds, and it occasionally received donations from the local priest.

The RHDS project soon advanced its own scheme for the distribution of medicines which eventually displaced the cooperative pharmacy already operating in Jeanty. Known as AGAPCO (an acronym for *Agence d'Approvisionnement des Pharmacies Communautaires*), this program established "community pharmacies" physically located in (but independent from) village dispensaries. In the AGAPCO plan, each pharmacy would be owned and managed by a committee of local residents. The DSPP furnished them with essential drugs through its own supply system. Each community pharmacy thus received an initial lump sum of RHDS money and purchased drugs according to an approved list from DSPP warehouses. As in the pre-existing "cooperative pharmacy" in Jeanty, the revenues from drug sales were supposed to purchase replacement stocks.

The problems with this plan soon became apparent in rural villages throughout the country. Money "disappeared," inventory was not renewed, profits were squandered, the prices paid by villagers gradually rose, and pharmacy managers had only a meager clinical understanding of the medications they sold. In response, health planners attempted to fine-tune the AGAPCO plan, as reported in numerous project documents (Rohde 1986; Bates *et al.* 1985; Bisaillon 1988). In Jeanty, however, people were dissatisfied from the very start, and they saw no improvement over the years. In their eyes, the state had simply taken over a thriving local institution and absconded with the profits meant for the community.

In early 1988, a group of young men in Jeanty described this takeover in blunt terms: "The state seized it. It was as if you had a business in your house, the state came in and substituted its own business for the one you had. That's how it happened around 1984 when the pharmacy was given to the state." Their attitude, shared by many other residents, fits squarely with peasants' long-standing suspicion of the Haitian state. This was the typical result of state intervention in local affairs: "That's why it doesn't have any medications now. It is up to the state to send medications, and they can just as well send some one year and then forget about it for two. Back then [before 1984] there were many more medications than now. Nowadays, the dispensary is just good for weighing babies, giving shots, things like that."

The bitter response of Jeanty residents belies the technical rhetoric of project documents, which glowingly describe the AGAPCO program as the introduction of a new pharmaceutical distribution system and the extension of urban-based medical services into underserved regions. However, neither the angry local critique nor the dry, neutral language of health planners fully explain the transformation of the AGAPCO program once it was implanted in Jeanty. What accounts for the scarcity of medications and the high prices paid by patients? The meager achievements of the AGAPCO community pharmacy in Jeanty reflect not theft by the state, but rather the efforts of several entrepreneurial residents to take control of this state-sponsored institution and work it to their own advantage. A handful of people have transformed the community pharmacy into a thriving private business actually outside the control of the DSPP hierarchy.

If dispensary patients do not benefit from the sale of medicines in the AGAPCO pharmacy, then who does? Villagers receive prescriptions as part of most general consultations.[4] The drugs themselves, however, come from two separate sources: the community pharmacy and a separate cache controlled by the resident nurse. The nurse usually receives certain medicines free of charge from the DSPP (which, in turn, received them as gifts from various international agencies). The nurse charges a token amount or nothing at all for these medications, depending on what she thinks the patient can afford and the medical importance of the drug for a particular patient. She devotes any profit from these sales to dispensary upkeep – buying alcohol, paint, soap, etc.

In contrast, villagers must always pay for drugs from the community pharmacy. Its director, Michelle Rosier, orders the drugs, sells them to patients, and maintains sole control over the use of profits. When Michelle is not in the dispensary, therefore, patients requesting drugs from the community pharmacy are told to go to her house, where she also keeps a small stock. Michelle also sets the prices for medications, and she almost never compromises. Even in Michelle's absence, the dispensary nurses have no authority to lower the price. Although the nurses do not publicly challenge Michelle's control, they freely criticize her in private. Interviewed in her home, one auxiliary nurse named Yves-Rose Gilbert states that the AGAPCO committee skims off the profits generated by the sale of drugs. Consequently, the fund is now in deficit, *and* there are far fewer medicines. Lucie Nemours, the resident nurse, ruefully observes, "It's called a community pharmacy, but I don't know how the community benefits." Nemours carefully distances herself from the pharmacy's operation, and she recalls being shocked and angry at the inadequate medication she found upon her arrival in Jeanty for her year-long rural residency. People voiced these criticisms with an air of disgust, and in light of the many problems with the "community pharmacy" reported from other Haitian communities (cf. Bisaillon 1988), their accounts of corruption in Jeanty are probably accurate.

Both the local nursing staff and international health planners trace this corruption to problems with the RHDS project itself. Thus, Yves-Rose Gilbert faults the AGAPCO-imposed "pharmacy committee." Although comprised entirely of villagers (in accordance with the RHDS blueprint), Michelle and the other committee members had no history of supporting either the dispensary or the prior cooperative pharmacy, and Michelle herself has no more than one month of cursory training. From its founding in 1984 until the period of fieldwork, the rest of the pharmacy committee contributed nothing to the management or financing of the dispensary. In an unpublished evaluation, an international consultant essentially agrees with Nurse Gilbert. Bisaillon (1988:5) lists several reasons for the failure of community pharmacies, including poor training of personnel about medications and embezzlement of funds caused by the absence of adequate DSPP supervision.

Gilbert (who has lived in Jeanty most of her adult life) blames the failure of AGAPCO on irresponsible and self-serving local residents, who followed the letter but not the spirit of the RHDS project. Bisaillon (a

6 Houses near the village center are usually more substantial than in the hills. This house is owned by a former Jeanty resident, now living in the USA, who rents it to two local families.

Canadian professor of pharmacy) blames the problems on a lack of adequate bureaucratic supervision. Their explanations arise from opposite poles of the international health enterprise in the late twentieth century: a rural villager at the lowest rung of the national ministry of health and a member of the exclusive cadre of international health consultants. Nonetheless, they both portray the failure of AGAPCO by the distance between the stated goals of the pharmacy (contained or implied in RHDS documents) and its operation on the ground. The problem, for both village nurse and international consultant, is the gap between planning and performance (cf. Justice 1986; Black 1991).

But most residents of Jeanty who use the dispensary do not consider the community pharmacy as an example of failed public health planning. People interact with Michelle just as they do with the itinerant pill-sellers, market women, and local shopkeepers who also sell proprietary medications. An ethnography of the circulation of pharmaceutical commodities throughout Jeanty suggests that "community pharmacy" now resembles yet another local venue for the sale of metropolitan biomedicines. Seen in this light, the "community pharmacy" represents neither the corruption of well-wrought plans for comprehensive primary health care nor the perversion of a public health ideal, but rather one of the many institutional routes for the diffusion of biomedicine in this rural area.

The itinerant pill-sellers who follow the circuit of agricultural markets are probably the most colorful of all vendors of biomedical products. During the twice-weekly market days in Jeanty, Joseph Jocelyn and his assistant hawk their wares while strolling among the crowded stalls. Joseph usually prefers dark glasses and an urban businessman's hat, which set him off as more sophisticated than most of the peasants he deals with. He keeps his medications in small vinyl suitcases at his side, and he also has two large glass jars slung over his shoulder and full of bright yellow-red and red-black antibiotic pills. In addition to this visual advertisement, he harangues the crowd with a small megaphone: "Buy Cafénol! Buy Valadon![5] It's good for all kinds of pain: in your knees, your arms, your stomach! Buy Tetracycline!"

Joseph can recite from memory virtually all of the medications he sells, and he easily lists the range of bodily complaints each one can treat.[6] However, most people who buy pills from him have already decided what they need and say no more during the purchase than "You have any Saridon? How much?" Joseph usually sells the pills individually and at reasonable prices: 5 cents for a single Cafénol or Tetracycline tablet (he also extends credit). He purchases most of his stock in bulk at pharmacies in Port-au-Prince or Les Cayes, paying, for example, 20 dollars for 1000 tetracycline capsules. This is his sole income, and he has practiced the trade for two years after having learned it as an apprentice under an established vendor in Port-au-Prince.

Villagers can also purchase the same proprietary medications from other vendors. Some market women sell such medicines along with small packaged foods, cigarettes, and matches. These women sit by their large decorated wooden boxes at the weekly markets and at church during Sunday Mass. The usual selection consists of tablets of Cafénol, Valadon, and Dolostop. Individually wrapped in brightly colored metal foil or plastic, they are easy to miss among the candies, cookies, and balloons for children. The five general merchandise stores, clustered near the market, also stock a slightly larger selection of medications. They sell not only the familiar caffeine and aspirin-based analgesics, but also antacids and anti-worm medication, usually in powder form. Unlike the itinerant pill-sellers, these market women and shopkeepers probably derive only a small portion of their income from the sale of pharmaceutical commodities.

As it currently operates, the AGAPCO dispensary pharmacy resembles not the product of formal development plans, but rather a sophisticated (and more profitable) version of these other village enterprises. In each case, the medications originate from outside Jeanty. Selling them to villagers represents the final step in a long series of transactions beginning with the manufacture of the substance (for the vitamin syrups, in Port-au-Prince, and for the others, in pharmaceutical plants throughout Latin America and the United States), continuing with its sale to large urban pharmacies and, finally, to the merchants who transport them to Jeanty. The community pharmacy thus relies on the same distribution system as the pill-sellers, market women, and small local shopkeepers.[7] The community pharmacy simply benefits from a certain economy of scale because the DSPP manages the original procurement and transport of medicines to Jeanty.[8]

The pharmacy, therefore, is not the chief purveyor of commoditized medical products in rural Haiti. It is not solely responsible for the disenchantment of healing relations which, according to some, occurs when the marketplace logic of buying and selling overtakes the multi-layered social relations of non-biomedical therapies (cf. Whyte and Van der Geest 1988). For buyers and sellers outside the pharmacy, medicines are already commodities: secular and disenchanted objects which dissolve long-standing local social ties and create exchange relationships based on anomic self-interest (see Taussig 1980:26; Brodwin 1992a). Even the technical efficacy of medicines is not particularly at issue in the exchanges at the community pharmacy and the marketplace. The vendors rarely know more than their customers about the medical effects of their product. Moreover, the transaction over medicines in each of these settings is anonymous. Most villagers do not personally know the vendor who sells drugs to them. The actual purchase is accomplished quickly and with little conversation, and ends with the individual paying for the product on the spot and then leaving to ingest or apply it elsewhere. This anonymity is the hallmark of the commoditization of pharmaceutical substances. Social relations between villagers and the vendor are primarily commercial; the personal quality of this relationship, in particular what buyers may think of the vendor's knowledge and expertise, hardly affects their interaction at all.

The differences which do exist between the community pharmacy and the other vendors of biomedicines primarily make the pharmacy more profitable, rather than separate it categorically from these other settings. For example, Michelle has a guaranteed market. Because of its location within the dispensary and its origin as a component of the RHDS program, the community pharmacy fills many of the prescriptions written by the clinical staff. Michelle need only wait in the dispensary (or at home) and customers will come to her, whereas Joseph Jocelyn must advertise and search out customers in the crowded market. Compared to other points of sale for biomedicines, the community pharmacy simply has greater capital, an advantageous location, and a director who knows the medications most often prescribed by the dispensary staff.

The underdevelopment of health

The situation in Jeanty is just a snapshot of the appalling maldistribution of medical resources throughout Haiti. Local residents know firsthand that they must go outside the village even for such basic services as blood and urine analyses. For most people, more advanced medical care requires several days of transportation and waiting for appointments, and it is prohibitively expensive. The state-assigned resident physician almost never appears at the Jeanty dispensary, and months may pass between the departure of one resident nurse and the arrival of the next. In some ways, the RHDS project has mitigated this maldistribution (through its well-attended maternal and child health clinics, for example, and the preventative care offered by CHWs), but in other ways it has worsened it. The AGAPCO program subverted a well-functioning pharmacy with deep ties to the local Catholic church, and this meant that far fewer drugs were available at prices that clients could afford.

What has happened to biomedicine in Jeanty shows that the under-development of health is also a local affair, and not just the dubious achievement of foreign imperialists, the national bourgeoisie, or misguided health planners. For the Haitian state (in particular, the Department of Public Health and Population), the RHDS project deepened its global position as a recipient of foreign aid, and especially as a dependent partner in development projects sponsored by the United States. The DSPP thus began with a strong rhetorical and financial commitment to rural primary care, but then neglected the project as it actually unfolded in Jeanty. The state's effect on rural health develop-ment in Haiti thus differs dramatically from the situation in other Latin American countries (cf. Morgan 1989). In Haiti, the state has *not* taken control of this rural health program in order to increase its domination of marginal groups or ward off potential threats to its legitimacy. Indeed, the state proceeded in just the opposite direction. Consistent with the centralization of political and economic power in Port-au-Prince, the state established routine forms of bureaucratic control in Jeanty, but then essentially withdrew from the field and left the ultimate shape of RHDS programs to the play of informal long-standing local interests.

What happened to the RHDS project in Jeanty is not reducible to either the hegemony of capitalist biomedicine or a remediable gap between planning and performance. It is impossible to parse what happens in the dispensary into discrete "foreign" and "indigenous" elements, and excoriate one or the other set. As the pharmacy came under the control of several entrepreneurial local residents, it lost many of its distinguishing features as a creation of national (and international) planning agencies. It now resembles yet another vendor in the informal commercial market for biomedicines in rural Haiti, but that market itself is the local node of an international system of commodity exchange. Jeanty residents have "localized" dispensary life according to the code of formal deference appropriate to other settings where they petition the representatives of national institutions who are themselves seeking to extend their power and legitimacy. The fate of the RHDS project in Jeanty emerged from precisely this dialectic between people's practical maneuvers for short-term gain and the constraining power of national institutions.

To trace the diffusion of metropolitan medicine requires abandoning a picture of Jeanty as a formerly bounded and self-reproducing micro-society that is currently penetrated by outside forces: biomedical, pedagogical, political, or commercial. To the contrary, Jeanty – like most rural communities in Haiti and the Caribbean as a whole – is a historical product of such outside forces. Any given arena of village life will show the stamp of supra-local institutions and ideologies. Biomedical services in the dispensary have thus been localized in terms of the other institutions – in particular, the schools and courts – which link Jeanty to the nation state and beyond. But it is the strategies and practices of particular individuals which animate these institutions and, as the next chapter shows, generate the moral meanings of biomedical power.

4 Medicalization and illness experience: two case-studies

Medical ideology in Jeanty

The diffusion of biomedicine in Jeanty has created not only new routes to material advance, but also new ways to think about the body and new treatments for disease. The everyday talk about illness is filled with references to microbes and infections, X-rays and injections. When people discuss cases of AIDS (*sida*) or tuberculosis (*tibèkiloz*), they do not regard these biomedical terms as puzzling foreign concepts which demand a cultural translation. No one questions a family's decision to spend enormous sums at local mission hospitals or to consult private physicians in Les Cayes and Port-au-Prince. However, the easy acceptance of biomedicine – illustrated in detail by the case-studies in this chapter – raises some troubling questions. Has the adoption of biomedical disease categories subverted the moral meanings of suffering? Has it deflected the possibility of political critique inherent in bodily disorder? Has biomedicine diminished the power and legitimacy of other healing forms? In other words, has biomedicine "medicalized" the concepts of affliction and healing practices in Jeanty?

The recent explosion of anthropological interest in medicalization grows from the basic constructionist insight that medical realities are social products and social accomplishments (see Conrad and Schneider 1992). While claiming simply to reflect objective facts of biology, biomedical discourses are in fact culturally constructed and historically contingent. Through the powerful philosophical doctrines of naturalism and individualism, biomedicine successfully hides its cultural scaffolding and political interests (Gordon 1988). However, medicalization is more than just an intellectual project. It advances several schemes of social control: the expansion of imperial or colonial rule (Vaughan 1991; Comaroff 1994), the bureaucratic regulation of marginal or "dangerous" populations (Foucault 1975; Rhodes 1991), and the reconstruction of everyday categories of suffering and bodily distress in order to hide the social origins of suffering (e.g., Lock 1986, 1988; Scheper-Hughes 1992a and b; Taussig 1992).

Studies of the "desocialization" of suffering, in particular, have criticized biomedicine for its tendency to reify sickness. Because biomedicine reconstructs disease as a neutral, autonomous biological reality, it prevents people from interpreting bodily disorder in terms of the lived world of everyday experience, including local forms of inequality and oppression. According to these authors, the reductionist and technocratic language of disease severs any connection people might make between disorder in the body/self and in the body politic. As human suffering is reified into disease entities, the social relations usually embodied in symptoms, signs, and therapies drop out of awareness (Taussig 1992:84). A recent case from northeastern Brazil exemplifies this process. Clinical biomedicine has reified pre-existing folk syndromes which had formerly traced the symptoms of irritability or madness to the underlying cause of hunger. Through reification, the profoundly social problem of hunger is isolated, denied, and replaced by a medicalized discourse on nervousness. Starvation and its effects on the body are seen not as a complicated political and social crisis, but as an individual disorder, a chronic feebleness which people self-treat with drugs or vitamins (Scheper-Hughes 1992a and b).

The case-studies of illness in this chapter show the microlevel negotiations, compromises, and coercions through which sufferers and their kin confront a new biomedical definition of their problem. As Scheper-Hughes notes, medicalizaton is a subtle process, but in Jeanty it does not always go in one direction, and people often accept biomedicine for reasons beyond its authority or technical efficacy. Residents of Jeanty draw freely on biomedical symbols and therapies without accepting its naturalistic ideology (the materialist, secular notion that removes illness from the realm of misfortune, social relations, or moral concerns; see Starr 1982:35–36). The mechanistic conception of disease within biomedicine does not supplant local constructions of the body and the moral meanings of suffering. The following illness narratives expose people's short-term practical motives for accepting a biomedical diagnosis and treatment; the result is a dialectical account of medicalization more in keeping with the indeterminate and shifting healing arrangements in Jeanty.

These cases describe a young woman diagnosed with eclampsia (a toxemia of pregnancy) and a man paralyzed from a motorcycle accident who was treated at several hospitals before returning home to Jeanty. The families and friends of these patients initially accepted the biomedical definition of the disorders, but then recast them in terms of local somatic and religious discourses. They constructed eclampsia as a disorder in the quality of blood – a reading which links interpersonal conflict and emotional shock to a wide array of physical symptoms and alterations in consciousness. They interpreted the paralysis as a sickness sent upon the patient by unknown enemies, perhaps through the agency of spirits of the dead. These constructions of the illnesses were not dislodged by the families' eager acceptance of biomedical treatment. This chapter shows why the discourse on blood and emotions was so appropriate for eclampsia, and how it encompassed the new biomedical term. It then describes how the discourse on sent sicknesses not only coexisted with biomedical treatment, but actually depended on it: the failure of medical practitioners to cure him was the best evidence that his affliction was due to other people's malign intentions.

Illness and the politics of (transnational) kinship

In 1988, Janine Dutoit was a 19-year-old woman living with her mother, her mother's four-month-old son, and two other male kinsmen in a relatively large but sparsely furnished home, about a ten-minute walk from the center of Jeanty. Janine attended the pre-natal clinics at the dispensary throughout her first pregnancy, which proceeded without apparent problem until the Friday night when she went into labor. Soon after the start of her contractions, she felt pains in her lower back; she began to suffer convulsions and she then lost consciousness. The woman Janine's family had chosen to attend the delivery called in a second midwife who immediately labelled Janine's condition as *eklampsi* (a Creolized version of the French biomedical term *éclampsie*) and insisted that her family take her to the state hospital in Les Cayes. Janine delivered her child and remained hospitalized for one week, although she cannot remember anything from this period. When she returned home with her baby, she continued to receive various types of herbal and biomedical treatments from her mother, midwives, other village practitioners, and the dispensary personnel.

Janine recounted her painful bodily symptoms and the social group which hurriedly mobilized around her at the start of the illness:

On Friday evening, I felt sick below my stomach, near my lower back.[1] They left to find a midwife. She said that it was just the labor pains for the child I was about to deliver. I began feeling the pain around eight in the evening. Around eleven, I was really beginning to suffer, but I still couldn't deliver the baby.

At midnight, I became *indispose*.[2] When the midwife saw that, well, she's not too skilled, and she said that it was *malkadi* [epilepsy]. At around two in the morning, they called Mme. Beaumont . . . As soon as she arrived, she saw that it was *eklampsi*, so at three o'clock they brought me across the Acul river.

During the *eklampsi*, I was breathing, but that was about all. My teeth were clenched together; I couldn't open my mouth. I was *indispose*: I had no strength left. It took six people to carry me to the Acul. They found a bus waiting there. When I arrived at the bus station in Aux Cayes, they hired another car for 20 dollars to take me to the hospital.

Although Janine describes her illness in strict chronological order, she actually remembers nothing from the time she became *indispose* late Friday night until the following Wednesday afternoon, after she had been in the hospital over four days. In her narrative, she interweaves memories of her own bodily experience with what she was told by the various members of the therapy managing group which gathered around her during this illness.

The classic definition of a therapy managing group is "a community of persons who take responsibility from the sufferer and enter into broker- age relationships with specialists," and it is comprised chiefly of "the family members who piece together the picture of therapeutic progress and decide the next step of action" (Janzen 1978a:7–8; 1987). Although the notion of therapy management is most often invoked in studies of African medical systems (Janzen 1987; Feierman 1985; Ranger 1992; Ngubane 1992), its theoretical ambit is much larger. Tailored to different settings, it suggests how medical knowledge is embedded in local social categories and articulated in particular social relationships (Janzen 1987).

The individuals who negotiated between Janine and the various local healers constituted a shifting and flexible therapy managing group along recognizably Haitian lines. To begin with, the boundary separating healing specialists and "lay" members of this group was blurred from the start. Mme. Beaumont, the midwife consulted by Janine's family at the start of the illness, proceeded to become a member of the group, and in fact determined its next step. She describes the scene upon her arrival at Janine's home:

I wasn't the first midwife. They came to me later. There was someone else who was working with Janine, named Chérie-Luise. This other midwife was palpating Janine's womb, and she said that Janine had *malkadi*. She didn't understand! When you have *malkadi*, you fall, you froth at the mouth.

I arrived at her house around five in the morning. Janine had become *indispose*; she was already stiff (*li vin indispose, li vin pran redi*). She had begun to eat her lips and her mouth was swollen. I asked, How did the sickness begin? I was saying to myself, it's a convulsion (*kriz*). But they told me it was *malkadi*. I told them, No, no, that's not it, that's *eklampsi*. You'll have to take care of that in Cayes.

. . . When you see that she can't swallow, and her mouth is swollen and her teeth are clenched, that makes it *eklampsi* . . . She was stiff. It was a nerve illness (*maladi ner*). The sickness came on her like the nerves.

In these accounts, recorded only a few days after Janine returned home to Jeanty, both she and Mme. Beaumont introduce a number of expressions to describe the illness. The meaning of some of these terms – *indisposition*, *kriz*, and *maladi ner* – are embedded in local understandings of bodily disorder and alterations in consciousness. The other terms – *eklampsi* and *malkadi* – refer directly to specific syndromes which are also diagnosed in biomedicine (eclampsia and epilepsy). *Malkadi* was a familiar disorder to many people in Jeanty, whereas both the word and the disorder *eklampsi* were virtually unknown before Janine's illness. Nonetheless, *eklampsi* was an especially persuasive and apt definition, and most people eventually accepted it as the name for her condition. Their reasons, however, do not fit the scenario of medicalization as desocialization. They have more to do with Janine's struggle for status in her kin group, her palpable experience, and its visible effects in her body.

Mme. Beaumont unequivocally classifies *eklampsi* as beyond the skills of local midwives and requiring immediate biomedical attention. Assigning this label to Janine's disorder justified taking her out of the village and to the state hospital in Les Cayes. Before dawn on Saturday morning, Janine was carried through the village and then across the shallow Acul river. The therapy managing group by then consisted of both midwives and Janine's "cousin," Juliette Dutoit, a woman in her late twenties. These were the people who accompanied Janine on the small van which was making its daily early morning trip from the river bordering Jeanty through several other hamlets in the neighboring parish and finally into Les Cayes. Despite Janine's rapidly worsening condition and Mme. Beaumont's insistence that she be brought immediately to the hospital, no private vehicle was available for the ninety-minute trip.[3]

Janine again provides a straightforward rendering of the unfolding events:

On Saturday morning, I went to the hospital with *eklampsi*. That same Saturday, I gave birth. There was someone else in my room with the same sickness. Both of them, the mother and her child, died. I almost died myself. When I arrived, the nurse and eight auxiliaries immediately looked for a private doctor. When he finally came, he prescribed a medication for 336 gourdes [$67.20]. Juliette bought it in a pharmacy. They gave the medication to me with an IV line (*sewòm*). After that, they did an operation and delivered the child. Beginning here in Jeanty, I was losing blood. When the doctor finished with the operation, I lost even more blood, and at the end, I didn't have a drop of blood left. The doctor prescribed another *sewòm* for 236 gourdes which could give me blood. If they hadn't given me that, I could easily have died when I was finished delivering my baby.

For one week, I was interned in the hospital. The price for everything came to 950 gourdes. The doctor didn't let me eat at all. It was only the *sewòm* [which nourished me]. During these days, I was in a state of *indisposition*. I came to on Wednesday. On Friday afternoon they sent me here [to Jeanty], even though I'm not really well. The sickness isn't over yet.

In her therapeutic narrative (see Early 1982), Janine progressively reveals both the medical procedures she was subjected to (particularly the direct infusion of liquids into her body) and their cost (astronomical sums for an ordinary villager). In fact, these two themes structured most of her own stories about her illness as well as the general discussions of her ordeal among other villagers over the next several days. These themes suggest why *eklampsi* – a totally unfamiliar biomedical diagnosis and literally a foreign word inserted into Creole – was so easily accepted by Janine and her therapy managing group.

Janine carefully recounts the costs of her hospitalization down to the last gourde ($0.20). She could afford this expensive biomedical treatment only because it was paid by Juliette Dutoit, the one member of the therapy managing group who is also kin. Although Janine's own household is quite poor, she is related to one of the wealthiest family groups in Jeanty. She gained access to its resources by invoking the traditional model of the *lakou*: a pattern of kinship, residence, and reciprocal obligations that has long structured social life in rural Haiti. The immediate crisis of her illness allowed Janine to re-animate the obligations between members of the same *lakou* and strengthen her connection to this leading local family, despite her personal poverty and the devastation in rural society caused by massive emigration abroad.

Janine and the rest of her household earn their livelihood in ways similar to most other villagers. The men are independent farmers (*kiltivatè*) who work various plots of land in the hills and along the Acul river. They own some of this land outright, and rent other parcels from wealthier residents of Jeanty (cf. Murray 1980). Janine's mother travels to the regional markets to sell the combined produce from their gardens. Janine ended school at age 16, and until her pregnancy, she helped her mother with child care or at her stall in the marketplace. She has never held any of the few salaried jobs (civil servant, school teacher, or auxiliary nurse) locally available to women.

Despite these meager resources, however, Janine and her household are all members of the Dutoit family. They live in one of the few large

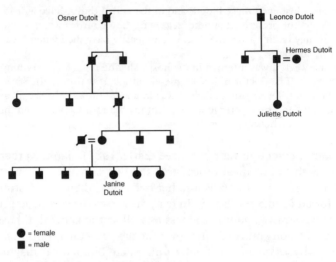

7 Kinship chart for Janine Dutoit

and sturdily private homes in Jeanty, located in the *savann Dutoit* (the Dutoit savannah). The center of the *savann* is a pleasant grassy clearing in the foothills just beyond the village center. A semicircle of six well-kept houses face this small field, and their occupants occasionally enjoy a cool breeze thanks to its slightly higher elevation.[4] An old and rutted road passes through the *savann* on its way from the center of Jeanty to the next parish to the north, and four or five similarly large homes line it on both sides. All of the residents of these houses claim membership in the Dutoit family. The *savann Dutoit* thus spatially unites a large kin group in a way similar to the *lakou*: a compound of huts occupied by an extended family which is the most commonly cited residential pattern in rural Haiti (Métraux 1972:256, Mintz and Price 1992:39; Bastien 1985:43–66).[5]

When Janine casually refers to Juliette as her cousin, she invokes both their relative positions in the extended Dutoit family (see Figure 7) as well as the cultural expectations for the use of family resources in response to illness. Figure 7 summarizes Janine's own explanation of social relations in the *savann Dutoit*. Like most kinship models, the diagram inscribes not objective genealogical space, but rather the interests of particular actors in claiming a certain kind of relationship.[6] In general, residents of rural Haiti establish kinship claims according to a bilateral system. People thus inherit land, partible wealth, and family spirits from both maternal and paternal lines (Murray 1977:312–13).

Family membership is determined, in the first instance, by tracing an agnatic or affinal connection to the founding members of the *lakou*. This general principle remains true despite (1) significant regional differences in the weight assigned to maternal vs. paternal lines (families in Jeanty exhibit a patrilineal bias), and (2) the extreme diversity in actual household composition, which can be male- or female-headed, monogamous or polygynous, and based on legal marriage or a consensual union (*plasaj*) (Lowenthal 1984:16).

Caring for a sick individual is a prime obligation for comembers of a *lakou*. Even non-resident kin (who may have joined another *lakou* after marriage) are expected to come with advice or specific services (Bastien 1985:65). In this light, it is clear that Janine chooses this particular genealogical map in order to demonstrate her ties to the Dutoit family and especially her legitimate reliance on Juliette Dutoit. For the most part, Janine reckons kin through men, in keeping with the traditional model of the coresidential *lakou* drawn by classic ethnographers of village Haiti. Herskovits described the ideal developmental cycle of the *lakou* as beginning with a single male ancestor and his wife, whose sons establish their households in the same hamlet "so that in time a group of immediate families related in the paternal line clusters about the dwelling of this original settler" (1937:123).

With minor modifications, this ideal model is repeated by residents of the *savann Dutoit* as they explain how they are related. The Dutoit group does not have a single ancestral couple, as recorded for Mirebalais (Herskovits 1937) and also the Marbial valley (Bastien 1985:45). Most people trace their ties to the Dutoit family through an original group of seven brothers, two of whom figure in Janine's account (Osner and Leonce). Any of their descendants can claim membership in the family. The boundaries of the Dutoit kin group are flexible and expanding, given the model of bilateral descent generally accepted in rural Haiti (Herskovits 1937:122).[7] However, even by exploiting this flexibility, Janine can claim only a distant relationship to the main Dutoit descent lines. Fortunately, the *lakou* model subordinates genealogical distance to coresidence in the family compound (or *savann*, in this case). Janine is therefore a full member of the Dutoit family, and she benefits from the powerful obligation for members of a family to visit, provide remedies to, and otherwise support a sick kinsperson (see Bastien 1985 and Coreil 1979).

The increasing poverty of rural society has actually strengthened Janine's position as a deserving member of the Dutoit family. Although all those living in the *savann* are Dutoit, not all of the Dutoit kin live in Jeanty, or, indeed, Haiti. The exodus of rural Haitians to provincial capitals, Port-au-Prince, and North America has profoundly affected this family,[8] and Dutoits now live in such centers of the Haitian diaspora as Miami, Brooklyn, Boston, and Montreal (cf. Laguerre 1984; Glick-Schiller and Fouron 1990). Indeed, Juliette – a school teacher and active community leader – is one of the few well-educated, ambitious, and high-achieving Dutoits who remain in Jeanty.

Janine is a poor relation of a wealthy family, but among the Dutoits it is increasingly only the poor relations who continue to live in the countryside (along with some of the elderly who simply do not want to move). Indeed, the youngest of the original seven Dutoit brothers left to settle with his daughter's family in suburban Montreal not long before Janine's illness. In better times, when most of the Dutoit family still resided in Jeanty, Janine would surely have received less money for her hospitalization, because the cash that Juliette used to cover her medical expenses came primarily from overseas remittances.[9] For a family with several members earning North American salaries, a $200 hospital bill is substantial, but not catastrophic.

Moreover, what wealth the family possesses in Jeanty remains relatively liquid. The potential gain from land acquisition and investment in village enterprises is small, given the destruction of the agricultural base and worsening poverty of rural Haiti (cf. Lundahl 1979). Remittance money is used either to support family members still living in the *savann* or to underwrite the costs of securing a visa and immigration papers for those next in line for residence abroad. The family's cash is thus more available for short-term expenses such as Janine's. Finally, even poor relations play an important role for the more prosperous Dutoits living abroad. People like Janine can be counted on to watch over the family's property and financial interests, and to welcome and take care of the relatives when they return to Jeanty for their two-week vacations from jobs in Cambridge, MA or Brooklyn, NY.

Labelling Janine's condition as *eklampsi* justified, indeed demanded, that she be hospitalized in Les Cayes. For Janine, however, the social significance of her hospitalization lies ultimately in the transnational extension of the Dutoit family and her own ambiguous position within it. Janine is a peripheral "cousin" and poor relation who remains in Jeanty, as the family expands and advances chiefly in North American cities. On the one hand, the relocation of the Dutoit family in the North American diaspora has given Janine a newly important role to play back in Haiti (and increased access to greater amounts of cash aid). But as the eldest generation in Haiti dies out, members of the core Dutoit households may effectively abandon the Jeanty branch of *lakou* entirely and leave Janine as bereft of options and resources as most other villagers. Janine's practical interest in accepting the biomedical treatment for *eklampsi* grows from a desire to shore up her tenuous family position. The enormous sums required to cure her *eklampsi* – which she emphasizes in her illness narrative – reanimate and publicly demonstrate her legitimate claim to membership in the *savann Dutoit*.

Blood, eclampsia, and embodied anger

Despite the recognized effectiveness of biomedical treatment, its notable expense, and even the medical origins of the word itself, the sense people made of Janine's *eklampsi* was not dictated by biomedicine. Janine's kin and neighbors instead reworked the meanings of her illness through a sophisticated local discourse linking powerful emotional states, movements of blood, and physical sickness. Their unanimous acceptance of the biomedical term *eklampsi* and their dependence on biomedical power to save Janine's life did not medicalize her condition, and an examination of how people actually deployed this discourse will suggest why.

Mme. Beaumont claimed that Janine suffered from *eklampsi*, not *malkadi*, and that she therefore required immediate hospital treatment. Her position convinced the therapy managing group to embark on this difficult and expensive course. Both of these illness names refer to diagnostic categories used in biomedicine. *Eklampsi* is a creolization of the French word *éclampsie*, which names a severe and sometimes fatal toxemia of pregnancy.[10] The symptoms villagers list as part of *malkadi* – eyes rolling up, frothing at the mouth, and loss of bodily control – indicate epilepsy, although I never heard anyone employ a variant of the French *épilepsie*.[11] Most people interviewed were familiar with *malkadi*: they knew how to protect persons with this disorder against accidental injury from burns or drowning, and they said that it rarely required biomedical treatment. However, the only people who initially knew of *eklampsi* were Mme. Beaumont and the nurse and auxiliaries at the dispensary. Janine herself reported that "it was Mme. Beaumont who said it was *eklampsi*. Before that, I didn't know what *eklampsi* was."

Introduced at the start of her illness, the term reappeared in later discussions about Janine's suffering after she returned home. Most villagers agreed that the *eklampsi* was caused by anger. "If you are pregnant," Janine told me, "and you become a little angry, you can get *eklampsi*." She gave an equally straightforward reason for her anger: she was upset that Mme. Beaumont, who had treated her throughout her pregnancy, was not called when she began to go into labor. Mme. Beaumont agreed: "It was a fit of anger that she had which gave her the

eklampsi . . . She was angry because she didn't want the other midwife."
Juliette Dutoit and other residents of the *savann* who knew Janine all gave
the same explanation.

They also agreed on the mechanical physiology of Janine's disorder:
the rise of blood in her body mediated the transformation of anger into
eklampsi. Janine put it this way several months later: "The *eklampsi* that I
had was blood which climbed into my head. At the time, it took me like
a crazy person; it seemed like I was mad." She recalled that during the
illness she lost consciousness and was frothing at the mouth, and then
concluded, " . . . even now, the same blood could still be in my head."
"*Eklampsi* is anger, it is blood," Mme. Beaumont told me. She continued
in even more graphic terms: when Janine first fell ill, "her eyes were as
red as that shirt," and she pointed to a bright red knit shirt worn by one
of her daughters: "So you see, Janine was really angry!"

In their discussions about Janine's illness, villagers inserted the novel
term *eklampsi* into a pre-existing discourse about intense emotions which
alter the quality and movement of blood through the body and thereby
cause physical disorders. This discourse and its associated cluster of
sicknesses has enjoyed the attention of recent ethnographers of illness in
New World African societies, especially Haiti. Certain strong emotions,
especially anger and shock, can cause a person's blood to heat, thicken,
or rise in the body. Blood can accumulate in the head, causing
headaches, stroke, or madness; it can lodge in the throat, causing
suffocation; or it can pass into the breast of a nursing mother, spoiling
her milk and causing illness in her baby. Blood can change color or
become too "sweet" or "sour" as a result of unsettling emotional
experience as well as exposure to certain "hot" and "cold" foods and
environmental agents. Finally, a deficiency of blood can cause loss of
consciousness and a host of other physical sicknesses.[12]

People freely drew on this loosely organized fund of images, meanings,
and associations in order to account for Janine's newly named disorder.
They invoked the language of strong emotions and the movement of
blood to explain its onset, its singular features, and its likely course. They
also routinely referred to conditions as *indisposition*, *kriz*, and *kriz de ner*:
stable illness categories that have coalesced from this general discourse.
They inserted *eklampsi* into the same series, and considered this novel
category as overlapping with, and in some cases identical to, these other
illnesses.

People familiar with Janine thus refigured a previously unknown biomedical illness category into locally meaningful terms. The creolized
medical diagnosis of *eklampsi* thus joins a host of previously documented
cases from Haiti, Latin America, and indeed throughout the world

where biomedical diagnoses are transvalued as they move outside the specialized setting where biomedical knowledge is produced.[13] What is most striking, however, is the source of authority for this discourse: why people's rendering of *eklampsi* in terms of anger, shock, and blood was so convincing. To account for *eklampsi*, villagers evoked a series of rich embodied experiences: the rising and falling of blood, the sudden changes in consciousness which they produce, the compulsion to react physically against aggression, and the body's vulnerability to social and environmental shocks. The discourse of blood, strong emotions, and sickness is so persuasive because of the palpable immediacy of all the major terms.

Recall Janine's description of the beginnings of her illness: she lost consciousness and was unable to remember any events during the following four days. Her body became stiff and was no longer under her control, so she had to be physically carried across town by several men. She presents these experiences as evidence that the *eklampsi* rendered her *indispose*. Indeed, the onset of *eklampsi* at pregnancy and in the presence of others, her extreme weakness, bodily collapse, and loss of sensible contact with her surroundings closely resemble the disorder of *indisposition* as experienced by residents of Port-au-Prince (Philippe and Romain 1979) and expatriate Haitians in Miami (Weidman *et al.* 1978). The chief symptoms of this widespread disorder include dizziness, extreme weakness and collapse, and sensory dissociation (temporary blindness and deafness). Most people attribute *indisposition* to perturbations of the blood caused by strong emotional states. Blood may become "too rich" because of a violent mood or unexpressed anger. Blood may "come up" towards the head, increasing in intensity or pressure, because of menstruation or sexual frustration.[14]

As she compared *eklampsi* in *indisposition*, however, Janine invokes the changes in blood not as a set of diagnostic criteria or a shared conceptual framework, but rather an unmistakable physical sensation:

When the blood rises in you, all of your body becomes bloated . . . You feel your flesh creep, and the blood rising up to your head; it can make your eyes red, and then you'll suffer from a headache. You feel your skin is heavy, because of the blood flowing through it.

All this is due to anger. A woman can become so angry, she won't have her period, because as the blood rises to her head, it can't circulate, it can't flow normally.

These palpable experiences and visible changes in the location of blood in the body lend to Janine's description of *indisposition* an immediate reality. This makes the illness category of *indisposition* an especially compelling analogue to the novel *eklampsi*. Applying this biomedical category to Janine's illness did not medicalize her suffering; to the contrary, the embodied vocabulary of blood and emotions successfully encompassed *eklampsi*.

Janine concluded that her *eklampsi* closely resembled *indisposition* based not only on the physical symptoms but also on the fit of anger which produced them. Anger caused by social conflicts as well as shock in the face of personal loss are the most common causes of blood rising up in the body (Philippe and Romain 1979; Charles 1979). Once again, in order to interpret *eklampsi* in terms of the more familiar condition of *indisposition*, Janine and other villagers invoke the pathogenic effect of strong emotions not as a conceptual framework or ethnopsychological trope, but rather as an embodied experience, every bit as palpable as the upward movement of blood.[15] For Janine, the anger you immediately feel when provoked or mistreated is an objectively justified and physically gripping experience:

> Suppose I'm in a quarrel with you, and I start to push you around. You didn't expect it, so you become irritated . . . If you are irritated, your blood becomes spoiled, and it starts to rise up through your skin[16] . . . You want to come back at me and fight me. It's just a reaction: I fight with you, you fight back.
>
> If you do fight back, you wouldn't have any problem at all [with your blood]; you just did what you were supposed to do. Neither one of us would have a problem, and we wouldn't be angry. But if you wanted to get back at me, if you say, "Hey, I'd really like to crush that person," but you feel you can't do it, then you would have a fit of anger . . . The blood will rise up in you, and maybe grab you in the throat, making you unable to speak.

Anger (especially in response to another's aggression) immediately affects the blood. If anger is not expressed, blood will rise in the body and cause various disorders along its path. In this account, Janine gives muteness as an example, but in her description of the onset of *eklampsi*, the blood travelled all the way to her head and caused convulsion and the loss of contact with her surroundings – a symptom which she claimed resembled madness (*foli*) (see chapter 7).

Kriz de ner was the second term (after *indisposition*) which people used as a gloss for *eklampsi*. The midwife Mme. Beaumont reported that Janine suffered from *kriz* (convulsions or seizures), and that her condition resembled the *youn ner*, which could be translated as "the nerves." Like *indisposition*, these terms are widely used in rural Haiti and elaborate more of the connections between blood, emotions, and consciousness. Villagers in Jeanty most often invoke the expression *kriz de ner* to describe two different extreme reactions to shock, best illustrated by the behavior of bereaved individuals when they are brought face-to-face with the reality of their loss at the funeral. On the one hand, it refers to dramatic and violent convulsions: individuals in the grip of such a *kriz de ner* typically writhe on the ground, at least partially dissociated from their environment, and shriek or scream, sometimes repeating short phrases such as "help me, help me" or "my brother, my brother." Friends and family members may forcibly restrain them but will rarely administer any popular treatments such as herbal teas or massage. The very same term describes people (disproportionately men) who simply collapse and lie motionless on the ground, although their body remains tense and seemingly on the verge of a violent outburst. To manage cases of this second type of *kriz de ner*, people poured herbal infusions over the victim's head (in order to lower the blood) or waved acrid smoke from burning cotton into his face (in order to force him to cry out). (The next case-study provides longer descriptions of such *kriz* at a village funeral.)

The shock caused by personal tragedy ushers in most episodes of *kriz de ner* (and it can cause other physical disorders as well).[17] This seems quite different from the anger, resulting from mistreatment or personal aggression, which can lead to *indisposition*. However, both of these disorders are discursively constructed through the same notions of blood and embodied through the same physical sensations. Changes in the condition and movement of blood are central to both disorders, and both typically lead to radical alterations in consciousness such as convulsions, collapse, and dissociation. Not surprisingly, therefore, accounts of *kriz de ner* overlap with what has already been quoted for *indisposition*. Luc Simon, a middle-aged man living in the first ring of hills above Jeanty, supplied the following explanation:

> *Eklampsi* is a shock. For example, you come to my house, and I pick a fight with you. You're in a state of shock which carries you off, and can even kill you . . . If you're shocked, the blood climbs up your body, and cause a fit of anger. They [shock and anger] act the same way. If you have a fit of anger, you could get *kriz de ner* or *eklampsi*.
>
> At a funeral, when people are crying, screaming, and throwing themselves on the ground, how do you feel? [I answer: I feel shocked, and sad, and it makes me think of people I knew who died]. You don't feel something rising from your feet to your head? You don't feel your blood start to tremble, that it goes "Zip!" up your body? You feel your blood rising, and you feel transformed from the way you were before.

Luc was teaching me about the relation between *eklampsi* and *kriz de ner*, and his interest in my immediate, visceral reaction to village funerals suggests the embodied quality of this discourse. The compelling association between strong emotions, the blood, and disorders such as *kriz de ner* is inscribed in concrete physical sensations, and these sensations can travel sympathetically between different people. The experience of witnessing other people's grief is enormously affecting, but not because it triggers memories of one's own past losses. The experience is rather an immediate bodily response to an unquestionably tragic event: a physiological resonance with other people's bodily displays of grief. Moreover, Luc spontaneously blurred the boundaries between different terms: *eklampsi* and *kriz de ner*, as well as anger and shock. Not everyone agreed with him (Janine, for example, preferred to cast anger and shock as two discrete influences on the blood).[18] People offered many such idiosyncratic interpretations without challenging the central tenet of this discourse.

Finally, people often applied the discourse retroactively, reinterpreting episodes of illness as the result of a fit of anger which at the time escaped the individual's awareness. Five months after Janine's baby was born, she was still suffering the physical effect of various shocks: her milk was spoiled, which caused her child to suffer chronic diarrhea. When I asked whether the incidents at the time of delivery were still involved, Janine replied that her spoiled milk could well have resulted from other shocks or losses: "You can easily forget the day. Everyday there's something which happens to shock you." Only later, she explained, can you draw the connection between a particular shock and an episode of illness. Luc also mentioned this delayed recognition of anger with the following example:

I spend the whole day in my gardens. I become angry because there isn't enough rain, or because someone stole my cattle. I come back to the house, and start to beat my wife. Other people will say, "When you found out that the cow was gone, that's when you became shocked, that's what caused the fit of anger. That is why you beat your wife when you returned home."[19]

For several months after Janine's delivery, villagers referred to her condition alternately as *eklampsi*, *indisposition*, and *kriz de ner*. Without exception, people interpreted the etiology, pathophysiology, and symptoms of *eklampsi* as congruent with these older and better known disorders. Even the nursing staff at the dispensary (who already knew the biomedical definition of the term) agreed that the *eklampsi* was a blood disorder caused by Janine's anger the night before she gave birth. People even linguistically assimilated the word *eklampsi* to the specific expressions already used in this discourse: some would say that "Janine had a fit of *eklampsi*," (*li te fe youn eklampsi*) just as she had a fit of anger or was in a state of shock (*li te fe youn kòlè*; *li te fe youn sezisman*)

To sum up: The illness category *eklampsi* has a number of obvious links to biomedicine. The term itself is a loan word from French biomedicine, and the midwife who introduced it at the start of Janine's illness considered it the sole province of professional physicians. Upon hearing this diagnosis, members of Janine's *lakou* immediately sought hospital-based treatment, despite its great cost. However, accepting this term did not medicalize the bodily condition. Janine, her healers, and her kin did not reify her condition by relabelling it as a neutral biological dysfunction. Calling it *eklampsi* did not individualize her illness and erase its social meanings.

People rather inserted *eklampsi* into the pre-existing discourse linking strong emotions to the movement of blood, physical sickness, social conflict, and alterations of consciousness. This is a Haitian variant of a pan-Caribbean, and perhaps pan-African-American discourse. In bringing it to bear on Janine's experience, people resisted the medicalization of her disorder. Why were they able to do this so easily? The first reason is fortuitous. The central images of discourse include some of the most dramatic problems which Janine experienced: loss of consciousness, convulsions, and bodily collapse. The several other disorders constructed within this discourse resemble Janine's condition, and their explanations also turn on blood and anger: both central components of Janine's difficult labor and childbirth. Furthermore, the discourse is quite open. It accommodates different interpretations and can be legitimately applied to a wide range of disorders, both at the time that people seek medical care as well as in later accounts of the illness.

But the striking openness and flexibility of this discourse do not fully explain its ability to encompass the new biomedical category of *eklampsi*. The categories in this discourse refer to sensible experiences: headaches, muteness, loss of consciousness, among many others. These are the inevitable reactions to social aggression and personal loss, and they are intimately linked with our emotional response to the same upsetting events. We can plausibly describe this framework as both "socio-somatic" and "somato-psychic" (see Farmer 1988). But it is the palpable immediacy of the movement of blood, fits of anger, and states of shock which makes this discourse so persuasive.

The local response to *eklampsi* in Jeanty resembles the fate of other biomedical diagnoses recently introduced elsewhere in Haiti. When the term *sida* (AIDS) first appeared in Do Kay (a town in the central plateau) in the early 1980s, people assimilated it to the same interpretative frameworks described in this chapter: disorder in the quality of blood, tuberculosis, and sent sicknesses caused by malice or jealousy (Farmer 1990). Although it fits some of these idioms better than others, Farmer concludes that people did not abandon pre-existing organizing principles in the face of this new disease (pp. 21–23). Singer *et al.* (1988), however, paint a classic picture of the medicalization of reproductive disorders among women in Jacmel. In adopting the term *fibrom*, a Creolized version of the biomedical diagnosis fibroma (a fibrous tumor), women relabel and reconceptualize the main features of *pedisyon*: a pre-existing illness category which carried several social and political meanings. *Pedisyon* (disdained by local doctors as a false folk belief) is thereby transformed into *fibrom*, a biomedical disorder which villagers claim only doctors can cure.

Where does *eklampsi* fit into this series? The case of *sida* represents the victory of a pre-existing collective logic over a foreign illness term. The case of *fibrom* illustrates the opposite result: the erasure of a prior medical notion (which imbricated bodily symptoms, emotional states, and social relations) and its replacement by a narrow, technically defined disease label. In the case of *eklampsi*, an older discourse successfully encompassed the new biomedical term. But this occurred not through any special quality of the pre-existing symbolic system (its "openness" or "rigor"), and not through the political resistance of villagers to medicalization. *Eklampsi* was inserted into the embodied practices of social life: a scheme in which bodily sensations anchor and produce social affects, and both are calibrated to the microlevel contradictions and blockages of social life in rural Haiti (see Bourdieu 1977:87–95; Csordas 1993).

Eklampsi is a metaphor for experiences of loss, social strife, and oppression, along with the related Haitian illnesses of *kriz de ner*, *indisposition*, and *move san* (see Farmer 1988). But such disorders are not just an idiom for (or oblique protest against) these experiences. They are the way people come to have the experience in the first place. Insufficient, spoiled, or rising blood causes discrete physical feelings (weakness, itching, tingling, headaches) and disorders in self/body experience (seizures, muteness, madness). These palpable experiences literally embody the anger, loss, and frustration of everyday life. In this sense, *eklampsi* has not been assimilated to a prior symbolic discourse. It has instead been recreated as a familiar bodily disposition through which people come to experience the objective social structures of Jeanty. Like the related disorders, *eklampsi* is a mode of somatic attention (Csordas 1990): how people first know about the limiting conditions of their lives, as well as how they communicate about these conditions and struggle against them. Residents of Jeanty have accepted the biomedical disorder *eklampsi* without medicalizing the illness experience or its meanings. This testifies not to the encompassment of a novel disease label by a pre-existing discourse, but rather to the existence of a particular constellation of bodily experiences and embodied emotions which allows people to perceive, appreciate, and express the objective conditions of their lives.

8 Friends help winnow corn and millet before market day.

When biomedicine fails

Dieusauveur was a 20-year-old man, originally from the parish of Jeanty, who was severely injured in a motorcycle accident while returning home from Port-au-Prince. The accident left him incapacitated: unable to walk, incontinent, and often in considerable pain. His family took him to several biomedical practitioners, but told me these treatments were ineffective. After several expensive and time-consuming trips to clinics and hospitals across the southern peninsula of the country, Dieusauveur returned to live in his brother's half-finished home on the fringes of Jeanty. He depended on a network of friends and especially family members to wash and feed him. During this period, he received several forms of healing, ranging from visits by the dispensary nurse and a lay "injectionist" to herbal remedies and Protestant prayer meetings. However, his condition worsened, and he died eight weeks after the accident.

Dieusauveur's death struck many villagers as especially tragic in light of the success he had already achieved and the social distance he had travelled from his family origins. The Martin family lives in the hamlet of Clermont, an area of steep hills exposed on one side to the salt air from the Baie des Cayes. Clermont is a poor area, even for the parish of Jeanty; its land is not particularly fertile, and it is located in an isolated part of the commune, far away from the major agricultural markets. Although it has a Catholic chapel, the residents of Clermont, according to the parish priest, are not active in formal church activities. The priest considers them somewhat backward (*yo pa eklere*), and he disparages both their continuing worship of the spirits and their gullible susceptibility to Protestant pastors.

Although he came from a family of poor cultivators, indistinguishable from their neighbors in Clermont, Dieusauveur completed three years at the Catholic secondary school in Jeanty. He had then enrolled at the national agriculture school at Damiens (near Port-au-Prince) in order to train as an agronomist, one of the few careers open to individuals with only a secondary education. Although his family contributed some money towards his schooling, he depended mostly on financial support from the Baptist church in Jeanty, where he and his family were members.[20] As a state-certified agronomist, Dieusauveur could join the lower tiers of the middle class and enjoy the secure, if meager, pay of a civil servant. This was quite rare for someone of his young age, rural background, and humble origins. (Indeed, the only other agronomist in Jeanty, who for several years received a salary as the state-appointed agronomist for the commune, is a married man in his mid-forties and the head of one of the town's wealthier families.)

At the time of the accident, Dieusauveur was returning from Port-au-Prince to spend the holidays of New Year's Day and Independence Day (January 2) with his family. His motorcycle spun out of control on an isolated stretch of road; no pedestrians or other vehicles were involved. Dieusauveur suffered very few external injuries, and he did not lose consciousness at the time of the accident; in fact, people said that he himself called out for help. His family was soon notified through messages sent to Jeanty with passing trucks and buses.

Dieusauveur's family immediately took him to l'Hôpital Bonne Fin, located in the mountains between Les Cayes and Port-au-Prince. Most villagers rank this hospital as the best (albeit most expensive) source of biomedical treatment outside of the capital, and they trust it far more than the state-owned hospital in Les Cayes.[21] L'Hôpital Bonne Fin is operated by the Mission Evangélique Baptiste du Sud d'Haiti (MEBSH), a large and well-established missionary organization from

North America, and both Haitian and white American physicians work there. It accepts primarily patients who have been treated first in the daily clinics held at "Cité Lumière," a Baptist compound to the north of Les Cayes. Since Dieusauveur and his family were members of the Baptist church in Jeanty, this was an obvious choice, and some of the church elders contributed funds for his treatment.

The narratives about Dieusauveur's illness circulating in Jeanty repeated and elaborated the story of the trip to Bonne Fin, and people sometimes added that the family consulted doctors in Port-au-Prince as well. These stories conveyed both that Dieusauveur's condition was serious and that his family took the appropriate steps to treat it.[22] Residents of Jeanty generally have high regard for private biomedical practitioners and foreign-operated mission hospitals. They said that Dieusauveur's doctors "tried everything; they took x-rays (*yo te fe radiografi*), they gave him strong medications." However, despite their sophisticated biomedical technology, considered far above anything available in Jeanty (and symbolized iconically by the use of x-rays), these doctors "couldn't do anything for him"; Dieusauveur "couldn't find an answer there."

For most villagers, these therapeutic failures did not indict biomedicine as a whole. People did not use Dieusauveur's case to launch a broader critique of biomedicine's truth claims, the skills of particular doctors, or the expense and inconvenience of hospital visits. Indeed, Dieusauveur himself continued to receive various biomedical treatments once he had settled into his brother's home after this initial period of fruitless hospitalizations. Lucie Nemours, the resident nurse in the dispensary, occasionally came to the house to apply new bandages to Dieusauveur's bed sores and to administer injections of penicillin from a vial which Dieusauveur's brother had purchased at a pharmacy in Cayes. The injections were more often performed by a middle-aged man from Jeanty, referred to as a first-aid worker (*sekouris*) or a technician (*teknisyen*) who came once every three days with his own syringe and needle.[23] People considered the inability of biomedicine to cure Dieusauveur not as a marker of biomedicine's weakness, but rather as a a sign that Dieusauveur's illness was an illness of Satan (*maladi Satan*), not an illness of God (*maladi Bondye*). This conceptual distinction took center stage as Dieusauveur's illness worsened.

I first met Dieusauveur in the half-finished home which his brother was building (with money provided chiefly by Dieusauveur's agronomist's salary). The house consisted of little more than cinder block walls with gaping holes for windows and doors and a tin roof. There were few indoor furnishings: pieces of lumber were strewn about the uneven dirt floor and extra cinderblocks served as chairs and tables for small oil-burning lamps. One room, however, was dominated by two beds: a large one where Michel Martin (the brother) and his wife slept, and a smaller cot where Dieusauveur lay day and night, usually wearing only a T-shirt and covered by a few thin blankets.

Dieusauveur was rarely left alone in this unfinished building. Michel and his wife lived there, and they welcomed a steady stream of other family members and friends. People came to check on his condition, chat with other visitors, or sometimes just sit in silence. For example, a schoolteacher from the village arrived at the house one evening accompanied by a Catholic sister. The two greeted Dieusauveur and then proceeded to ask Michel whether his brother had control over his bowels or could feel anything in his legs. Once Michel had answered most of their questions, one of women turned to Dieusauveur and said, "That's good, you're getting a little better." They continued to ask about the family's visit to Bonne Fin and to rank the abilities of the local dispensary staff.

In the midst of these visits and vigils, Dieusauveur received various types of healing. People occasionally brought large bunches of leaves and herbs, tied by a cord or vine, to be divided into smaller bundles and boiled as infusions over several days. Such therapeutic teas are a core element of domestic health care in rural Haiti. Michel graciously accepted these gifts, although he often didn't know exactly which plants were included. On one occasion, Michel and another young man from the village looked over a bunch of leaves brought by a neighbor. As they began to call out the names of the ones they recognized, Michel told me with a bemused expression, "Everyone knows a different sort of leaf, and each one is good. It's like if you put a problem on the blackboard, everyone will have a different way of figuring it, but they get to the same solution."

Small informal prayer meetings also grew out of ordinary social visits, and these represent perhaps the most basic type of religious healing I witnessed in Jeanty. For example, by sundown one day, Michel's house was filled with at least fifteen people, including many young adults who had returned from Port-au-Prince because of the threat of political violence.[24] As darkness descended, individual conversations diminished and we began to listen to one of the preachers from the Baptist church as he sat speaking quietly with Dieusauveur. They were talking about his fevers and the partial return of feeling to his legs, but when they finished, the preacher turned to the group and asked us to pray.

The people there had come at different times, did not all know each other, and comprised both Catholics and Protestants (including the daughter of a Protestant pastor and members of some of the leading Catholic families). Nevertheless, we easily joined to sing a short hymn and recite the 23rd Psalm, both in French. The preacher then began an impromptu prayer addressed to Dieusauveur. Although he spoke this time in Creole, he employed a formal style and a practiced soothing delivery for his message of moral uplift. "We hope God is with you, on your bed," he began. "Do not become discouraged, we pray that God will give you his protection tonight, and enable you to keep hope." As he spoke, everyone in the room knelt on the floor or stood with their heads bowed and one hand covering their eyes and recited their own prayers, also in Creole. Our voices merged into a low drone in which individual words were indistinguishable. When these prayers ended after about ten minutes, the preacher led the group in reciting the Lord's Prayer (in French). Dieusauveur then quoted a line of Scripture, and everyone went over to shake his hand before leaving. What began as a random group of friends and neighbors who had assembled to visit the ailing Dieusauveur ended as an impromptu prayer service for healing.

Kriz and the discourse on sent sickness

Dieusauveur's condition gradually declined in the following weeks. People said that he was suffering from two types of fever, hot fever in the afternoon, which caused him to perspire, and cold fever in the evenings, causing chills. Neither the herbal nor the biomedical treatments could restore control over his lower body. Nonetheless, his death on a humid morning in late February came as a shock to many villagers. Kinsmen, neighbors, fellow members of the Baptist church, and even those who didn't know him very well at all keenly felt its tragedy, and the strength of their reactions was nowhere more evident than at his funeral, held the day after he died.

A large crowd gathered behind the four men who carried the coffin from Michel's house past the savann Dutoit and across a dry riverbed into the center of Jeanty. Once the procession reached the Baptist church, the men placed Dieusauveur's coffin near the altar, between a raised platform where the church dignitaries sat (around twenty men dressed in somber suits and ties) and the pews which were packed with mourners. The small church was hot, crowded, and noisy, and the emotional pitch was high and unpredictable. At the front, a young woman was circling the coffin, crying, and speaking to Dieusauveur in a barely controlled voice, "I won't see you anymore, but just the other morning we were talking together . . . " Children from the different schools in Jeanty had been let out to attend the funeral, and they crowded in a large semicircle around the coffin watching her in fear mingled with curiosity.

The formal funeral service began when a young man (a preacher, who also taught at the Baptist secondary school) rose from his seat among the dignitaries, walked to a lectern in the front of the platform, and led the congregation in a series of slow, stately French hymns. He had to repeat the name of the hymn several times to be heard through the scratchy loudspeakers and over the din of the mourners. In addition to people shuffling, fanning themselves, and trying to comfort troublesome babies, the loud sobbing of women rose and fell. They often repeated a particular phrase – "it's not true, it's not true, it's not true" or "Oh my God! Oh my God!"[25] – while they wept, taking a short breath after each phrase as if they were gasping for air. The hymns could not drown out their gasping and weeping. The preacher somehow managed to hold the room's attention during the Scripture readings which he interspersed with the hymns. He introduced each reading by announcing the main theme (e.g., "Physical death and spiritual death, in Luke, chapter two") and naming the church elder who would read it. Different men on the platform then stood to read the passage aloud, usually in halting and barely understood French.

The mood of the room changed dramatically when the preacher moved to the side of the lectern and began a review of Dieusauveur's life. Speaking for the first time in Creole, he recounted Dieusauveur's success in school in Jeanty, his agronomy training at Damiens, and he described the support Dieusauveur continued to give to his family while living in Port-au-Prince. As his talk progressed, women began to have *kriz*: in one of the front pews, a woman bolted up from her seat and started to jump in place, gradually turning all the way around. Her jaw was clenched shut, and her bulging eyes seemed locked in a steady stare. Two people immediately tried to calm her by holding her arms and leading her back to the pew. Behind me, a woman broke out into uncontrollable rhythmic screams, fell down and started to writhe on the floor. As the schoolchildren gazed at this commotion, some of them began to cry, and others were quietly muttering "Dieusauveur" to themselves.

The preacher seemed determined to contain the situation, and he stubbornly persevered with the details of Dieusauveur's life. However, people's agonized screaming interrupted him, destroyed his concentration, and captured the complete attention of the other mourners. More and more women abandoned themselves to their grief, and their wailing soon drowned out the preacher's voice entirely. As this groundswell of cries gathered force, each additional voice made further wailing both possible and inevitable. The preacher soon gave up trying to control the service, and the crescendo of screams dominated the room for several minutes. In the midst of it, at least fifteen women were going into *kriz* in the aisles, shaking violently and rolling on the floor. The Baptist church dignitaries sat impassively on their platform, virtually helpless in the face of this collective performance of shock and grief.

Finally, some of the church leaders managed to organize a group of four women to lead the congregation in the same type of slow, stately French hymn that began the service. These songs (plus the screech of feedback from the sound system) reintroduced some order to the room, although during the final few measures of the last hymn, one of the four women directing the singing started to shriek in short, repetitive bursts. She ran off the platform, overtaken by a *kriz*, writhing and falling to the floor, before she was finally led out a side door by several men. The preacher took the microphone again and implored, "Try to calm yourselves, try to have strength." However, most people by now seemed to have spent their energy, and the preacher was able to complete the narrative of Dieusauveur's life, deliver a quick sermon (devoid of any local references, in order to avoid new outbursts), and conclude the service with only a few more interruptions.

After filing out of the Baptist church, we formed a ragged procession to the Martin home in Clermont where the actual burial would take place. The group dispersed along the narrow path and mourners either walked in silence or talked quietly among each other in the stifling midday heat. After an hour-long walk, I climbed over the last ravine and saw the coffin sitting in front of the largest of a cluster of wattle and daub houses belonging to the Martin family. A few women had begun to wail again, and the emotional pitch intensified several minutes later when four men carried the coffin down a short hill where a large new concrete tomb awaited. People's screams again reached a crescendo as they ran after it crying and reaching to touch it. The men set the coffin on the ground before the freshly painted tomb. One of them opened it, leaned over Dieusauveur, and placed something on his body. He then urgently shouted at people to stand back, and he flung a small brown bottle in front of him, shattering it against the tomb (see page 105, below). The men proceeded to hoist the coffin into the tomb, and a mason plastered shut the small opening.

The crowd then retraced their steps to the Martin *lakou* and tried to escape the sun by packing into the one-room house. At the start, an eerie silence and calm prevailed, probably due to utter emotional exhaustion. But as various Martin relatives walked around serving Coca-cola, beer, and sweet warm coffee, a quite ordinary social mood gradually appeared.

The mourners chatted privately in normal tones, and it seemed that the long funeral was finally over. However, as I started the long walk back to Jeanty I heard a low cry from behind a house near the tomb. Here, away from the crowd and after the main events of the day, I witnessed for the first time a man having a *kriz*.

One of Dieusauveur's brothers, Arnaud, lay face down on two straw mats covering the ground. He was surrounded by four people: one man was sitting on his calves and another on his waist, holding Arnaud's arms crossed around his back. While a third man knelt next to Arnaud, cradling his head, a woman held a small tuft of smouldering cotton to his nose. Arnaud occasionally jerked his face away to avoid inhaling the acrid smoke. Despite these movements and a few low moans, his eyes were closed, his face expressionless, and he seemed unconscious. He maintained his body in a state of extraordinary tension: as one of the men tried with great difficulty to unclench his fists, and Arnaud seemed engaged in a sort of motionless struggle with his restrainers.

After about 15 minutes, while still lying face down and without any apparent change of his body or greater awareness, Arnaud began to say a few things in a plaintive, although clear voice, "You won't be giving me courage any longer, Dieusauveur . . . That's the way life is." He let out a few more quiet, muffled moans. A woman who was standing there observing the scene told him, "Scream out, scream out if you can." The men gradually relaxed their hold on Arnaud, and managed to prop him upright. The muscular tension and powerful resistance he offered earlier had disappeared, and they were replaced now by an extreme lassitude. Arnaud could barely find the energy for even small bodily movements; to remain sitting up, two men were forced to support him around the abdomen. Finally, the men began telling him to "Stand up, so you can see where you are." Arnaud stood up with assistance and slowly opened his eyes, but he seemed confused and remained silent for several more minutes before the group made their way back up to the house.

These dramatic *kriz* represent people's immediate reaction to Dieusauveur's death. Some of the mourners were so strongly affected because they knew him and had closely watched the course of his illness. Others were aware that Dieusauveur had achieved a rare success and had become an important source of support to his family, and they reacted to the tragic loss of a successful son of Jeanty. However, to conclude that their *kriz* were produced by personal grief reflects the dominance of interior psychological states in Euro-American notions of bereavement and mourning (Lutz 1985). Without exception, people in Jeanty understood *kriz de ner* as the inevitable and immediate response to loss. *Kriz* are related to *sezisman*: they are produced by blood rushing to your head when you witness a great tragedy or suddenly learn of someone's unexpected death. For this reason, the English word "shock" better conveys the quality of people's explanation of *kriz* than "grief." Shock connotes the physiological reaction (with psychological correlates) to an identifiable event. Similarly, *kriz* are unmediated bodily responses to loss; they are not the by-product or visible expression of "grief" conceived as a purely psychological state.

But although *kriz* are naturalized as a consequence of the movement of blood, not everyone is equally susceptible to them. Luc once told me that certain people are more easily irritated (they are "a little bit wild"), and their blood rises with less provocation. Several villagers (both male and female) explained that women are more often subject to *kriz* because "their blood is weaker" than men's. Although the intricate links between gender, blood, and vulnerability to *kriz* have yet to be explored, Dieusauveur's funeral already reveals a striking paradox. Although women's constitutional weakness accounts for their greater tendency towards *kriz*, Arnaud was counselled to cry out as part of the management of his condition. Men may be more resistant to *kriz de ner*, but when they get one it is more serious, and must be "treated" by inducing them to adopt typically female behavior.

The *kriz* caused by Dieusauveur's tragic death illuminate the interpretations of Janine Dutoit's *eklampsi*, and they also provide an important contrasting case to the states of dissociation experienced by religious healers (chapters 5–7). Many of the villagers who considered Janine's *eklampsi* as a sort of *kriz de ner* did not personally witness its onset, but they were familiar with *kriz* from attending funerals such as Dieusauveur's. In fact, individual mourners underwent such *kriz* during every funeral I attended which was held for someone who either was young or met death in an especially tragic way: e.g., a successful Dutoit man who died of AIDS, and a father of three who was gunned down by the army during the election day violence on November 29, 1987 in Port-au-Prince. The only funerals I attended *not* marked by these emotional outbursts were for an older man, whose burial on the next election day (January 17, 1988) was sparsely attended, and for the elderly, infirm wife of one of the senior Dutoits. In the second case, despite her husband's renown in the village and the presence of a huge number of relatives, no one had a full-blown *kriz de ner*, because of the woman's age, obvious record of accomplishments, and declining health. Moreover, having a *kriz* is unrelated to the action of the various supernatural entities – Christ, Satan, the Holy Spirit, spirits (*lwa*), or other nameless malefecent spirits – which can be incarnated in devotees or in the victims of spiritual attacks. No one judged the mourners at Dieusauveur's funeral "possessed" *despite* some striking resemblances with incidents described in later chapters.[26]

However, the way people interpreted Dieusauveur's afflictions is intimately related to an elaborate quasi-religious discourse about human jealousy, malice, and the illnesses which one's enemies can cause. This talk of illnesses of Satan and illnesses of God (*maladi Satan* and *maladi Bondye*) was invoked to assign a specific meaning to the failure of biomedicine to cure Dieusauveur, and it also underlies the claims to religious healing power examined in the rest of the book.

On the morning of the funeral, François Lesage, a young man who had accompanied me several times to Dieusauveur's home, stated his suspicions:

It was the way he died. It was an accident, but he wasn't injured, not in his head or in his legs[27] . . . Maybe it was somebody else who sent something on him. But only if you visited a *houngan* could you know what happened. His family would have to go to a *houngan* to check things out, to see whether he died from a proper cause or whether somebody did him in.

Other people in the village also speculated that the "chief cause was a devil." When a local *doktè fèy* or herbal practitioner (literally, "leaf doctor"), heard the circumstances of the accident, he responded without missing a beat "It's an *ekspedisyon* [a "sent sickness"][28] . . . There are people who can put out a magical force on you; so now they sent something upon Dieusauveur to make him fall off his motorcycle." Another young man, briefly visiting home from Port-au-Prince, suggested that jealousy lay behind the *ekspedisyon*: "If you buy a car in this little underdeveloped country, people are jealous of that, and they can make the car crash and kill you." In the context of Haiti's pervasive poverty, jealousy is an understandable and inevitable danger of any economic advance.

Throughout these discussions of Dieusauveur's death, villagers invoked several versions of the same general model of "sent sicknesses." When I asked them to explain this model, they invariably began with a basic distinction between two different kinds of illness. Some illnesses come about when people driven by jealousy or desire for retribution "send something on you," while others are caused by unremarkable bodily processes, such as an infection or a change in the condition or quality of blood (see Brown 1991:347ff). However, people referred to this distinction in remarkably diverse ways, even in the context of the single case of Dieusauveur.

Some of these terms refer explicitly to the maleficent motivations of other people. For example, that Dieusauveur died without an identifiable illness or visible injury suggested to François that somebody sent something on him (*se youn lòt moun ki te voye youn bagay sou li*). He cast the basic distinction as one between a "proper death" and "somebody doing him in" (*si se te youn bon koz mouri, oubyen si se te fe yo te fe-l*). Other young men in the village also alluded to an illness sent on you by other people (*youn maladi voye sou ou pa lòt moun*). They opposed this to an illness which comes naturally, which they termed an "illness of your body" or "of your blood" (*youn maladi ki vini natirelman; youn maladi kò-ou, san-ou*).

Another set of expressions index the means by which one can send a sickness. People referred to Dieusauveur's affliction as an illness of Satan (*maladi Satan*), but in this usage, Satan does not designate the spiritual actor in the French Catholic cosmology – the incarnate image or icon of the universal principle of evil. A Satan rather refers to what is sent by somebody else: an invisible entity which can take up a place in your body and kill you. The complementary term illness of God (*maladi Bondye*) simply denotes all other kinds of illness; I never heard people say either that God sent an illness upon someone or that God is generally responsible for human afflictions.

People also commonly used the term *maladi mò*, which Métraux translates as a "dead illness," based on the etymology of *mò* from the French adjective *mort* (Métraux 1972:274ff). But the use of this word in an expression such as "they sent 3 dead upon him" (*yo te voye 3 mò sou li*) suggests a looser translation of *maladi mò* as an illness caused by the spirit of a dead person. In this usage, the *mò* (like Satan) represents the spiritual entity which is sent upon the victim and causes his misfortune, illness, or death. Sometimes this term is paired with the specific disease which the spirit caused, such as tuberculosis (*mò tibèkiloz*). Other times it denotes the identity of the spirit: a spirit of a child is *youn mò ti moun*, and the spirit of an adult, *youn mò gran moun*. The compound expressions *maladi mò ti-moun* thus refers to an illness caused by the spirit of a dead child that was sent to the victim. Thus any disease, even one with a known and accepted biomedical diagnosis (e.g., tuberculosis) can be sent upon its victim through the action of a *mò*.

The act of sending a Satan or *mò* is termed an *ekspedisyon*, as the *doktè fèy* explained for Dieusauveur's case. While Metraux, relying on an account from Marcelin (1947), glosses this simply as getting rid of the victim, in Jeanty the term means the dispatching of a spirit, and it is synonymous with a *renvoi*. People also mentioned a series of specific mechanisms or material routes for *maladi mò*: a powder hit and a lamp hit (*kou d poud, kou d limyè*). A powder or an oil lamp is ingeniously hidden so that the victim encounters them in her daily rounds. When she comes into contact with these physical agents, these traps (*atrap*) cause illness and death in the same fashion as a *mò*.

Although most people used such expressions to account for Dieusauveur's illness, they invariably added that these were just their own speculative conclusions. Only an *houngan* skilled in the buying and selling of spirits could divine the true cause of his death. However, as François Lesage explained, this was unlikely to happen for Dieusauveur because his family was Baptist, and "Protestants don't believe in taking a case like that to an *houngan*. They believe that prayer alone would work, but we know that what you need to take off the magic (*retire majik*) is a *lwa*." The following chapters will discuss these religious, moral, and medical issues in much greater detail: the procedures followed in consulting an *houngan*, paying him to retrieve a *mò* from the cemetery, and sending it against one's enemy, as well as the moral commentaries offered by both Catholics and Protestants about such practices.

However, long before Dieusauveur's family reached the point of deciding between consulting an *houngan* and relying on prayer, they had brought him to several well-equipped biomedical settings. Their complaint that the doctors could not do anything for him took on a special meaning in light of the general distinction between *maladi Satan* and *maladi Bondye*. When explaining the difference between these two categories, people routinely said that biomedicine is powerless before a *maladi Satan*. Janine Dutoit's remarks summarize the conventional opinion:

> If you're sick, and it was someone else who sent it on you, the doctor in the dispensary can't do anything for you . . . Even if you go to the dispensary, or Aux Cayes or Bonne Fin, you can easily spend a lot of money, and still die . . . You have to find a *ganga* [= *houngan*].

Jean Milot, an herbalist from a neighboring parish, told me that the hospital can treat illnesses of your body or your blood, such as "coldness" (*fredi*), tetanus, weakness (*feblès*),[29] but it can't treat *maladi majik*. Only after someone has been treated by a *houngan* should he go to the hospital "in order to get serum, to recover, to regain his strength."

The failure of biomedicine is the chief empirical marker of the categorical distinction between *maladi Satan* and *maladi Bondye*. As a particular episode of illness unfolds, therefore, people cannot know its status until they have finished with biomedical treatment. I interviewed explicitly on this point. Since the victim remains unaware of the maleficent motivations of others and the actions of an *houngan*, and even the poisonous powders and lamps are carefully hidden, how do you decide whether an illness has in fact been sent by someone? The answer was straightforward: you take it to the dispensary, and if the nurses or doctors can't do anything for you, then it's probably a *maladi Satan*. In fact, the failure of biomedicine encourages people to look carefully at other types of evidence: people start to inquire whether the victim habitually had conflicts or troubles with others, or has given her enemies a specific reason to try to do her in. (The suspicion of guilt accompanying "sent sicknesses" will be taken up in following chapters.)

The determination that a specific illness is humanly caused is thus made after the first stage in the help-seeking process: that is, after the biomedical definition of the problem and treatment fail to produce a cure. Dieusauveur's family had hoped that he could be treated success-fully at l'Hôpital Bonne Fin, but not only from an obvious desire to restore his health. If biomedicine was effective, they could safely assume that his illness was not caused by the malicious intentions of others, and even more, that he was not a deserving guilty victim of their pathogenic attack.

However, biomedicine could not save Dieusauveur's life, and the hurried grave-side ritual over his coffin suggests the moral implications of this biomedical failure. From a distance, I could see only a man placing something alongside Dieusauveur's body, closing the coffin, and then smashing a small bottle against the concrete base of the tomb. Other villagers attending the funeral informed me that this was a *senp*.[30] Through the ritual of including a *senp* in the coffin, Dieusauveur's body was protected against theft from the tomb. In one of the glosses of *maladi mò*, the victim is not actually killed, but rather only stunned (*etoudi*). The same people who sent the *mò* upon him then return to the grave, retrieve their victim, and either keep him as a slave or give him to the *houngan* as a required payment for other benefits, such as the victim's wealth or job that the *houngan* had granted them. By approving this *senp*, Dieusauveur's family wanted to guard him from such a fate.

Dieusauveur's death was a powerful event, and people responded through both the unmediated physical reaction of *kriz de ner* and the talk about Satanic illness. The rest of the book will examine the intricacies of this discourse: the way it organizes the practice of herbalists, midwives, and *houngan* – religious specialists who serve, and embody, various African-derived spirits (chapters 5 and 6); and the quintessential moral questions of innocence and guilt which it poses for healers, patients, and their kin (chapter 7). Based on the fundamental vocabulary presented above, these chapters will elaborate the contests for healing power and moral worth which follow on the failure of biomedical treatment, as well as people's practical defense against the pathogenic effects of human jealousy and malice.

Part II

The moral discourse of medical pluralism

5　The Catholic practice of healing

The morality of healers in rural Haiti

The actions taken to treat Janine Dutoit and Dieusauveur Martin exemplify how people negotiate between several different medical idioms over the course of a single illness episode. The case of Dieusauveur, in particular, demonstrates how much is at stake in naming a disorder and explaining what caused it. Not just his health, but also his moral status – whether he was an innocent or guilty victim of a *maladi Satan* – hung in the balance during the help-seeking process. However, healing practitioners themselves also move between several different conceptions of the source of therapeutic power. The struggles of these healers to authorize their own therapeutic knowledge and challenge the legitimacy of competing options is the topic of this chapter.

Jean Milot, a *doktè fèy* (herbalist), and Mme. Marie Beaumont, the midwife who originally diagnosed Janine Dutoit's disorder as *eklampsi*, enjoy secure reputations as effective healers among many residents of Jeanty. By narrating their life-histories and accounting for their particular skills, these healers take up a specific position in a plural moral universe. That is, they each appropriate a certain notion of upright ethical action in order to authorize their own therapeutic practice as both effective and morally correct. Like many other healing specialists in rural Haiti, they stake their moral claims in religious terms; in particular, by drawing on the several discourses of popular Haitian religion about the moral value of angels and spirits.

Residents of Jeanty consult a remarkably large array of non-biomedical healers. In fact, the local plural healing system includes the entire range of the practitioners mentioned by other Haitian and American anthropologists working in southern Haiti: midwives, bonesetters, herbalists, injectionists, *houngan* and *mambo* (male and female specialists in serving the spirits), and Protestant pastors (see Coreil 1979; Clerismé 1979; Conway 1978). Each researcher proposes different criteria to classify these healers. Conway privileges theories of etiology; according to him, religious specialists such as *houngan* and pastors are "personalistic" curers, who treat diseases caused by human or non-human agents, whereas herbalists and midwives are "naturalistic" curers (cf. Foster 1976). Coreil groups them into primary, secondary, and tertiary levels, based on the disorders treated, the cost of treatment, and practitioners' technology and level of training (Coreil 1983). Subsuming Haiti in the entire Afro-Caribbean region, Laguerre proposes three categories of "folk" practitioners: non-religious curers (including midwives and bone-setters); faith healers, inspired by God or spirits; and other morally ambiguous servitors of the spirits who both heal and cause illness (Laguerre 1987:55). Finally, Hess classifies non-professional healers into three sectors – domestic medicine, Creole medicine, and mercantile medicine – based on the social context of their practice and the disemic codes of Haitian culture (Hess 1981, 1983).

According to all of these schemes, herbalists and midwives are secular healers, in contrast to the religious specialists who rely on the power of either the Christian god or the *lwa* (African-derived spirits who populate the Vodoun cosmology). However, when I began my fieldwork in Jeanty in 1987, herbalists and midwives invariably mentioned an invisible spiritual entity called an *anj gadyen* (literally, "guardian angel") from our very first conversations. They referred to the *anj gadyen* in order to trace their career as healing specialists and to account for their unique healing power.

Although they construct the *anj gadyen* in different ways, their talk about it accomplishes much the same purpose. Catholic herbalists and midwives invoke the *anj gadyen* as part of a strategy to differentiate themselves from the immoral *houngan*, who serve not beneficent angels but rather the satanic *lwa* (also excoriated as "dirty spirits"). They invoke a fundamental ideological and moral divide – pitting Satan against Christ, and the *houngan* against Catholic healers – which in fact underlies the distinction between *maladi Bondye* and *maladi Satan* discussed in the last chapter. This is how herbalists and midwives justify their moral worth, legitimate their therapeutic power, and decide whether to run the moral risks of treating sent sickness.

Condemning the spirits

Take the example of Jean Milot, a 65-year-old Catholic herbalist who lives with his wife just across the shallow river bordering Jeanty. His home is sparse but large enough to house several of his four children when they return home between attempts at finding work in Les Cayes or Port-au-Prince. Of all the herbalists and midwives I interviewed, Jean

9 A woman selling herbal remedies in the market stretches after a
long morning sitting next to her table of bottles and dried leaves.

has the most personalized reading of the *anj gadyen*, and his position on the *lwa* exemplifies a widespread Catholic reading of the moral components of the self.

Jean begins his explanation of the *anj gadyen* (or *anj*, meaning simply "angels") by depicting them as the seat of individual autonomy and judgment:

> Each child of God has an *anj*, which was created with you, which directs you. The *anj* will tell you what to do, it will protect you. For example, the *anj* brought you here to my house. If you didn't have the *anj* which God placed in your head, you wouldn't know which route to take.

However, the *anj* (which Jean also refers to by the synonymous term "good soul," or *bon nanm*) does not alone make up the person. It is joined by a bad soul (literally, *gwo nanm*, or "large soul"), and in this Manichean reading of the self, the two souls coexist in the same individual's body. The *bon nanm* represents the source of virtuous and effective action, whereas the *gwo nanm* is the cause of immoral behavior:

> Each person has a *bon nanm* and a *gwo nanm* . . . The two are together in your body. The *bon nanm* was given to you by God, and it doesn't do things which are not good . . . The *gwo nanm* represents the other side of you . . . If you do something which is bad, it is the *gwo nanm* which makes you do it.
>
> But then you think about it, you mull it over, and you say that you shouldn't have done that. That's when the *gwo nanm* leaves your body, and the *bon nanm* appears. It understands the sin, it understands that you shouldn't have done that . . . When the *bon nanm* re-enters you, you see clearly.

This style of psychological and moral theorizing may well have characterized rural Haitian life throughout much of the twentieth century. The *anj gadyen* which Jean describes is roughly equivalent to the *ti bon anj* (the "small good angel"), a standard category of Haitian ethnopsychology mentioned by most researchers along with its complement, the *gwo bon anj* (the "big good angel"). Drawing on field-work in the late 1940s, for example, Métraux writes that the *ti bon anj* watches over the sleeper and, after death, accounts for the sins of the person who was in his charge (1972:303, 258). The *gwo bon anj* is made of grosser stuff; it is almost a material presence in the body. The *gwo bon anj* can be removed from someone's head and stored in a bottle to protect it from enemies, and after death it can linger, ghost-like, in the places the person lived (1972:306, 258).

Maya Deren provides a more speculative, metaphysical reading, but it better captures the moral concerns expressed by Jean and other healers. The *ti bon anj* represents an impersonal conscience or the universal commitment towards the good. It is detached from the pressures of daily

life, and impervious to development and corruption. The *ti bon anj* is thus
a constant of the human condition (Deren 1953:26). The *gwo bon anj* is
a person's soul understood as the repository of her history, abilities, and
intelligence. The activities of daily life – including the possibility of
mental confusion or evil – depend on constant communication with the
gwo bon anj (1953:27, 35).

To return to Jean Milot's own words, recall that he describes the *gwo
nanm* as the complement, and moral inverse, of the Catholic *bon nanm*
(the *anj gadyen*). He traces a person's decision to act unethically and then
re-evaluate one's sin to the waxing and waning influence of the two souls.
These ethnopsychological categories thus carry a moral force. They
constitute the self as both a purposeful agent who exercises full self-
control, and an ethically upright, morally correct person.

Jean thus deploys the moral rhetoric of good souls and bad souls (*bon
nanm* and *gwo nanm*) in several ways. He first describes the chaotic and
meaningless behavior typical of someone under the exclusive domination
of the *gwo nanm*:

> The *gwo nanm* is crazy. When people start to run around, to break things,
> to roll on the ground, they call him a crazy person. It is the *gwo nanm* that is
> directing him. The person doesn't have his *bon nanm* any more.
> If you didn't have the *anj*, you could have ended up in the river [separating
> Jean's house from Jeanty]. The *gwo nanm* would leave you in the water; it's an old
> soul, an old rebellious soul[1] . . . I know that the Christian *bon nanm* is in you,
> because you are writing down everything I say. If the *gwo nanm* were in
> you, you'd be writing nonsense.

According to Jean, the *gwo nanm* is responsible for people's unruly,
disordered behavior. But it also incites immoral or unethical conduct: it
leads you to do "something bad," "something which you shouldn't
have done." In this respect, the bad soul is both a morally inflected
component of the self and a personified spiritual being. Jean identifies the
gwo nanm as an "old rebellious soul," and opposes it to the Christian *bon
nanm*. On another occasion, Jean classified the *gwo nanm* as a "rebellious
angel," and then proceeded to say that a rebellious angel is a Satan. The
bad soul (and, likewise, the guardian angel) represent more than
conventional names for ethical principles; they are spiritual entities with
their own quasi-autonomous existence, and Jean embeds them in the
conventional moral structure of village Catholicism: the opposition
between Catholic worship and the service of the spirits, or *lwa*.

Haitian religious pluralism is enormously complex, comprising the
formal, state-sponsored Catholic church, numerous Protestant sects,
and that syncretic amalgam of West African practices and French
Catholicism which most non-Haitians know as Vodoun (but is usually

referred to in Creole by such terms as "to serve the spirits [*lwa*]" or "to serve the mysteries"). These different components cross-reference each other and even share key icons and forms of worship. However, Jean (like most other residents of Jeanty) repeatedly insisted to me that he is a Catholic who emphatically does *not* serve the spirits. The particular position he takes up in this plural religious landscape deeply informs his healing practice and the ways he makes it morally legitimate.

Jean stridently defines himself as a Catholic herbalist as opposed to an *houngan*, the expert in serving the *lwa*. He extends his discourse on angels, spirits, *bon nanm*, and *gwo nanm* to describe the source of his healing power and the origins of his career. To begin with, Jean relies on the *anj* in the preparation of specific herbal remedies:

> When you come to me, I consult you, I see what you have. We agree to meet tomorrow, for you to bring me money for the medication. Tonight, I'll see what I should do with you . . . When I sleep, the *anj* bring me all the ways to treat somebody. I can even answer them, saying "I'll do it." As soon as I fall asleep, I see how to act, which medications to buy.

The *anj* do more than simply bless the remedies or generally ensure that his therapeutic actions will be effective. According to Jean, the *anj* tell him which *fèy* to use for each specific case. Thus he once stated that because of the knowledge of the *fèy* possessed by his *anj*, "it really isn't me who treats people, it's the *anj kondiktè*" (the "conducting angel," a term synonymous with guardian angel).

The *anj* glossed as distinct spiritual beings also appear in Jean's story of the beginnings of his career as a *doktè fèy*. Jean underwent two types of apprenticeship. He first learned about treatments from his mother, a midwife and sometime herbalist. When Jean was in his early twenties, he began to substitute for her in deliveries and cases of illness. When she died, he continued to treat some of her old clients. He later learned how to use "magic" to treat "Satanic sicknesses" from an *houngan* named Luc Sinwa.

Although Jean gained his empirical knowledge from these apprenticeships, the immediate impetus to begin work as a *doktè fèy* was a call from his *anj*:

> I began treating people when I was 30 years old. An *anj kondiktè* told me how to do it while I was sleeping. I didn't want to do it at all, but then one day I injured myself with a knife while I was working. I saw in my sleep that it was the *anj* who had made me cut myself, because of my refusal to do the work they wanted.
>
> [Why didn't you want to do what the *anj* showed you?] All of my children are in Catholic school, and my wife takes communion and makes confession! So I don't want to have anything to do with that stuff. But when I saw that it was something serious, that they wanted me to be a doctor, I stuck to it.

Why did Jean originally refuse to follow the calling of his *anj kondiktè*? Jean mistook the *anj* for invisible beings of another sort – that is, for *lwa* who wanted him to serve as a devotee or *houngan*, engaged in the elaborate ceremonies of temple-based Vodoun, providing food to nourish the *lwa* or even lending his own body for them to possess. His refusal typifies the public repudiation of the *lwa* common among Catholic villagers. For Jean, the spirits stand for everything opposed to the kind of upright life which is sustained by participation in the Catholic sacraments. His refusal to work for the *lwa* thus testifies to his own moral virtue.

However, Jean eventually decided that the call he heard in his sleep came from his guardian angel, not the *lwa*, so he began practice as an herbalist, not as an *houngan* who serves the spirits. He continues his moral denigration of the realm of the *lwa* as he contrasts his own healing practice to that of an *houngan*:

> People who are *houngan* make good money. They push away God, and take up with Lucifer, with Ogoun,[2] in order to become wealthy. An *houngan* will make 200 gourdes, you'll only make 50. But you're better than he is. It is only in this world that the *houngan* has his mandate; after death, he's nothing. He's going under the feet of Lucifer . . . But if you are an herbalist, it's the work of God that you're doing.

The *houngan* literally sell themselves to the Devil. They may earn more money in this world than an herbalist, but they will be robbed of the afterlife in heaven that a good Catholic can expect. By demonizing both the *lwa* and those who serve them, Jean positions himself squarely on the side of the Catholic God. Jean originally opposed the good soul to the bad soul as two components of the self. He now extends the moral polarity to guardian angels (the effective source of his healing power) and the *lwa* (relied upon by the maleficent *houngan*).

Jean Milot here takes up a position I encountered often among the Catholic residents of Jeanty. If villagers approvingly regard the *anj gadyen* as the source of morally upright action, they take just the opposite position towards the *lwa*. For many people, the *lwa* represent the antithesis of Christian virtues. They often responded to my inquiries about the *lwa* with an incredulous question of their own: why was I interested in such dirty, Satanic matters? Even asking about it placed me under suspicion. They (half-jokingly) accused me of using the information to send a sickness upon someone or even to try calling the *lwa* myself.

In countless conversations, people expressed their visceral disgust with the *lwa*. Most people easily identify the *lwa* with bad souls. They use the term "Satan" to denote not only the *lwa* but also the *houngan* who serves them, the maleficent spirit they send upon their victim, and the resulting afflictions ("Satanic sicknesses").[3] In general, most people describe *houngan* as dirty, untrustworthy characters who invoke their spirits primarily to send sickness, but also for other immoral and unsavory purposes which no upstanding Catholic would even care to speculate about. Moreover, simply by opposing an *houngan* (e.g., by treating a sent sickness the *houngan* has caused), an innocent Catholic lays him or herself open to vicious and lethal counterattacks. Because of this danger, Jean refuses to treat *maladi Satan*, even though he knows how.

Why did people loudly demonize the spirits in my presence? A full answer begins with how people assimilated their relationship with me to the sedimented religious history of Haiti. In Jeanty, most people perceived me as a high-status outsider; someone with as much money and education would presumably practice only formal Catholicism. Denouncing the *lwa* is the same strategy they adopt in dealing with the only other foreigner living in the village, the French Catholic priest. Many people figured that I subscribed to the same hostility towards non-Catholic practices that has typified the colonialist European clergy (and Europeanized elite) in Haiti for most of the past 200 years (see Métraux 1972:323–59; Breathett 1983). In their dealings with me, they understandably choose the Catholic-inflected condemnation of the *lwa* as the appropriate idiom to portray themselves as reputable and morally trustworthy people.

However, publicly denouncing the spirits is a strategic move with several local benefits, as well. The Catholic church is one of the most powerful sources of formal social value and prestige in rural Haitian society (and far more legitimate than its closest rivals, the government and army). Most residents of Jeanty (approximately 85%) are Catholics who attend Sunday Mass and, if they can afford it, are baptized, confirmed, and married in the church. They want to keep up their reputations as good Catholics not only for me, but also for their neighbors and perhaps themselves. The strategy of condemning the *lwa* thus emerges not only where Haitians confront higher status (hence, presumably Catholic) foreigners, but also in many other contexts of village life where people position themselves as more enlightened (*eklere*), more educated, or more powerfully connected than their peers.

Their public rhetoric notwithstanding, people's actual religious practice follows quite another course. In their declarations in front of me or other villagers, people pose the choice in dichotomous terms: you can serve either Christ or the *lwa*, and in serving one, you repudiate the other. Obviously, this argument does not merely describe the situation; in its stark oppositional logic, it reproduces the condemnation of African-derived religious practices which the Catholic church has issued for several hundred years. In private interviews, however, many residents of Jeanty freely describe themselves as Catholics who also serve the spirits. In Jeanty (and throughout rural Haiti), people's actual religious behavior fits along a continuum, where most people attend some combination of both services for the *lwa* and formal Catholic Mass (cf. Drummond 1980). Their behavior does not fit the standard public rhetoric, which casts these as mutually exclusive and contradictory practices.

But religious pluralism in Haiti is more complex than the public denunciation, yet private approval, of services for the spirits (*pace* Desmangles 1992). In fact, people continue to denigrate the *lwa* and *houngan* even when they admit to *houngan*'s healing power and recount their own attendance in his consulting room. These particular denunciations result from the way people apply the formal moral code and social prestige of Catholicism to their immediate lives; the way they use it to figure their own innocence and guilt. I first encountered this attitude indirectly, in the form of resistance to my (awkward and probably impolite) questions. On one occasion, an elderly woman, the senior member of a prominent Jeanty family, denied any knowledge of the *lwa*. When I persisted and asked whether she ever visited an *houngan*, she quickly and defensively replied "Why should I? I don't have problems with anybody!" She took my question as a challenge, but not only about her formal religious affiliation. Apparently, I had accused her of something, and her response reflects the general understanding of why one might consult an *houngan* or know about their activities.

I was told that people seek out an *houngan* for one of only two reasons: to send an affliction upon an enemy, or to learn the cause of one's own affliction. Either motive can endanger one's public reputation not only as a faithful Catholic, but also as a morally upright person. Obviously, trying to send a sickness paints one as willing to murder others for personal gain, since jealousy over material resources (money, jobs, possessions) is one of the prime reasons to send a sickness. But merely consulting an *houngan* for one's own affliction can also carry a moral stain. Since the *houngan* is the only specialist who can identify a sent sickness, seeking him out suggests that one has potential enemies, who might have good cause to launch a malicious spiritual attack; for example, to revenge for a prior wrong. According to this cultural logical, merely having (or acknowledging) enemies holds one up to suspicion of guilty or immoral activities in the past. This explains perhaps the most common response to my question, have you ever visited an *houngan* for a sickness? "No, I'm innocent. I don't need to."

This concern with innocence and guilt pervades people's attitudes towards *houngan* and their healing powers. Any engagement with an *houngan* entails a suspicion of guilt. To hold the *houngan* in utter disrepute and loudly to proclaim one's ignorance of them powerfully attests to one's innocence. This is why *houngan* are despised and conventionally associated with the figure of Satan, the inverse image of Christian morality (cf. Hawkins 1984:349ff). Because the *houngan* owes his special maleficent power to these spiritual beings, people identify the *lwa* as satans, as well, and denigrate them in equally strong terms.

Jean Milot thus explicitly locates his therapeutic practice within the plural religious landscape of rural Haiti by invoking the conventional moral divide between Christ and Satan and stridently denouncing *houngan* and *lwa*. This strategy conforms to (and reproduces) the long-standing condemnation of African-derived religions by the national Catholic elite. Claiming a Catholic religious identity is a route to prestige and respectability through the espousal of European cultural practices that is common throughout the Caribbean (Wilson 1973). But this is not just a matter of claiming an external and visible religious affiliation. Jean is also protecting his reputation as a decent and ethically upright individual. Both motives inform his boast that he resists the temptation to reap the same profit as an immoral *houngan* – that he relies only on the angels' power to heal, not the satan's power to send sickness.

Calling the spirit: Mme. Beaumont and Erzili

Marie Beaumont is perhaps the most reputable midwife in Jeanty, and most people refer to her respectfully as Mme. Beaumont. She is a vigorous 55-year-old woman who lives with three daughters, her husband, and her husband's father in a large home near the center of Jeanty. She adopts yet another morally inflected position towards the *anj gadyen*, the *lwa*, and their influence on human behavior. In many respects, her position overlaps with the one taken by Jean Milot. However, Mme. Beaumont surveys these issues from a privileged perspective: unlike Jean, she can become possessed by various *lwa* virtually at will. On several occasions, Mme. Beaumont was entered by Ogoun and Erzili (two of the most important *lwa* in Haiti), and I was able to speak extensively with these embodied spirits.[4]

Mme. Beaumont considers herself a good Catholic, and both she and her daughters actively participate in church groups. Although she acknowledges that the *lwa* enter her, she refuses to draw upon their power in her healing practice. This is a contradictory and problematic position to occupy. Simply by having *lwa*, she risks being associated with other types of dirty, Satanic activities, such as the immoral and disorderly behavior caused by the bad soul (*move nanm*) and the *houngan*'s malign skill at sending sickness. In her discursive attempts to resolve this contradiction, she invokes two different accounts of the *lwa*: one rooted in the Catholic oppositional scheme also invoked by Jean Milot, and the other in the domestic cult of ancestors – a core component of popular Haitian religion. She selectively draws from both these religious idioms in order to narrate the origin of her healing practice and legitimize it as morally correct.

Mme. Beaumont's contradictory position first appears in her talk about the *anj gadyen*. She describes the *anj* in the same personalized terms that Jean employed, but her experience of them is even more vivid. Mme. Beaumont relates how she learned the skills of a midwife from the *anj* who came in her sleep:

> I saw people telling me, "do it this way, do it that way" . . . In my dreams, the *anj* gave me a scissors to cut the umbilical cord, they gave me thread to tie it off. I saw it as if in broad daylight with my eyes wide open. Each night I was doing a delivery, so finally I said to myself, "Okay, I'll make that my profession."

Like Jean Milot, Mme. Beaumont was initially confused about the identity of these beings who spoke to her in her sleep. Were they *anj* or *lwa*? Jean decided that it was the *anj*, after all, who wanted him to do the godly, beneficent work of a herbalist, not the *lwa* calling him to the Satanic activity of serving the spirits. But when I asked Mme. Beaumont the same question, she did not make as sharp a distinction. She told me, "Yes, the *anj* is like a *lwa*," and then hastened to add

> But I don't accept it. If I wanted it, that would be that. But I don't want it. The situation would be the same with my child: if she wanted to serve the *lwa*, she would serve the *lwa*, but she doesn't want to . . . If some guy comes to chat with me and I want to talk too, I'll answer him. But if I don't want to talk, I don't respond. It's the same thing.

Mme. Beaumont easily allows that the *anj* who instructed her in the midwife's trade resembled *lwa*. However, she adopts a position which successfully deflects the moral taint usually created by traffic with the spirits. In a partial break with the conventional Catholic scheme, Mme. Beaumont does not demonize the *lwa*. Merely having spirits does not mark her as evil, in league with Satan, and opposed to the godly Catholic realm. She chooses another strategy to establish her moral worth: she privileges not the absolute opposition between *anj gadyen* and *lwa*, but rather how she responds to the spirits' calls that she serve them as a mambo.

On this point, Mme. Beaumont is absolutely clear: she has decided not to serve the *lwa*. As she says above, this is simply a matter of choice, and no more difficult than refusing to interact with other human villagers. The *lwa* are not so powerful that they can force Mme. Beaumont's devotion against her will. Although she definitely has *lwa*, she retains the ability to refuse to serve them as a *mambo*, that is, to draw on their power for religious or therapeutic ends.[5] Through her vehement refusal to serve them, Mme. Beaumont distances herself from the evil and disorder which, according to the formal Catholic viewpoint in Haiti, inevitably result from contact with the spirits.

Mme. Beaumont thus moves away from the broad Catholic condemnation of the realm of the *lwa*, and into a more pragmatic discourse about vulnerability and protection from specific malign influences. She does not claim that the *lwa* are intrinsically evil, but rather that the *houngan* are tricky and unsavory characters, and that any engagement with them carries certain risks. Unlike Jean Milot, she does not condemn the *houngan* categorically for relying upon the spirits. Indeed, she acknowledges that by calling up their *lwa*, *houngan* enjoy certain powers that she lacks. This is chiefly the power to treat cases of Satanic sickness, and Mme. Beaumont reports her standard piece of advice for victims of this class of disorders: Go back to the *houngan* who sent the sickness upon you, so he can take it off again. Nonetheless, she generally thinks it is wiser for most people to avoid dealing with *houngan*.

However, Mme. Beaumont employs an even more persuasive strategy to ensure her moral worth. She does not classify the *lwa* which enter her as members of the same set which includes Satan, the *gwo nanm*, and the crafty and untrustworthy *houngan*. On the contrary, she locates them in her very own family. "These *lwa* come from my family line, they come from my ancestors," she repeatedly told me. Mme. Beaumont here embeds the *lwa* in a radically different framework from the conventional Catholic scheme. She defines the *lwa* in terms of the family cult of ancestral spirits, a vital component of religious life for many Haitian villagers which lies entirely outside of both formal Catholic worship and attendance at the *houngan*'s healing ceremonies. By invoking the ideology of the domestic cult of ancestors, Mme. Beaumont can escape the Catholic rhetoric of moral condemnation.

Students of Haitian religion often distinguish between the domestic forms of worship vs. public temple-based cults. Most classic works (e.g., Métraux 1972; Deren 1953; Simpson 1970; Bastide 1971; Rigaud 1953) focus primarily on the public cults. These seem to be more common in Port-au-Prince and the surrounding area (the Cul de Sac Plain) than in other regions of the country. They involve more elaborate and expensive rituals as well as a social hierarchy comprising *houngan* and several lower grades of devotees who enter through initiation rites. The detailed classifications of various *lwa* and their traits presented by the above authors reflect the knowledge of the *houngan* leaders of these public cults (cf. Métraux 1978; Courlander, personal communication). However, the meanings Mme. Beaumont assigns to the spirits arise from the domestic form of popular Haitian religion, which in rural areas is essentially a localized ancestral cult (cf. Herskovits 1937; Murray 1977; Lowenthal 1978; Smucker 1984).

In this cult, the *lwa* are conceived of as quintessential local spirits, associated with one's ancestors and tied to one's family lands. Ancestors further than two generations back (one's grandparents' generation) typically become assimilated to the "generalized archetypes" of *lwa* mentioned in most accounts of Haitian religion: Ogoun, Erzili, Damballah, etc. (Smucker 1984; Brown 1991). "Serving the spirits," in this context, means satisfying the sensual desires of the spirits and fulfilling one's familial obligations to the ancestors. The *lwa* are not demonized as the moral inverse of *anj gadyen*; on the contrary, people grant them a series of ordinary human traits. Métraux, for example, writes that they are "wily, lascivious, sensitive, jealous, and subject to violent attacks of rage which are quickly over . . . " (1972:94). In Jeanty, people assume that these *lwa* have much the same tastes as human beings: they enjoy drumming and dancing at the ceremonies held in their honor as well as the sweet foods and alcoholic beverages which people place on small household shrines to their family *lwa*.[6] If neglected for too long, a *lwa* can bother various family members by causing sickness or a run of misfortune which continues until the schedule of offerings is resumed (cf. Lowenthal 1978)

Mme. Beaumont cannot help that her family's spirits chose her (or that they continue to "dance in her head"), but she refuses to satisfy them with ceremonies, feed them with offerings, or do the *mambo*'s work of divination and healing (cf. Brown 1991:203ff). Within the Catholic framework, it is easy to understand her rejection of the *lwa*; they represent the undesirable inverse of Catholic virtues. However, within the idiom of the cult of domestic spirits, she rejects the *lwa* for a less momentous reason: she simply doesn't like them. They are attracted to her, but she does not return their attention. This is a legitimate idiom for one's relationship to the *lwa* within Haitian popular religion. The *lwa* are attracted to her for obscure and capricious reasons, so her refusal of them is equally uncomplicated: "The *lwa* exists, but I don't acknowledge it as my own.[7] It's like a child who was born without a father . . . I don't recognize it as my child . . . I make the *lwa* into an orphan."

Mme. Beaumont claims that she has abandoned the *lwa*, but the *lwa*

has not abandoned Mme. Beaumont. She says that she refuses to nurture
it or even to acknowledge that she is related to it, and for her, that settles
the case. But because she does not demonize *lwa*, Mme. Beaumont made
no attempt to hide her ability to call the spirits, either from me or from
the many other villagers who have personally witnessed the *lwa* "dancing
in her head." Not surprisingly, when her *lwa* speaks it offers quite
another opinion on Mme. Beaumont's rejection of it. It also reveals that,
contrary to all of her protests, Mme. Beaumont does rely on the power
of the *lwa* when faced with difficult deliveries.

I never needed to request explicitly that Mme. Beaumont call her
spirits. Instead, during our long conversations in the sitting room of
her house, either she or her husband would nonchalantly suggest that she
call the *lwa*. The first time this happened, Ogoun was the *lwa* who spoke
to me. When the suggestion was made again during the next interview, I
said I had already spoken with Ogoun. Mme. Beaumont asked me, "Is
there another one you need? Do you need Erzili? You'll really have to pay
her well; she won't come for free! Ogoun was angry at the old 1 dollar
you gave the last time."

Mme. Beaumont can call up Erzili with minimal preparation or ritual
apparatus. She simply had her husband fetch a cup of water and then
walked with it to the narrow porch in front of her house. She dripped the
water three or four times on the ground, saying "Erzili, there is someone
who is calling for you." She came back inside, returned to the chair where
she had sat throughout the interview, took off her eyeglasses, and closed
her eyes. As she sank back into the chair, the mood of the room seemed
to change. The laughing and teasing between me, Mme. Beaumont,
members of her family, and mutual friends ceased and gave way to a
quieter and more serious and respectful atmosphere. After only a few
minutes, Mme. Beaumont (or, rather, Erzili) looked up and shook both
left and right hands with everyone present.[8]

The impression that a spirit had actually entered her was sustained in
several ways. Erzili began speaking in a soft whisper, far meeker than
Mme. Beaumont's confident and brash style. (This voice fits with the
usual characterization of Erzili as the apotheosis of sensual feminine
grace and beauty, cf. Métraux 1972:110; Desmangles 1992:131–44;
Brown 1991:225–46.) She always referred to Mme. Beaumont in the
third person, as "my horse." This is one of the most common analogies
for a spirit entering a human being: the *lwa* "mounts his/her horse."
When Erzili decided to leave, she closed her eyes and settled back into
the chair. After several minutes, Mme. Beaumont opened her eyes and
asked for her eyeglasses, as though she had just taken them off. She
noticed me seated in front of her, and asked, "You're still there? You

haven't left yet?" Her speech and behavior were enormously convincing; the entire performance supported the notion that a separate spirit had temporarily inhabited her and then left her with no memory of its actions.

I was thus able to interview Erzili on the same range of topics as the other healing specialists in Jeanty: I asked her what herbal remedies she knows and what sicknesses she is able to treat. However, the *lwa* soon brought the conversation around to her own central themes: her annoyance that Mme. Beaumont refuses to work for her, and her fond memories about the better days when she was served by the midwife's grandparents:

> I'm not in the habit of treating people. My horse [i.e., Mme. Beaumont] doesn't want to do it. I could take off an old Satanic sickness . . . If you're sick, I could tell if it's a Satanic sickness upon you. I could take it off today, and tomorrow you'd go home.
>
> If my horse wanted to do it, I could make her a big-time *mambo* . . . If my horse wanted to receive me, the way her grandmother did, she would be really wealthy . . . But she would rather talk with the white foreigner to make her money. Because you're a little rich kid. You're like the snake that swallowed the frog.

Erzili here boasts about her healing powers and complains that they are wasted by Mme. Beaumont's refusal to become a *mambo*. (She also teases me about having a huge income unrelated to my skills or anything I actually accomplished in the village.) She seems absolutely mystified by her horse's decision, and elsewhere she calls her horse stupid and lazy. But the *lwa* is not genuinely vindictive. Although Mme. Beaumont has abandoned her, Erzili will not revenge herself upon her horse or her horse's children. The *lwa* says that she would only punish someone who had once served her but then stopped, and that exempts Mme. Beaumont.

Despite her poor treatment from Mme. Beaumont, the *lwa* has not abandoned her. In a story about a delivery in Jeanty, Erzili describes how she entered Mme. Beaumont, and thereby actually saved her life. This story sheds new light on Mme. Beaumont's vehement claims that she refuses to call upon the *lwa*'s power in her healing practice.

Erzili relates that her horse went to the home of a pregnant woman a few months ago to attend a delivery along with Octavia, another prominent midwife in Jeanty. The woman delivered her child without complications, but then could not deliver the placenta, and soon afterwards went into convulsions, lost consciousness, and died. Erzili claims that the death resulted from a sickness sent upon her by some enemy in the village:

> [How did you know it was a sent sickness which troubled her?] She delivered easily, without any problem. And she had delivered her two other children with

no problems. But that night, when she delivered, a sheep and a goat died right in the middle of things . . . I don't know why [she got the sent sickness]. She could have sworn at somebody, caused trouble for some people. That could have made them get her. She was pregnant, so she was easy to do in.

According to Erzili, as the woman lay dying, the same maleficent force was not satisfied with killing its original target and attacked Mme. Beaumont as well as Octavia, and the two midwives were overcome by nausea and vomited. At that moment, Erzili entered her horse and Octavia's *lwa* appeared as well. Erzili says that they would have been killed without the protection which she and Octavia's spirit provided.

This story reveals the complexities of Mme. Beaumont's relationship with her *lwa*. To begin with, the account replicates some aspects of the oppositional Catholic moral scheme. Erzili characterizes the episode as a Satanic sickness, probably sent by human enemies who sought revenge for the victim's own hostile and immoral actions. However, since Erzili herself told the story, she casts herself in the opposite role from the one the *lwa* conventionally plays in the Catholic idiom. Most villagers would classify the *lwa* as an intrinsically evil analogue to the *move nanm*, a member of the same ungodly set as the dirty *houngan* and Satan. In the story which Erzili tells, however, she is the protector from evil rather than its source.

During the delivery, the *lwa* actually plays a role closer to the *anj gadyen*, ensuring that no harm comes to Mme. Beaumont. Erzili even remarks, "If my horse had truly not accepted me in her head, she would have died along with the mother of the child."[9] However, the protective presence of the *lwa* does not ultimately challenge Mme. Beaumont's vehement position that she does not serve the spirits. As Erzili recounted the events of the delivery, she never once described her horse calling upon her. She instead characterized her relationship with Mme. Beaumont in the following ways: "I helped my horse do a delivery; when she's involved in her work, I come; If I see it's something my horse can't do, I enter her." Erzili comes of her own volition, not in response to Mme. Beaumont's request. In this way, Mme. Beaumont preserves her identity as a midwife, not a *mambo*; as someone who may receive the spirits' protection, but does not actually serve them.

The Catholic discourse of healing power

Because of their reliance on the empirical techniques of herbal medicine and midwifery, Jean Milot and Mme. Beaumont seem to differ categorically from the range of religious healers in rural Haiti: *houngan* and *mambo* who draw their therapeutic power from the spirits, Protestant pastors who heal when possessed by the Holy Ghost, and lay Catholic groups who rely on prayer and exorcism in their ceremonies for the afflicted (see chapters 6 and 7). Nonetheless, their own life stories and accounts of treating clients suggest that it is wrong to classify them as secular healers. Jean and Mme. Beaumont take up a definitive and emphatically non-secular position in the plural Haitian religious system.

To begin with, they continually impressed upon me that they are good Catholics: neither servitors of the spirit nor members of Protestant sects. More importantly, in the very descriptions of their healing practice, Jean and Mme. Beaumont invoke a range of invisible spiritual beings: guardian angels, good and bad souls, the *lwa* as malevolent "dirty spirits," and the *lwa* as ancestral shades. They draw on this religious rhetoric both to explain the origins of their healing careers and to account for the power of their treatments. They compare themselves to other healers not as secular vs. sacred, but rather as inspired by angels vs. servitors of the spirits. Finally, they invoke the same morally inflected ethnopsychology to portray their practice as motivated by the principle of mature, orderly, and controlled behavior.

At this point, however, their strategies diverge. Jean and Mme. Beaumont each propose a different reading of the competing sources of healing power. They both locate themselves in the morally superior position, but in the context of two different arrays, that is, two different conceptions of self and spirit. The herbalist and midwife do not merely occupy different positions within the same ethical and religious framework; they actually imagine and inhabit different moral worlds.

Jean Milot assumes and recreates the conventional moral divide of village Catholicism. He constructs the guardian angel in specifically Catholic terms, as the moral inverse of the *lwa*, in order to characterize himself as a morally correct healing specialist, as opposed to the dirty *houngan*. His rhetorical strategy emerges from a series of related oppositions, and he clearly positions himself on the right-hand, and morally superior, side of this array.

Satan	vs.	*Christ*
Lwa (anj rebel)		*Anj gadyen (ti bon anj)*
Bad soul (*move nanm*; *gwo nanm*)		Good soul (*bon nanm*)
Serving the *lwa*		Attending Catholic Mass
Houngan (religious specialist)		Catholic priest
Houngan (healer)		Catholic herbalist/midwife
Maladi Satan		*Maladi bondye*

These oppositions, however, do not depict the "underlying symbolic structure" of healing power in Jeanty. It is not a model of all possible positions, which allows the anthropologist to locate particular individuals according to their religious affiliation or therapeutic practice (she either serves the spirits or attends Mass; he practices as either an *houngan* or an herbalist). On the contrary, this diagram simply denotes – in more formal and explicit terms – the way that Jean Milot authorizes his healing practice as effective and morally correct. The diagram itself already announces a determinate position vis-à-vis the source of morality and healing power. It is the conventional Catholic framework invoked by Jean Milot and many other villagers in front of particular audiences.

To array these terms as a series of mutually exclusive and binary oppositions is an accomplishment, a particular way to affirm one's innocence, not a neutral description of the shared deep structure of belief. It is only one of the many possible crystallizations of the syncretic religious system in Jeanty. This conventional moral divide is convincing, and many Catholic villagers accept it – certainly in public and often as a guide to private action as well. Because this divide animated so many of my conversations about the *lwa* with village residents, I present it here in its unvarnished form: a moralistic dichotomy between good and evil which allows no compromise.

This picture of religious practice, however, differs dramatically from the usual perspective in Haitian ethnography. Most anthropologists take one of two approaches to popular religion in Haiti. The first approach privileges people's psychological ease in moving between Catholic and neo-African elements and inventing new hybrid forms (Herskovits 1937; cf. Apter 1991). The alternative is to focus on the relative insignificance of Christianity for believers, who are depicted as moving below the surface of Catholic icons and rituals in order to reach a putatively more authentic African core (Desmangles 1992; Brown 1991). These views of religious practice complement the two major models of Haitian religious syncretism: a genuine fusion of formerly distinct elements vs. a stratigraphic juxtaposition in which the original content of each element is preserved (for hundreds of years, in the case of inherited West African components) (Brodwin 1994).

What accounts for the difference between these classic approaches and the oppositional model presented here? Regional variation may play a part; people in villages like Jeanty, with its enthusiastic and highly regarded priest, may simply come closer to the formal ideal of *Katolik fran* ("pure Catholic") than in other places. Equally important, however, was how I chose to interpret people's talk about their religious practice. Most people initially assimilated me to a well-known social category, almost a stereotype: the high-status and presumably Catholic foreigner (a plausible guess, since I lived in the same compound as the priest at the start of fieldwork). This kind of person would expect vehement denunciations of the *lwa* and would make an appreciative audience for them. People's protests of moral innocence and their claims never to have served the *lwa* were appropriate to the stereotypical role people assigned me.

However, the dialogical situation of fieldwork was more complicated than this. The strident disdain for the *lwa*, after all, is not a recent foreign importation. The Catholic church has been part of the fabric of Haitian society since the French colonial regime 300 years ago, and it remains the major legitimate institution in the countryside. The stereotypical foreigner who is disdainful of *Vodoun* is just an extreme caricature of one of the many voices which make up the cultural conversation in current-day Haiti. Moreover, this is a voice that everyone can adopt, and speaking it carries certain benefits. In particular, it can bring one closer to the socially dominant code of value and respect, a code which many people have partially internalized.

In the face-to-face situation of fieldwork, therefore, people ran the risk of losing status if they did not denigrate the *lwa* in the strongest terms. They would potentially lose status not only in my (stereotypical foreigner's) eyes, but also in the eyes of other villagers and perhaps by their own standards as well. For this reason, I did not take their claims to be good unalloyed Catholics as an attempt to manipulate me or deceive me about their true religious identity. Indeed, I do not assume that there exists a single religious identity in Haiti behind the multiplicity of specific practices and expressions of faith.

The elaborate oppositional array depicted above (p. 125) is neither a neutral description of the underlying religious structure nor a way to disguise the true affiliation or beliefs of particular speakers. Although it answered the exigencies of the moment (that is, when a presumably Catholic foreigner started asking about *Vodoun*), it is constructed out of the dominant code of morality in rural Haiti, and it represents a legitimate and stable position to occupy in this plural religious system.

However, there are other ways in Jeanty to imagine a moral world and to ally oneself with the morally correct sources of therapeutic power. Mme. Beaumont, for example, chooses a strategy which differs from the schema presented above. The crucial point for her is not whether she has *lwa* (which she freely admits to), but whether she chooses to serve them. Although she partially accepts the conventional Catholic moral divide, a more permeable boundary separates her from the paradigmatic chain originating with Satan. First of all, simply having *lwa* does not constitute a moral stain. Secondly, when the *lwa* do enter her, they do not demonically impel her to perform immoral acts. They instead assist in her work, exemplified by Erzili extending protection and even healing power to her. In their separate ways, Jean and Mme. Beaumont authorize themselves as ethically upright actors who have made the right choice among competing moral worlds. The *houngan* and *mambo*, profiled in the next chapters, actually do the same thing, but by proposing a moral world which moves even further away from the conventional Catholic reading.

6 *Houngan* and the limits to Catholic morality

The dirty *houngan*: a Catholic perspective

From my very first days in Jeanty, I was eager to begin speaking with *houngan* and *mambo*: individuals who call up the spirits and explicitly rely on their healing power. Years of graduate training in anthropology had not suppressed my typically American fascination with the exotic side of popular Haitian religion.[1] Luckily – for both my research and my reputation in the village – my desire was frustrated at every turn. Because of the conventional public disdain for the *lwa* and those who serve them, people rarely admitted to any knowledge of local *houngan*. In fact, several months passed before I managed to make contact with *houngan* who lived nearby, who were willing to speak with me, and who knew the handful of people who helped me throughout my research. I thus had ample time to become familiar with the range of attitudes held by Catholic villagers towards the *houngan*.

In public, villagers invariably discussed the *houngan* in terms of the Catholic moral framework presented in the previous chapter. Most villagers insisted that they never visited one or even knew anything about their practice. Often their denials were angry and defensive, as though I had accused them of engaging in criminal activity. Indeed, from the conventional Catholic perspective, any contact with an *houngan* carries a suspicion of guilt. *Houngan* are known as specialists in *maladi Satan*, and consulting them raises the possibility that one either is a "guilty victim" of such a humanly caused illness, or else harbors malicious designs to send a sickness upon someone else.

However, to consult an *houngan* for healing poses not only a moral threat, but also an immediate physical threat to one's health. The majority of villagers genuinely acknowledge and fear the *houngan*'s malign ability to send sickness. As I heard many times, "The *ganga* who treats you could well be the same one who made you sick." This dangerous, ambivalent power both to harm and to heal also contributes to the devaluation of *houngan* expressed by the majority of villagers. Most

129

people I spoke with basically agreed with the conclusions of one young man: "If you don't need anything from a *divinò*, you wouldn't go to one."

How, then, did residents of Jeanty understand my own desire to meet with an *houngan*? People occasionally teased me about my motives: What do you need from those people? I was asked. Do you want to buy a powder to do away with someone? Do you want to "buy points" to become rich?[2] While they usually meant this as a joke, at times people genuinely wondered whether I might cross the line and come to "serve the spirits" myself. On several occasions, both virtual strangers and some of my closest friends asked me whether I wanted to purchase the services offered by an *houngan* (e.g., killing an enemy or quickly amassing great wealth), to join the group of men informally associated with particular *houngan*, or even to begin practice as a *divinò* myself. These were not inquiries about my religious affiliation or the cognitive content of my beliefs; they instead concerned my personal morality. For example, Gisèle, a young woman who worked in the priest's compound, had repeatedly warned me against visiting the *houngan*. When I asked her why, she answered from the familiar Catholic position: "That's not something I believe in. I don't like it, I'm afraid of it . . . Why do want to talk to those people? Do you want to work as a *divinò* when you return home?" I said no, I did not want to become a *divinò*; I simply wanted information about their practice. Taking a cue from her talk about beliefs, I told her I was not afraid of *houngan*, because I don't believe in Satan. She quizzed me closely on this last point:

> You say you don't believe in Satan, but if someone told you to do something that was bad, you wouldn't do it, would you? [I answered: No, I wouldn't.] So, that is what causes you not to believe in Satan. But if someone ordered you to do something that was wrong, and you did it, then you would believe in Satan.

Gisèle's concern about my visiting the *houngan* was essentially a question about my moral scruples. I missed the point at the time, because Gisèle and I used the concept of "belief" in fundamentally different ways. By saying I did not believe in Satan, I tried to locate myself outside the conventional Catholic universe. I meant that I did not demonize the people practicing as *houngan* or consider them to have Satanic powers. Because I did not subscribe to local understandings of the *houngan*, I did not fear them as dirty and dangerous figures (see Good 1994:14–16).

In the questions she posed to me, however, Gisèle used the notion of "belief" to mean loyalty to an ideal code of behavior. Gisèle herself does not believe in Satan, but this does not mean that she dismisses the influence of Satan as the spiritual principle of evil or of satans as the media for the *houngan*'s pathogenic attacks. She has not forsaken the map of the spiritual world proposed by village Catholicism. To disbelieve in Satan means rather that she chooses not to act in "Satanic" (that is, evil or sinful) ways. Gisèle locates herself in the local moral system which gives a paramount place to individual choice. She discusses "belief in Satan" in much the same way as other residents of Jeanty talk about the decision to follow an *houngan* or remain a "pure Catholic," and as Mme. Beaumont discussed receiving or resisting her family *lwa*. According to Gisèle, all humans must actively choose whether to act in moral or immoral ways. In asking me whether I believed in Satan, Gisèle wanted to know which decision I would make. From her standpoint, the question of belief in Satan therefore does not turn on one's cognitive assent to a certain account of spiritual reality, but rather one's moral assent to an ethical ideal.

The social context of *houngan*'s practice

Only by accompanying people to the consultation rooms of local *houngan* did I eventually learn the other possible responses – besides moral devaluation – to the realm of the spirits. The people who introduced me to *houngan* were two relatively poor young men who, while nominally Catholic, rarely attended Mass in the central church. These two individuals, along with my research assistant and occasionally other mutual friends, always accompanied me to interviews with the local *houngan*. Although they never exactly pledged me to secrecy, they did ask that I not tell too many people where we were going. They knew that other residents of Jeanty could easily assume that I intended to purchase immoral and dangerous services from the people we visited.

There are fewer *houngan* in Jeanty than either herbalists or midwives. Everyone can name a different expert in the use of *fèy*, and dispensary staff can list at least twenty women who practice as midwives in the commune. However, extensive interviews with people who serve the *lwa* revealed a much smaller number of *houngan*: only eight individuals from both the commune of Jeanty and contiguous parts of the neighboring commune of Torbec, roughly the entire area within a two-hour walk from the Jeanty marketplace. Many more people recognized the names of these eight *houngan* if directly asked, even when they claimed never to have visited one.

Again in contrast to both herbalists and midwives, most *houngan* live relatively far from the village center. The *houngan* from Jeanty live in isolated hamlets past several steep hills, while those in Torbec live far from the few passable dirt roads traversing the Cayes plain. Only one of these eight *houngan* makes his home in the village center, and even he does not have an extensive local following (he prefers to hold all of his ceremonies for his *lwa* in the distant coastal town where he stays most of the year). I was told that most *houngan* did not dare establish themselves in the village center: the Catholic priest is too popular, people said, and villagers would become angry if an *houngan* openly attempted to raise his visibility by moving down from the mountains.

The homes of *houngan* are relatively large, but the only visible sign that their owners serve the spirits is a separate open structure with thatch roof supported by a well-worn central post and ringed by benches at the perimeter of the hard-packed dirt floor. These open-air rooms, called *pewon*, resemble similar sanctuaries, or peristyles, found in temple-based cults in Port-au-Prince (cf. Métraux 1972:77ff; Deren 1953:36, 47; Courlander 1960:129 and *passim*). In Jeanty, they are the site of elaborate and dramatic rituals for the *lwa* involving animal sacrifice for a family's ancestral spirits as well as the embodiment of the *lwa* by their human devotees (cf. Lowenthal 1978). These ceremonies are probably the most important of the *houngan*'s religious tasks. Some families in Jeanty honor their *lwa* only once a year, or even once every several years, and they typically spend enormous sums to purchase sacrificial animals and pay for the *houngan*'s service. Other major ceremonies take place according to a ritual calendar which overlaps with the cycle of Catholic holidays (these ceremonies are concentrated in late summer, coinciding with several Patron Saints' festivals, and from All Saints' Day until the new year). Finally, people will also pay for a large ceremony in order to propitiate the *lwa* judged responsible for a particular case of *maladi Satan* (this occurred during the illness described in the following chapter).

Such ceremonies – lasting anywhere from a few hours to several days – are rich, multilayered collages of possession, dance, and spirit songs interwoven with the rituals of sacrifice to the *lwa* and other acts of devotion. These complex social performances offer a condensed version of the symbolic world of popular Haitian religion, especially its African-derived theological and aesthetic base. However, the ceremonies do not provide a very good window into the moral and ideological motives of the people who come to them for healing. By the time they arrive, ritual participants have already decided that their affliction is a *maladi Satan*. The crucial questions of innocence and guilt are investigated in an earlier stage of the help-seeking process: the individual consultations, divinations, and small-scale treatments that take place in a small room in the *houngan*'s home.

These private consultations have rarely been the topic of ethnographic study. Most anthropologists of popular religion in rural Haiti focus chiefly on the elaborate quasi-public ceremonies. For example, Métraux

(1972) devotes seven pages (out of 366) to the sending of *maladi Satan,* and little more than two pages to private divinations: the topics which occupied the bulk of my interviews with six different *houngan* over the course of several months. My interest in private consultations meant that I witnessed only a handful of actual treatments. After all, resorting to an *houngan* for an illness is a risky business; a stranger would never be welcome to sit in. Someone unknown to the family can legitimately observe an individual's treatment only when it takes place during a larger ceremony, where the person receiving healing may well be indistinguishable from other participants. Moreover, it meant that most *houngan* assimilated me to the category of client: someone who comes to address personal questions to the *lwa*. I was not considered a potential devotee who wants to take part in the dancing and singing in order to invite a *lwa* to enter his head. But I was not the novelty that I seemed to herbalists and midwives – someone who came only for an interview, instead of a consultation based on genuine need.

I thus approached the *houngan* like any other villager who required the spirit's assistance, and they responded to me in kind. For example, during our first visit with St. Denis, a 63-year-old *houngan* living in the Cayes plain, I introduced myself and my range of interests: the use of *fèy* for healing sicknesses, the reasons why people visit an *houngan,* and the causes of *maladi Satan*. St. Denis quickly rattled off a list of the various *fèy* and their uses, and then turned to my friends and inquired, "For these other questions, does he want me to call up the mysteries?" Whereas herbalists and midwives gain their expertise from the *anj gadyen* who speak to them during sleep or through apprenticeship with older practitioners, the *houngan* rely entirely on the *lwa* for their knowledge and healing power.

I soon learned to state at the very beginning that I was interested in a consultation. This immediately thrust me into the role of a client who goes to the *houngan*'s private consultation room in order to speak with a *lwa*. Without exception, the *houngan* I interviewed were perfectly content with this arrangement. Indeed, the few times that I spoke with them when they did not have their *lwa*, they had little to say about their religious role or healing skills.

Almost all of my interviews with *houngan* took place in their dark and cramped consultation rooms, usually located in one corner of the *houngan*'s home. These rooms can generally hold no more than four or five people at a time, perching on a low bench or the few chairs which line the wall. The *houngan* sits at a small table or desk crowded with an assortment of old bottles and clay jars (*govi*), rocks caked with wax drippings from innumerable candles, a small bell and a worn deck of cards, and sometimes a few polished stones. Some *houngan* decorate the walls with *veve*: abstract symbolic emblems of particular spirits drawn in charcoal (cf. Métraux 1972:163ff; Brown 1976). Others affix images of various Catholic saints, especially those considered the analogues of *lwa*, such as St. Patrick, St. James, and the Virgin Mary. These prints are usually blackened by smoke and barely recognizable.

Invoking and embodying the *lwa*

Louis Narcisse was a middle-aged man who had complained to me for several months about his painful muscle aches and fatigue. When he told me he was afraid he might be suffering from a *maladi Satan*, I offered to accompany him to an *houngan* and pay for his consultations.[3] Louis knew the name of André Chavannes, an *houngan* living across the river in a neighboring parish, and we arrived there for the first consultation one day in the early afternoon. André greeted us at the door, and after the necessary introductions, led us into his small consulting room and sat at his table. It was covered with a heavy red cloth, and an assortment of small bottles filled with remedies lined the back. Among the clutter of other objects, including a few decks of cards and a kitchen knife, was an old battered French book, missing its cover and with mouldering yellow pages. The book contained Catholic prayers and devotional passages written in both French and Latin.[4] On the floor next to his table were some items left over from the treatment of other clients. These illuminations (*iliminasyon*), as André called them, were used to prepare herbal remedies. A bowl full of a viscous mixture of pounded leaves was draped with folded white cloths and sat in the center of a ring of empty cola bottles. Bunches of *fèy* and a mortar and pestle leaned against the wall.

As André settled in his chair, he lit an oil-wick lamp (called *tèt lamp gridap*, these are widely used in rural households). He rang a small bell, then tidied up the table in a cursory fashion, arranging the playing cards in a single pile and placing his bell on the top. Sitting upright in his chair, he crossed himself, rang the bell again, and began rapidly to whisper a Catholic prayer in Frenchified Creole. When the prayer was finished, he reached over for one of the bottles, uncorked it, and inhaled it once through each nostril. He then took the red kerchief from the back of his chair, wiped his face on it (it was getting hot in the small, airless room), and laid it across his shoulders.

Although André was engrossed in these various activities connected with calling up the *lwa*, there seemed no alteration in his mood or the quality of his consciousness. He yelled out to his wife to buy a cola

10 An *houngan* (male specialist in serving the spirits), right, and his friend give an impromptu performance of the singing and drumming which call down the spirits.

bottle's worth of rum and laughed when he overheard his neighbors complaining about their losses in the lottery. However, the next stage – the actual entering of the *lwa* – involved a more drastic change. With the red kerchief draped on his shoulders, André closed his eyes, leaned over the table, and buried his head in his hands. After mumbling a few more prayers, he began to induce a series of long guttural belches and coughs. These became progressively more violent over the next ten minutes: André began to moan and gasp for air between the coughs which wracked his entire upper body. Finally, after one last fit of coughing, belching, and gagging, it all abruptly stopped, and André leaned silently back in his chair, his eyes still closed.

He soon began to rock back and forth and softly whistled, a serene smile on his lips. For several minutes, André sang a spirit song (*chante lwa*), and then he opened his eyes, straightened his back, and looked sternly up again at the wall in front of him. He crossed himself, rang the small bell, and then turned to us with an entirely new expression. He noticed our presence, as if for the first time, and formally greeted us while shaking our hands in the distinctive crosswise fashion often used by people with *lwa*. From this moment until the end of the consultation (which lasted about an hour) we communicated only with his *lwa*, who was named Byenzomal.[5] André Chavannes, the spirit's "horse," seemed completely absent. When he had finished the divinations and given to Louis the names of several remedies to purchase, Byenzomal rang the bell again and announced, "We're through." Louis and I left the room to sit on the small porch in front of the house. After no more than five minutes, André emerged and joined us. He acted exactly as before the consultation; his *lwa* had entirely disappeared.

Each of the six *houngan* I interviewed employs slightly different technical devices to call up his spirits, but these are no more than variations on a theme. The spirit never enters all of a sudden; the *houngan* must first take several steps to invoke it. André Chavannes did this, for example, by crossing himself, ringing a bell, and singing spirit songs (*chante lwa*). Other common techniques include pouring a few drops of water on the ground or wafting smoke through the room. Following these ritual actions, the *houngan* induces a trance using one of several techniques. André's fits of belching and coughing ranked among the more dramatic; other *houngan* would rap themselves on the head, stare blankly into a glass of water or candle flame, or pray intensely with their eyes closed.

Many formal elements of these consultations with *houngan* recall the description of Mme. Beaumont calling up her *lwa*, Erzili (see the previous chapter). For example, Mme. Beaumont as well as most *houngan* follow the same two-step procedure of first inviting the *lwa* and then inducing a trance during which the *lwa* actually enters them. However, Mme. Beaumont did not make use of special ritual instruments; she simply walked outside and poured water on the ground as an offering. The *houngan* rely on more elaborate actions in order to invoke their spirit.

The midwife and the *houngan* also used the same performative techniques to sustain the impression that the spirit had temporarily dislodged its human host. Whenever the spirit first appeared during a consultation, as when Erzili entered Mme. Beaumont, we invariably began a new round of introductions and handshaking. Other people in attendance always addressed the *houngan* by the name of its spirit, and sometimes they could not even remember the *houngan*'s own name in discussions held the next day. Even the *houngan* considers himself totally absent when the *lwa* enters. For example, André had invited me to attend the treatment of a young woman at his home one evening, but when I arrived, I was barred from entering by the woman's family. When I later mentioned this to him, he excused himself by saying, "Oh, I didn't know you had come. After all, I wasn't there."

Mme. Beaumont and the *houngan* thus subscribe to the same stereo-typed codes governing the interaction between individuals and their *lwa*. However, the *houngan* are first and foremost religious specialists. Consultations with them thus take place in a markedly different moral universe than interactions with any other type of healer. *Houngan* draw both their power and knowledge from the *lwa*, the spiritual entity usually demonized by Catholic herbalists and even more stridently by Protestant pastors (see chapter 7). Moreover, they specialize in the treatment of *maladi Satan*. While certain herbalists also claim to heal this class of illness, the treatment offered by *houngan* stands apart. Compared to the healers profiled in the previous chapter, the *houngan* take a very different position regarding the powers and moral valence of the *lwa*, and they advance a different, but equally convincing reading of *maladi Satan*.

Divination, illness, and healing

The *houngan* explicitly rely on their *lwa* for the central activities of a consultation: divining the cause of an illness and carrying out the treat-ment. Through these activities the *houngan* and their clients jointly construct the reality and power of the spirits in a way that modifies or subverts the conventional Catholic moral divide. To begin with, *houngan* creatively rework the Catholic attitude in order to escape the moral stain associated with the realm of the *lwa*. At other times, however, they exit this Manichean discourse entirely. They rely on a different form of therapeutic power whose limiting conditions are not innocence and guilt, but rather success or failure in the pragmatic task of protecting clients from the swirl of malevolent forces around them. Through these two discursive and ritual strategies, the healing practice of *houngan* constitutes an alternative moral universe to the one proposed by village Catholicism.

The two most common techniques of divination involve ordinary playing cards and Catholic prayer books, and André Chavannes' use of playing cards is fairly typical. Soon after the *lwa* Byenzomal entered André, he turned to Louis and asked, "You came for a lesson?" Byenzomal then took a stack of playing cards in his hands, crossed himself, returned the cards to the table, and had Louis cut the deck. After crossing himself again, Byenzomal laid out the cards in six haphazard rows, occasionally announcing the card's suit and number. Once the cards were arrayed on the table, the *lwa* gazed over them while reciting a rapid and unintelligible prayer. Without breaking his concentration, he asked Louis a few questions about his symptoms, and eventually began to scribble in a small notebook. Although his "writing" consisted entirely of cursive zigzag lines, Byenzomal was engrossed in it. He finally looked up and listed for Louis the *fèy* and other ingredients he must buy to prepare the appropriate herbal remedy.[6]

How the *houngan* derives particular messages from a given combination of cards is basically a mystery to the client.[7] On a few occasions, they would use simple verbal or visual puns to explain their "discovery" that a client suffered from sent sickness. If the ten card (*dis*, in Creole) appeared, they would point to it and say, "You have a conflict with someone" (*ou ap dispite ak moun*), punning on the word *dis*. If the queen appeared, they would cite this as evidence that the client has a problem with women. In general, however, there was only a tenuous connection between the technique the *houngan* used and the state of affairs he divined.

This is also true of the other popular divination practice: the interpretation of religious texts. Olivia, an elderly loquacious *divinèz* living in Torbec, once described how she uses her books – the same genre of old, well-thumbed religious publications that André Chavannes used – to determine whether a client's illness is due to an *ekspedisyon*:

> It's the *kondiktè* who tells you everything. You open the book. The *kondiktè* makes the sign of the Christian cross, and as he's holding the book open, he recites three Pater Noster prayers by heart . . . Wherever you opened the book, that's where you'll read it. If it's an evil-doer, you'll know it. If it's from your family, you'll know it . . . If the illness is not a good illness, you'll see it on the page where you opened the book.

Olivia here refers to her spirit as a *kondiktè* (similar to Mme. Beaumont's *anj kondiktè*), and she claims that by interpreting particular passages, the spirit can answer a client's most important questions: Do I suffer from a *maladi Satan*? Is it due to an enemy sending something upon me? Or is it due to an ancestral spirit? Even in this brief description of her divination technique, Olivia foreshadows her moral position toward the *lwa*. She refers to her spirit as a *kondiktè* and cites its reliance upon Catholic devotional practices. This exemplifies the first discursive strategy by which *houngan* mark their divergence from formal Catholicism. Her actual use of this Catholic text for divination provides many more examples.

As she took out an old, battered book from a compartment inside her consultation table, Lak-an-syel (Olivia's spirit) announced: "I must find what you need. I must find the explanation. When you open it, that's what I'll find inside . . . I am going to tell you what medication you use for a painful illness, for a *limyè*, for a *poud*." Lak-an-syel then passed the book to the people sitting around the room. It was entitled *L'Ange conducteur des âmes dévotes* (*The Conducting Angel for Devoted Souls*), printed in 1921 by Imprimerie Henri Deschamps, one of the largest publishing houses in Port-au-Prince. It contained a rich, baroque assortment of Catholic prayers and meditations, and Lak-an-syel had us each open to a page at random and read aloud. We thus took turns reciting snippets of funeral prayers for the salvation of the departed soul; devotional passages for members of religious orders, in which one consecrates one's body and spirit to Jesus; and rosary meditations on, for example, the fifteen principal mysteries of Our Lord, each divided into three parts.

However, Lak-an-syel's interpretation of these passages bore practically no relation to their orthodox Catholic content. For example, one of the men in the room began to read in halting French, "My God, I acknowledge I am with you with all my being, with all my heart . . . ," and before he could go further, Lak-an-syel broke in with her interpretation:

The person who is sick, it's a superstition illness. But if he has confidence in God, you can fix a bottle of medication for him, find a tea to give him. Okay, go ahead, read again.

The man resumed with the next prayer, "My soul, my body, belong to you. Lord, remove my sins, and make me know in what condition . . . " Again Lak-an-syel interrupted, enthusiastically seizing on these words:

Hold it! Hold it there, okay? Did you hear? "Make me know in what condition" he arrived at this stage. "Make me know in what condition" the illness came upon him. Did you hear? It's telling me, it's showing me the way . . . The illness is a strong one; it's a sort of vengeance . . .

The trigger for her was the word "condition," since one category of *maladi Satan* comprises those which the *houngan* sends on the victim as a condition for granting some other boon to the original culprit. That is, the illness is the payback in the Faustian bargain which the victim had earlier made with "satan" (that is, the *houngan*) in order to carry out some act of evil.

Lak-an-syel then began exuberantly to sing a spirit song, and several others in the room joined in or simply hummed along. When this song died down, the consultation continued as before: as people read fragments of prayers, Lak-an-syel would concentrate intently and occasionally nod in assent. But her interpretations – explanations of the various reasons for a *maladi Satan* and innumerable recipes for herbal cures – were virtually unrelated to the actual prayers in the text.

The interpretation of playing cards by the spirit Byenzomal and of

Catholic devotional readings by Lak-an-syel exemplify the irreducibly mysterious process of divination. The underlying rationale for the *houngan*'s explanations remains hidden. Although their divinations are carried out in plain view, *houngan* rarely explain the correspondence between a particular card or prayer and the determination that the client suffers from a sent sickness or requires a particular remedy. Moreover, the clients in a consultation rarely ask for such an explanation or challenge what the *lwa* says. Indeed, reading the cards or interpreting the book of prayers most often seems a pretext for the spirit convincingly to "discern" that the client suffers from *maladi Satan* and needs the *houngan*'s treatment. This is, in fact, the conventional response, and one which the client had probably already assumed.[8]

Moreover, people do not always understand much of what the *houngan* does say during the divination. I carefully interviewed on this point, since I thought that my own language skills were not advanced enough to catch important allusions or side comments. People attending consultations usually told me that the *houngan*'s prayers (and some of the spirit songs) were simply incomprehensible, and that only someone who also has a *lwa* could understand them. André Chavannes himself gave the same answer: when I asked about his notebook filled with squiggles, he replied that only he could read it.

People's conviction that the divinatory songs and prayers are unintelligible except to other spirits supports the entire complex of attitudes towards the *lwa*. The position that ordinary humans cannot understand what the spirits do during divination or say in their prayers contributes to the collective construction of the *lwa* as non-human repositories of special knowledge. However, it also buttresses the authority of the *houngan*, because it endows whatever they say during a consultation with the quality of revealed truth. Unlike expertise with *fèy*, this knowledge is not a matter of empirical practice or apprenticed learning. Because the knowledge is secret, and originates in a spiritual entity which enters only a certain select few, it also remains unquestioned. Indeed, while the clients at a consultation often confessed to me that they did not understand what the *lwa* said, they never openly questioned the results of divination.

Although people attending a consultation rarely contest the *lwa*'s interpretations, they do sometimes dispute something more basic: the very authenticity of the *lwa*. For example, the young men who accompanied me to consultations often argued later whether the *houngan* "really had *lwa*." Those *houngan* who did not genuinely have *lwa* were judged as charlatans. To make this crucial distinction, these young men relied on the same rhetorical markers of the *lwa*'s presence that are described above. Did the *houngan* induce trance in a sufficiently dramatic, or even violent, fashion? Were the changes of voice and mannerism which signal the arrival of the *lwa* sufficiently obvious and long-lasting? Their attitude reveals a third possible position to take towards the *houngan*: not the formal Catholic moral denunciation nor the respect and fear of the client, but rather an iconoclastic skepticism.

Houngan's moral claims

People's reactions to the *houngan* when they are sitting face-to-face in the consulting room differ remarkably from the disgust and moral disdain which they express during conversations at home, with their family, or while socializing with friends. During the actual consultations for healing, clients ask questions, listen in respectful silence, and accept the explanations that the *lwa* gave them. Only occasionally do they become impatient when the *lwa* wanders too far from the topic at hand (usually after drinking the rum which clients purchase for him as an offering). Their reactions to the *houngan* run counter to the attitudes prescribed by the conventional Catholic oppositional scheme. Even in discussions held after the consultation was over, when people argued over the interpretations they received or the genuineness of the *houngan*'s spirit, they never excoriated them as dirty, disreputable, or anti-Christian.

Moreover, the *houngan* themselves do not fit the stereotype of an evil, satanic figure, implacably opposed to Christian morality and actively subverting the lives of upstanding Catholic villagers. To the contrary, their practice is overflowing with Christian imagery, Latin prayers, and references to the beneficent power of God. If they do not consider themselves the inverse of the Christian image of virtue, what position do the *houngan* adopt towards the dominant Catholic moral perspective?

Most *houngan* in Jeanty draw deeply from the Catholic symbolic and cosmological system. They incorporate its images and vocabulary in their divination practice, and they understand *maladi Satan* – the disorder they are typically called upon to heal – in ways familiar to any Catholic herbalist (or, indeed, ordinary villager). The icons of saints staring down from the walls, the books of devotional prayers which the spirit interprets, and the ritual actions of crossing oneself and reciting Latin prayers all surround the standard divination procedures with elements of village Catholicism familiar to most rural Haitians. (In fact, ever since the Second Vatican Council in the early 1960s fostered the acceptance of French [and, more recently, Creole] as liturgical languages, the *houngan*'s consultation room and *pewon* have become the only places in the country where parishioners can hear sections of the Latin Mass.)

Moreover, most *houngan* are aware of their disreputable public image, as figured by the Catholic moral divide, and in numerous ways they try to justify their activities and dispel the moral taint surrounding them. Olivia once justified her practice with the following explanation:

> Myself, I don't get mixed up with killing people. I don't get mixed up with evil-doers, who send sickness by hiding *limyè* and *poud* for their victims. If an evil-doer comes to buy something from me, I won't give him a thing. I serve in the name of the Lord our God, along with a *kondiktè* . . . who tells me to follow the right road.
>
> All those *houngan*, all those *divinò*, they cry out "Bravo!," they yell out this and that: that doesn't concern me. I go the way God directs me. I'm not going to tell you, "I'm the best *divinò*, everybody is rushing to my house, I killed people." I don't get mixed up with that.

By referring to the Christian God and to the *kondiktè* as ethical guide, Olivia seems to locate herself squarely within the standard denunciation of the realm of the *lwa*. She exemplifies the first discursive strategy by which *houngan* establish their moral status: replicating certain aspects of the Catholic discourse, but then defending the speaker from the suspicion of guilt which usually accompanies serving the spirits. Olivia thus acknowledges that she is a *divinèz*, but asserts that her practice serves benevolent ends: she practices in the name of God, not like those other *houngan* who openly boast of their malign powers.

This same strategy informs another way for *houngan* to assert their moral virtue: to claim that their *lwa* is inherited, not purchased, and that they do not practice simply for monetary gain. All the *houngan* I spoke with claim that their *lwa* came from their family: it was either the same *lwa* that an ancestor also served, or itself the spirit of a deceased ancestor. In contrast, they pointed out, the other maleficent and immoral *houngan* purchase their *lwa*. Inheritance from one's ancestors is the only legitimate, morally correct way to acquire the *lwa*. While no one claims that purchased *lwa* are less genuine or powerful, they do say that people purchase a *lwa* for one reason only: to make money from this investment by holding ceremonies, "selling points," or "sending sickness," i.e., by selling their clients the means to acquire riches or to kill an enemy.[9] By claiming that their own *lwa* is inherited implicitly protects the *houngan* from the widespread suspicion that they have no moral scruples and use their *lwa* only to make a profit (cf. Brown 1991:231).

For example, Olivia builds on these fundamental moral distinctions in order to differentiate herself from other merely mercenary *houngan*:

> There are all types of invisible spirits. There's one which comes if the client makes a sacrifice, and there's one which is a *kondiktè* of God. This is the one who shows you the road to follow . . . I wouldn't do a sacrifice just to make a lot of

money. That doesn't interest me. If someone comes with just 5 cents, I'll work for 5 cents.

Olivia reproduces one aspect of the Catholic oppositional scheme, while modifying it to support her claim to be a morally upright practitioner. Like virtually every other *houngan*, Olivia continually emphasizes that she works not for her own benefit, but under God's guidance; that is, her practice involves not sending sickness, but rather healing the sent sicknesses which afflict her clients. She acknowledges that she serves the *lwa*, but not for personal gain, that is, not just for the fee that a client would pay for an animal sacrifice to the spirits.

Olivia refers to her spirit as an *anj kondiktè*, although this "angel" has all the characteristics normally ascribed to a *lwa*. Olivia told me that she had to call up her angel, or her master, in order to read the cards, and that during this divination process, her angel takes over her body. From the Catholic perspective, the *anj kondiktè* (or *anj gadyen*) represents the source of ethical behavior; it exists as a quasi-separate moral guide within each individual. Because Olivia calls up the spirit for the righteous goal of combatting *maladi Satan*, she uses exactly the same Catholic vocabulary to describe her *lwa*. She thus refers to her spirit as not only a *lwa* and a mystery (*mistè*) (the conventional terms), but also a master, a conductor, and an angel (*mèt*, *kondiktè*, and *anj*). Her spirit, she says, is an *anj* who determines if a given illness is good or evil by reading the cards or interpreting the book. Only the *kondiktè*, she says, can tell her what to do to treat someone with *maladi Satan*. She thus appropriates this Christian imagery in order to cast her own healing practice as beneficent and morally correct.

The treatment of sent sickness

The *houngan* creatively modify sections of the dominant Catholic discourse in order to escape the moral blame usually associated with having *lwa* and engaging with sent sickness. They thereby position themselves, at least partially, as pure-hearted religious specialists within the familiar world of village Catholicism. However, in their actual treatment of *maladi Satan*, they abandon this discourse and exit the Catholic moral landscape entirely. In doing so, the *houngan* do not thereby take on all the demonic qualities popularly attributed to them: after all, that would root them only more deeply in the conventional Catholic moral divide. They oppose *maladi Satan* with a battery of supremely pragmatic techniques. In the fight against sent sickness, their spiritual power and cunning is more important than their superior moral position.

Olivia's description of sent sickness superficially resembles the standard Catholic reading:

There's a kind of stomachache which isn't an illness of the person's body. It's an illness forced on him by Satan: what they call a persecution illness. It's something they give to him in a drink, or in his food, or in his cigarette. That's the magic part.

But there are defenses against it . . . you can empty out the person: take what was inside, put it outside. After that you can send him to the doctor to examine him, to see if he is weak, to give him a shot or some vitamins to make him stronger.

In this passage, Olivia starts by invoking the same demonizing rhetoric as most other Catholic villagers, but unlike her neighbors, she does not take the next step and associate *maladi Satan*, as a physical illness caused by human enemies, with the image of Satan, as an essentially immoral and evil principle. At no time did Olivia or the other *houngan* use my questions about *maladi Satan* as a springboard for strident denunciations of Satan or any of the other terms linked to Satan in the standard oppositional scheme: the bad soul, the "dirty" *lwa*, and the people who traffic with the *lwa*. *Houngan* rather understand *maladi Satan* as simply a practical and recurring problem of social life, an illness requiring especially powerful treatment, and not one term embedded in a larger calculus of personal innocence and guilt.

Unlike most Catholic villagers, *houngan* do not position themselves as morally virtuous by denying all knowledge of *maladi Satan*. They instead straightforwardly discuss lists of techniques to treat sent sickness once it has occurred, and offer bits of savvy advice to avoid becoming a victim in the future. In fact, *houngan* talk about their treatments for *maladi Satan* in the same matter-of-fact way that herbalists talk about *maladi Bondye*: they list innumerable recipes along with the indications and mode of usage for each concoction. However, although the *houngan*'s remedies include various *fèy*,[10] they typically use these in conjunction with another class of substances called "pharmacy remedies" or "magical waters and powders" (*renmèd famasi, dlo majik, poud majik*). The way they deploy "pharmacy remedies" in order to treat sent sickness illustrates how the *houngan*'s therapeutic authority depends on their practical skills and knowledge rather than a superior position in the conventional moral divide.

The *houngan* usually mentions magical waters and powders at the end of the first meeting with a client. After divining that someone indeed suffers from a sent sickness, the *lwa* tells the client to purchase different ingredients and bring them to the next consultation.[11] Many of these ingredients are ordinary medicinal leaves and roots, which clients either find in the wild or purchase at the twice-weekly village market. However, a number of other ingredients can be purchased only at the commercial pharmacies in Les Cayes (hence their popular name, "pharmacy remedies"). Despite their name and despite their point of sale alongside standard pharmaceuticals such as aspirin or antibiotics, these "pharmacy remedies" do not share the same secular, disenchanted attributes of other biomedical commodities.[12] This much is obvious in the list of the most common "pharmacy remedies":

Disgust powder	*Degoutans*
Repulsion powder	*Repiyans*
Push-away powder	*Repouse*
Stand-back powder	*Kanpe lwen*
Leave-me-alone powder	*Lese m atò*
Chase powder	*Chase*
"What I say, goes" powder	*Sa m di, se sa*
Send-it-off powder	*Expedye*
Cure-all powder	*Geri tout*
Strong water	*Dlo fò*
Death water	*Dlo mò*
Gede water	*Dlo Gede*

"Pharmacy remedies" are effective only for cases of sent sickness, and people explained their therapeutic action in simple and unambiguous terms which incorporate the remedies' actual names. Stand-back powder makes Satan stand back from you. Send-it-off powder removes whatever sickness is upon you, and returns it to the person who originally sent it. Chase powder chases down the Satan that is making you sick. Death water (or *Gede* water) is effective if you have the spirit of a dead person upon you (the *Gede* is a class of *lwa* associated with graveyards and the dead).

Houngan routinely include these substances in their more elaborate remedies for sent sickness. Olivia (or rather her *lwa*, Lak-an-syel) once explained to me: "For a dead spirit, you buy sugar and a head of garlic and mix them together. Add "Stand-back" and "Chase" medications, mixed with water . . . You massage the person, and if the illness returns, you go back and massage some more . . . Little by little, that which is upon him must get out, because the mixture isn't good for it." Other *houngan* provide countless similar prescriptions, often combining "pharmacy remedies" with several other healing techniques. For example, to treat a woman whose illness was due to a *limyè*, André Chavannes prepared seven packets of herbal infusions, sacrificed a chicken to his *lwa*, and then mixed "Push-away" powder with some other proprietary pharmaceuticals for the patient to drink.

What accounts for the effectiveness of these magical waters and powders in the treatment of sent sickness? These substances are material symbols through which the *houngan* creatively enact their fight against the invisible sources of affliction, such as spirits of the dead or *limyè*. When the water or powder is physically applied to someone's body, the direct command present in its very name – Stand back! Leave me alone! – acts on the malevolent spirit that is causing the sickness. The symbolic effectiveness of these "pharmacy remedies" thus depends on the metonymic transfer of their qualities to the patient. Through this tangible, physical medium, the *houngan* substantialize their religiously based authority to repel the cause of the patient's sickness.

The *houngan* or *mambo* can actualize the power resting in the names of these substances in several ways. They can include the magical powders in an herbal infusion; they can add the waters to the oils used to massage a patient; they can slap a handful of magical powder on someone's arm or back; they can hold open a bottle of magical waters for someone to inhale, or offer a pinch of powders to snort in each nostril.[13] Administering this treatment, in whatever form, constitutes a type of symbolic action which the *houngan* undertakes with a single goal: to repulse the sickness that was sent upon the patient (cf. Tambiah 1985:103).

However, the ritual potency of these "pharmacy remedies" arises from more than the metonymic transfer of a verbal command (implicit in their names) to the spirits assailing the patient. This treatment orchestrates two other sensory modalities – smell and touch – which also contribute to its symbolic effectiveness. Several of these magical waters have quite pungent, foul odors. "Stand-back" typically smells like a mixture of ammonia and gasoline. Bottles of "Disgust" and "Repulsion" purchased by my research assistant smelled of rotting vegetables and perhaps fecal matter. This extraordinarily disagreeable odor is an integral part of their power to repulse evil spirits. Recall that the "satan" sent upon a victim is a spirit of a dead person, and that it yet retains some human attributes (for example, when afflicted by a spirit of a dead baby [*mò ti moun*], the sick person will be unable to speak). Presumably, the spirit also retains its sense of smell, and it will have the same immediate reactions as we do to these waters: it will instinctively "stand back" when it gets a whiff of this water on the skin of their victim. It will be driven away by "disgust" from the person it is causing to fall ill.

The transfer of the symbolic power of these waters to the patient thus arises from both their physical presence on the body and their smell, which envelops the person and repels the spiritual attack. In the case of magical powders, however, physical contact alone is sufficient. The magical powders usually do not give off the same foul odors, yet they are

11 The *houngan* and *mambo* carry out healing consultations while seated in front of a small table. This one features a bell and whistle to call the spirits, playing cards for divination, and soot-blackened icons of Catholic saints, each corresponding to a specific *lwa*.

deemed equally powerful protection, and even people who are not the victims of sent sickness often ask to receive this sort of "treatment." For example, the topic of magical powders came up during a long consultation/interview with Nouvel, a spritely *houngan* from an isolated mountain hamlet in Jeanty. In response to several requests from people who had accompanied his client that day, Nouvel eagerly moved from one person to another with handfuls of a brown granulated powder, which smelled vaguely of cinnamon. He took each person's arm in one hand, and with the other slapped the powder into the crook of the arm, simultaneously pronouncing the name of the powder along with a short cryptic phrase: "Disband-from-the-field, it's for you to disband" (*Kase kan, se pou ou kase*).[14]

This scenario is typical of the many times when the various people sitting in the consultation room – my research assistant or friends and kin of the *houngan* – would request a pinch of magical powders when the *houngan* took out a small sample from his table to show me. These magical powders have a combined curative and prophylactic effect, typified by people's explanation of *kase kan*: "Once you have this upon you, Satan cannot do anything to you. Satan has left the field." These powders act almost like a physical shield: when applied to the surface of your skin, they protect you against an attack from a satan originating anywhere in your social world. The command implicit in their name and animated by their physical placement on the body shelters it from the external causes of illness.

The preceding section has focussed on the "inner frame" of the *houngan*'s magic: the techniques to animate various inert substances and then enlist their power in the fight against the client's sent sickness (see Tambiah 1985:35). The *houngan* synchronize linguistic devices (the names of these magical powders and waters) with non-verbal stimuli (certain smells and physical sensations). By orchestrating these different media, the *houngan* generate a powerful discursive frame in which they carry out their therapeutic work. This frame allows them to actualize the rhetorical force implicit in the remedies' names, and thereby transfer their attributes to the patient.

However, these semiotic strategies also expose the "outer frame" of ritual: the local contexts in which *houngan* practice as healers and the way they deploy their healing power to take up a position within the competing moral and ideological frameworks of rural Haitian society. How do the treatments offered by *houngan* relate to the other ways they serve the spirits? What connections exist between the use of these magical substances and the religious construction of personal power and vulnerability? In light of *houngan*'s actions to treat sent sickness, how does their overall account of affliction constitute an alternative discourse to formal Catholicism?

As we have seen, the *houngan* straddle the conventional Catholic moral divide. On the one hand, they do not demonize the *lwa*, and they openly describe themselves as specialists in sent sickness. On the other hand, they replicate the standard division between the *anj* and the *lwa* – good vs. evil sources of healing power – in the distinction between inherited and purchased spirits. However, their actual treatment of sent sickness goes beyond the Catholic discourse entirely. Most *houngan* take a pragmatic and morally neutral approach to sent sickness. They do not regard it with the same disdain and fear expressed by most Catholic herbalists and ordinary villagers, and they do not suspect its victims of having brought on the spiritual attack by some evil action of their own. *Houngan* never mention the client's conduct or personal moral virtue when they explain the properties of the "pharmacy remedies" and actually administer them.

The contrast with the standard Catholic responses to sent sickness could hardly be more stark. The standard Christian response is directed internally, and it addresses the moral status of the victim. The success of "pharmacy remedies" is technical and directed outwards towards the pathogenic actions of maleficent "satans." The *houngan* thereby abandon the dichotomous moral scheme presupposed by most Catholics. The *houngan* do not bother to invoke Christian icons in order to oppose the malevolent spirits which cause sent sickness. To the contrary, they use the same substances to cure *maladi Satan* which Catholics associate with its cause.

Whenever I explained my field research to friends and associates in Jeanty, I volunteered to show them examples of what I was interested in. On these occasions, I would play a snippet of a "spirit song" I had recorded on cassette tape, pass around the medicinal herbs people had given me, and, on one occasion, even open up the bottles of "pharmacy remedies" I had purchased in Les Cayes. Their disgusting smell evoked people's visceral disgust with the realm of the *lwa*. "Get it away; it smells like Satan," one woman had shrieked, literally running away from me as I stood with the bottle in my hand. She had immediately reacted to the magical water as a concretized "inverse image" of the Christian god (see Hawkins 1984). "Pharmacy remedies" thus repel a spiritual attack in the same way the attack was sent. The work of healing which is accomplished through these substances is almost a mechanical affair: rubbing "Stand-back" water on your body will force Satan to stand back; drinking a mixture of "Push-away" powder will force the Satan inside you to leave. When ritually animated by the *houngan*, the power contained in these substances has no particular moral valence: in the hands of one *houngan*, it helps send the sickness, in the hands of another, it becomes the medium for a cure. As the *mambo* Olivia herself says, "You have to fight fire with fire."[15]

Consistent with the general this-worldly orientation of popular Haitian religion, *houngan* do not assimilate their action in the face of sent sickness to cosmological principles of good and evil. Their practice instead depends on a ritualized technology which the non-believer may gloss as "magic," but which rests on fairly clear principles of attack, repulsion, and protection. The *houngan* cast these principles in materialist, not moralist metaphors. They hold a coherent theory about sent sickness, but one which does not address the personal innocence or guilt of the sufferer. Their advice about avoiding sent sickness thus highlights the pragmatic dangers of social relations and one's personal vulnerability to an enemy's attack. For example, Olivia once specifically warned against this vulnerability:

> You have a fight with a friend, but it passes, and five, six, or even seven years go by. But as they say, "The war is over, and the hatred is still there." This means that the day you forget about it, that's the day they'll get you . . . You might have become friends again, but watch out when you're with him. That's the time for him to do you in.

Olivia does not react to the presence of potential enemies and their power to cause harm by classifying them as dirty and Satanic, and positioning herself as morally superior. She rather offers sensible advice such as the above warning, which shares the same empirical and practical orientation as the "pharmacy remedies."

Many people regard the *houngan* as effective healers, but for a different reason than the Catholic herbalists and midwives. The perceived efficacy of the *houngan*'s treatments does not arise because they reproduce the general cultural order (as exemplified by the conventional moral divide of village Catholicism). Nor do these treatments facilitate the maneuvers of people to present themselves as ethically upright actors. Their perceived efficacy comes from another source entirely. These treatments enunciate the generally accepted truth that all social intercourse is dangerous and the source of chronic personal vulnerability. Therefore, one must in certain cases abandon the struggle for the moral high ground and seek potent remedies, even if they are located in the formally disdained neo-African section of Haitian culture. This is, in fact, the major symbolic statement about the social order made by the *houngan*'s healing rituals. The conflict-ridden and pathogenic quality of everyday life drives people to have recourse to the *houngan*'s treatments. But these treatments are located in precisely that realm of Haitian culture which is demonized by formal Catholic rhetoric. The treatments thus expose the limits and existential weakness of the major legitimating ideology and institution in rural communities.

Beyond good and evil?

The *houngan* adopt a pragmatic, almost mechanistic, orientation to the same range of social and human problems which others address through a calculus of innocence and guilt. This is illustrated by the *houngan*'s reliance on a powerful external technology of healing, instead of addressing their clients' conduct or interior moral status. It also explains why they treat cases of sent sicknesses with substances popularly linked with dirty, murderous behavior. In short, the *houngan* are not concerned with the moral valence of the "pharmacy remedies," nor of the *lwa*, nor of the victims of sent sickness. Their healing power depends on cunning and the adroit use of practical skills, rather than their superior position in the conventional moral scheme.

As religious practitioners and as healers, the *houngan* take a this-worldly approach to ordinary human desires and afflictions, and this fits with the general theological framework and ritual practices of popular Haitian religion. During ceremonies for the *lwa*, for example, the spirits enter the bodies of their human hosts (their "horses") and are fed, cajoled, and ultimately satisfied and appeased by other people attending the ritual. Indeed, the functional goals of large ceremonies (healing or honoring one's family spirits) as well as their aesthetic organization depend on invoking the spirits to leave their mythic home in *Ginen* or the bottom of the sea and appear in the midst of human activity and answer mundane human needs (cf. Lowenthal 1978, Murray 1977:502ff). After they have "mounted" their human "horse," one can address the spirits directly and enlist their help to further one's own designs. This differs remarkably from the distanced, otherworldly framework of formal Catholicism, in which the priest mediates all contact with God,[16] and in which the God rules over the most general processes of life and death, but is deaf to most specific appeals from human beings (Métraux 1972:327).

Although the work of herbalists and midwives is shot through with moral and religious concerns, the community still regards them primarily as healers. The *houngan*, however, are considered first and foremost as religious specialists, although healing plays a major role in both their ritual practice and conceptions of spiritual power. In both cases, however, these practitioners take up a particular position against a wider background of competing ideological and religious frameworks. Their contest for healing power and moral authority sets the stage for another window on the plural medical system of Jeanty: the way victims of sent sickness negotiate these shifting discourses of innocence and guilt, and vulnerability and protection. The story of Jerline Liron in the next chapter describes the management of a sudden and disturbing case of *maladi Satan*. It also introduces a third moral discourse – fundamentalist Protestantism – which is currently transforming the ideological land-scape of rural Haiti and challenging the healing powers claimed by both servitors of the *lwa* and pious Catholics.

7 Religious healing and the fragmentation of rural life

A case of sent sickness

The Manichean moral divide of formal Catholicism pervades the public debates about religion in Jeanty (and much of rural Haiti). The domestic cult of the ancestors and the worship of the *lwa* is the chief alternative discourse, and it both overlaps and subverts the formal Catholic perspective. The previous chapters have traced the actual strategies used by particular herbalists, midwives, *houngan*, and ordinary villagers to negotiate between these competing moral worlds. The positions they adopt towards their personal religious affiliation and the forms of healing power fall along a continuum: from virtuous Catholics who publicly demonize the *lwa* and disdain those who serve them, to the *houngan* who abandon the conventional moral divide altogether in the practical fight against sent sickness.

This chapter will explore both the ideologies of healers and the treatments they offer through the unfolding course of a serious, potentially life-threatening illness. Jerline Liron was a talented and ambitious young woman afflicted by a sent sickness, caused by the maleficent spirit of a dead child (a *mò ti moun*) which inhabited her body. Members of her therapy managing group deployed several medical idioms and bodily techniques as they struggled to heal this affliction and control her violent and disorderly conduct. Their responses are rooted in formal Catholicism, service to the spirits, as well as fundamentalist Protestantism, a relatively new presence in rural Haiti which is currently destabilizing and transforming the plural forms of religious healing. As her illness progressed, adherents of each religion advanced competing conceptions of the invading spirit, and they recommended different therapies in order to drive the spirit out. Moreover, their suggestions had profound implications for Jerline's innocence or guilt, and these moral questions structured both people's debates about her condition and the actual course of treatment.

The ways people arrived at the etiology of *maladi Satan* for Jerline's condition recall the speculation surrounding Dieusauveur Martin, the successful son of Jeanty who died after a freak motorcycle accident (see chapter 4). This etiology posed implicit dangers to Jerline's moral status, and these ultimately arose from the system of moral oppositions which locates *maladi Satan* in the same paradigmatic chain alongside the *houngan*, the *lwa*, and Satan himself (see chapter 5). When Jerline's family consulted an *houngan*, he treated her with "pharmacy remedies" and other techniques based on the same principles of symbolic effectiveness (see chapter 6).

This case-study also introduces the healing practice of two new groups of religious specialists: lay Catholics and Protestant fundamentalists. Once members of Jerline's family had settled on the diagnosis of *maladi Satan*, they invited a group of lay Catholics to meet regularly at the Liron house for singing, prayers, and dramatic exorcisms. Although this group (comprised mostly of women) operates outside the control of the parish priest, their exorcism rituals symbolically enact the conventional Catholic oppositional scheme. The members of this group collectively construct the entity assailing Jerline as Satan: an invisible evil spiritual being which can temporarily efface the autonomy and self-control of its victim. In general, their position fits squarely within the dominant Catholic perspective. While the spectacle and intensity of their exorcism rituals contrast starkly with the orthodox masses sung in the central church, they do not challenge any of the main tenets of formal Catholicism.

The group of lay Catholic healers carried out their combined religious and therapeutic treatment of Jerline either inside her home or under an adjoining thatch arbor. Drawn by the singing and prayers, a small crowd of onlookers usually gathered at the house and discussed the case among themselves. One day, however, several of them loudly interrupted the proceedings with an angry and damning challenge. "Satan is upon this entire house!" they said, peering into the room where Jerline sat. "You can't save the child without leaving Satan once and for all."

These accusations were levelled at Jerline's family by members of a local Pentecostalist church, and they are the leading edge of the general fundamentalist critique of Haitian Catholicism. Their challenge forced Mme. Liron to defend both the treatment she chose for her daughter as well as her own tenuous position within competing religious discourses. The escalating exchange of accusation, defense, and moral self-justification illustrates several profound transformations in Haitian religious idioms of healing power and moral authority.

Symptoms, experience, and moral danger

In 1988, Jerline Liron was a 19-year-old woman, the elder of two daughters. The household – two daughters, their mother and stepfather – was poor, even by the standards of rural Haitian society. They lived in a crumbling wattle and daub home located in Torbec, on the edge of the floodplain of the Acul river.[1] The produce of their small gardens barely yielded a profit at the Jeanty markets where Marie, the mother, set up her stall. The family usually could not find the money for a new coat of whitewash on the clay walls of their house or to fix the thatch roof. Moreover, the Liron family had recently moved to this area from a coastal town 30 miles away. This meant they could not depend economically on either networks of mutual aid with nearby relatives or the patronage of leading village families.

However, the family did have one secure source of income. Jerline held a salaried job as a teacher in a Protestant church school across the river in Jeanty. The 50 dollars she earned monthly was of crucial help in buying the family's food. Since her salary ultimately came from a North American missionary organization, this money flowed into the household like clockwork for ten months of the year, despite political turmoil, hurricanes, or crop failure. It provided a meager, though important cushion against economic failure for her family which already existed on the margin of survival.

Jerline is an extremely able and intelligent person. Not only is she literate, but she also held one of perhaps only twenty salaried jobs among the 3000 residents of Jeanty. She was the economic mainstay of her family. However, there was scant evidence of her talents and accomplishments during the violent convulsions which gripped her at the height of her illness, and which left her totally disoriented, unable to speak, and needing to be forcibly restrained. Moreover, her intelligence, her skills, and her job as a schoolteacher made Jerline a prime target of jealousy, and hence, a likely victim of *maladi Satan*. Jealousy is a prime motivation for someone to send a sickness upon an innocent victim and lay claim to their wealth or position in life.

Marie Liron gave the following account of the beginning of her daughter's illness. Jerline was returning home from the Ebenezer Bethel church school where she taught when she stopped at the market in Jeanty to buy some food and other provisions. According to her mother, when she was at the market, she saw a shadow pass before her eyes, which made her afraid. However, she continued home and cooked the midday meal for her household, usually the largest meal of the day. She finished eating, made some juice for herself, and started to leave to buy some ice.

At that point, before she could even drink her juice, "the illness came upon her," and Jerline started to shout for help.

Later that day, even after the illness began, Jerline was able to talk with her family. She told them that someone had sent a spirit of a dead person upon her. However, even this simple ability to concentrate, to speak, and to remain socially engaged soon disappeared. When I arrived at her home two days later, I learned that she had barely slept at all for the previous two nights, and that the state I found her in had continued basically unchanged since the sickness began.

When I entered the family's three-room house, Jerline was lying on a straw mat placed on the floor in the center of the bedroom. She had a wild look in her eyes, and her face registered no recognition of any of the people present: neighbors, her family, my research assistant, or me (and we had been frequent guests at her house for a number of months). Her appearance was disheveled: her hair was unwashed and uncombed, her dress dirty and ragged. Both her arms and feet were bound, one piece of cloth tying the ankles to each other and another tying the wrists. In addition to these restraints, she was constantly held by one to four people. For example, one man would cradle her from behind, with his arms around her and his legs crossed in front of her torso. Often, a second person held her arms in place, and a third person, usually Jerline's sister, grasped her legs to keep her from thrashing too violently.

While sitting or slouching back into the arms of one of her restrainers, she would alternate periods of calm (lasting from one to ten or fifteen minutes) with violent spasms. During the calm periods, Jerline's breathing was often labored, and she would murmur with every exhalation. She would either roll her head around, with glassy eyes, glancing about the room (although not showing any recognition), or stare disconsolately in front of her. The violent spasms almost invariably began with a piercing, blood-curdling scream. She would throw her head back and start to thrash or writhe her entire body, often violently. It often demanded the strength of four people to hold her down. Even then, she would try to shake them off, at one point screaming "Let go of me, so I can leave" again and again.

During the first few days, she was usually conscious but dissociated from her surroundings. She alternated between violent agitation and extreme fatigue. The first periods were the most dramatic. Jerline seemed out of control, her body wracked by convulsions, shrieking in pain, as if tormented by some unseen figure, unable to recognize her family, striking and biting those who held her. To my eyes, her expression and actions contained no hint of her former self (although later events would prove me wrong). During the calmer periods, when her consciousness seemed to clear, she could speak normally to her family and to me, although with little affect and great effort.

Jerline's extraordinary condition raised a number of pressing questions: What kind of illness is this? What is its name? Is Jerline present or absent in her body? What is the identity of this invisible being also present in her body: the spirit of a dead person? As people debated and discussed these questions, Jerline's moral status – locally expressed in terms of her innocence or guilt – hung in the balance.

Everyone who saw Jerline immediately concluded that she was crazy or mad (in Creole, *fou* [adj.] and *foli* [noun]). People described Jerline's condition as a *foli* for several reasons. Her wild appearance and violent behavior broke all rules of female modesty and appropriate conduct, and they also contrasted dramatically with her own reputation as a good daughter and effective wage-earner. Many people specifically mentioned her dissociation, loss of self-control, and inability to recognize family or friends as prime characteristics of *maladi foli*. Her condition thus differed categorically from the types of legitimate dissociation in an *houngan*'s consultation room or at the quasi-public ceremonies for the *lwa*, when African-derived spirits enter the body of the devotee. Jerline's illness took place outside of any ritual context and her behavior contained none of the characteristic signs of these spirits: certain dance steps, songs, or mock aggressive and erotic interactions with spectators. Thus, the bodily techniques to control Jerline's fierce convulsions – especially the binding of her hands and feet – resembled the restraints used to manage several other villagers commonly known for years to suffer from *foli*.[2]

The construction of Jerline as a crazy person (*moun fou*) or afflicted by *maladi foli* dominated talk among her family and friends for the first two days or so. However, these terms have a number of different meanings and implications. To say that Jerline was mad merely delimited a still quite large field of competing definitions of her disorder. Was the madness the result of a knowable human cause, traceable to some disturbance in her social relations, or was it rather a "natural madness," a madness that some called a "true sickness"? These were the first questions raised by Jerline's condition, and they seem to pose a straightforward choice between the etiologies of *maladi Satan* and *maladi Bondye*. Ordinarily, people strongly prefer to consider a given illness as a *maladi Bondye*. They can thereby avoid consulting an *houngan* and escape the suspicion of guilt which usually accompanies sent sickness (cf. chapter 4).

In the case of *foli*, however, either choice implied some risk to Jerline's moral status. To call her disorder a "natural madness" would have

12 Most families rely on a large mortar and pestle to grind coffee and cornmeal for home consumption.

implied the long-term and irreversible loss of her "good soul," one of the central components of the self (see chapter 5). Perhaps nine or ten other individuals in the village, I was told, no longer had their "good soul" upon them. This explained why, even after many years, they remained socially isolated, threw rocks at people for no reason, spoke words that made no sense or scrawled random markings on walls. One villager told me this sort of "natural madness" can make your head empty.

Jerline's family rejected this reading and chose instead to frame her madness as caused by other humans, in particular, by the spirit of a dead child sent by an enemy to kill her. What were the moral implications of their choice? In this case, surprisingly, regarding Jerline's case of *foli* as a *maladi Satan* had definite advantages. To begin with, it accounted for her sickness not by the loss of her "good soul," the emptying out of the self, but rather by the presence of another spirit, which seemed temporarily to displace or overpower the good soul. At the very least, saying that Jerline had a "dead one upon her" kept her intact. It preserved her as a full person – one who still possessed this core component of control and social awareness. Moreover, it gave the family hope for, as one person informed me, "if you have a 'natural madness,' that's worse. But if you have a dead one upon you, they can take it off again." Unlike a natural madness, a *foli* due to *maladi Satan* can be cured.

However, this understanding of Jerline's sickness carried its own set of moral dangers. If she has a satan upon her, who sent it, and why? Having a sent sickness makes people suspect you are guilty of malign intentions towards others. For example, someone can send a dead spirit upon you as a retribution for your own previous attempt at killing some-one else. You could have stolen money from the *houngan* who arranges such matters, and who is now seeking revenge. It could have been intended for some other guilty party in your family, but was then deflected onto you. Finally, someone jealous of your good fortune could be planning to kill you and then take possession of your money or job.

Therefore, to say that Jerline's sickness was sent upon her by someone else left unsettled the question of her innocence or guilt. Innocent people, I often heard, are generally less likely to become victims of sent sickness. In fact, by the second day of Jerline's *foli*, people began to debate why she would have a dead spirit upon her, since she *seemed* such a good person. Jerline's family combatted these implicit suggestions of guilt by seizing on the final scenario mentioned above: someone else wanted her steady job as a schoolteacher. This person then consulted an *houngan* to send a dead spirit upon her, kill her, and thus allow him to take up her old job himself.

For the simple naming of Jerline's sickness, therefore, the moral stakes were high. Did she continue to possess one of the core components of the self, the "good soul"? Yes; she suffered from the type of *foli* caused by a human enemy. Was she to blame for this madness? Did this sickness implicitly establish her guilt? No, her family claimed; she was the innocent victim of another villager's jealousy, that is, of a pathogenic attack via a *maladi Satan*.

However, a *maladi Satan* is not just an etiologic concept with moral overtones. A "Satan," in this context, refers to what is sent: the invisible entity which can take up a place in your body and eventually kill you. It refers to an embodied malevolent spirit which causes visible disorder and suffering as it assails its victim. This meaning of "Satan" was implicated in the talk about and practical management of Jerline's body during these first few days of her sickness.

A shifting crowd of people began to gather at Jerline's house: friends, people from the neighborhood, and members of a lay Catholic prayer group invited by Mme. Liron.[3] These people actively debated the identity of this indwelling entity, and they used a number of expressions whose meanings overlapped: someone had sent Satan, a satan, the spirit of a dead person, or a bad soul (*move nanm*) upon her. Specifically, most people concluded that she had the spirit of a dead child upon her: they explicitly compared Jerline's inability to speak with that of a baby or small child. In this analogy, the spirit of a dead child metonymically transfers its qualities to Jerline. This particular embodied spirit explains not only Jerline's loss of comprehensible speech, but also other behavior, such as biting or striking those who held her, which clearly contravenes the norms for a healthy mature adult.

The techniques used by Jerline's family to control her body also support the formulation of "the spirit of a dead child upon her." The very physical restraints employed (cradling her from behind, for example) recall how one would control a child: that is, to keep her from physically harming herself. Moreover, no one ever referred to these practices as a punishment, and I never once saw any display of anger towards Jerline. She was held no more responsible than a child for her loss of bodily control or even the physical attacks on her caretakers.

Jerline and this spirit coexisted in the same body: this much was implied by the conventional idioms people used as well as the commentaries I heard, for example after the following incident. On the second day of her illness, Jerline sat on the floor moaning softly, with labored breathing, and wearing an expression both sad and exhausted. She reached for a few bits of chalk lodged in the crumbling wall. A man handed this to her, and she leaned over and wrote in flawless script and grammatically correct French: "Essayez de deserrer mes dents" (Try to unlock my teeth). The man who was holding her legs read this over a few times and then said out loud in Creole "She wants you to unlock her teeth." He asked for a spoon, which Marie Liron quickly retrieved for him, and he commenced to force it between Jerline's lips and teeth, which were indeed clenched shut. After they managed to open her mouth, Marie called for a bowl of food which she placed on the floor before her daughter.

Imagine the impression this made among people who knew that Jerline is a schoolteacher, and therefore one of the few people in the village with a mastery of French: a language which most people can neither understood nor write. All who were present took this scenario as evidence that Jerline still inhabited her body, since it was obviously *Jerline* who wrote that, not the spirit which had been sent upon her. The particular message implied two other things about her condition: (1) she retained an awareness of her body, at least enough to know that it was no longer under her control, and (2) she was minimally aware of her social surroundings; she knew there was someone to read her message and to bring her food.

So, both the dead spirit and Jerline continued to inhabit the same body over the course of her illness. I later asked a friend who usually accompanied me to the Liron home, "So, it isn't Jerline who is screaming like that, who's biting people, who's struggling so much?" His reply was clear, "No, it's the dead spirit that is upon her; it's not Jerline. But she can see people." And indeed, a few days afterwards, during the first conversation I had with her since this all began, she told me, "I saw you there, Paul. I knew that it was you." So, the local phenomenological account of her condition (as well as her own reported experience) cast her as present in her body but not in control of it; as crowded by this other entity. The other inhabiting entity did things for which she was not held responsible, but did not entirely efface the core of her identity or her awareness of her surroundings.

Calling the *lwa*; exorcising the spirit

The Liron family is Catholic; in fact, compared to many families in the region, it is relatively devout. The youngest daughter Ti-Rose regularly sings with the choir in the Catholic church in Jeanty, and when Jerline became pregnant six months after her illness, her mother exhausted her meager savings to pay for a church wedding before Jerline gave birth (in order, as Marie put it, "to save Jerline's communion," since illegitimacy would bar her from this sacrament). Nonetheless, once Jerline's mother and the other members of her therapy managing group decided that her condition was a *maladi Satan*, they lost no time in consulting two local *houngan*. Each of them gave slightly different accounts of Jerline's affliction.

On Saturday morning, two days after the illness began, Marie's husband visited St. Denis, a *divinò* who lived only twenty minutes away. St. Denis called his *lwa*, Alicia, who stated that Jerline's illness was ultimately caused by someone jealous of her job as a schoolteacher, but that the spirit of a dead person was not to blame. The *lwa* instead traced her illness to a poisonous powder which Jerline's enemy had hidden on a piece of furniture at her schoolhouse (a *kou d poud*). When I talked with St. Denis several days later, he repeated this assessment of Jerline's condition, but he already knew that the family did not accept it and had begun to consult another *divinò*. He did not know the identity of this new *divinò*, although he assumed that Marie had returned to the village where she was born to choose someone who was already known by her family.[4]

In fact, Marie only crossed the Acul river and walked up into the hills of Jeanty in order to consult the next *houngan*, an elderly but vigorous man named Pierre Morin. Morin's treatment of Jerline required several visits over a number of weeks. He agreed to come down to the Liron home and meet Jerline during the first, most violent phase of her illness. At this initial consultation, he called up his *lwa*, Nouvel, and then established (through divination with playing cards) that someone had sent a dead spirit upon Jerline. He instructed Marie to buy certain herbs as well as protective charms (in Creole, *gad*, or guards) to repel the satan. These were chiefly small items for Jerline to wear, such as a tooth putatively taken from a human corpse and tied to a leather necklace, and several wooden match sticks to put in her hair. Nouvel also told the family to trace an abstract design (*veve*) consisting of two overlapping arrowheads, pointing upwards and downwards, above all of the doors and windows of the house,[5] and to keep the house totally shut when the spirit came upon Jerline and made her scream.

Nouvel carried out his main treatment of Jerline during three subsequent consultations: the first one held a week later at the Liron household, and the following two held after about a month at Morin's home in the hills of Jeanty. These consultations were elaborate and time-consuming affairs, some lasting over four hours, and they seemed to follow no set order. Once the *lwa* had been invoked, Nouvel would alternately sing spirit songs, rapidly recite French prayers, and administer the specific remedies for Jerline's sent sickness. Morin is a spritely, trickster-like *divinò*, and the same character shows through when he has his *lwa*: he often leapt from one activity to another, answered my requests for explanations with jokes or puns, and would sometimes need to be reminded by Marie to get on with the treatments.

During most of Nouvel's treatments, Jerline did not need to be bound or restrained. Five days after the onset of the *foli*, her convulsions started to subside and she was able to talk and recognize a few people. Although she was still weak, she could cooperate with Nouvel and communicate with those around her. In contrast to the first few chaotic days of her illness – when Jerline was surrounded by a crowd of kinspeople, friends, and onlookers, and the entire household was in a constant state of frenzied activity – the *houngan*'s treatments were private affairs. Only Jerline, her mother, stepfather, sister, and fiancé, my research assistant, and I were present. Nouvel's own pace of work, as well as Jerline's improved condition, gave a deliberate and even relaxed quality to these consultations.

The treatments themselves involved a heterogeneous collection of healing techniques. Nouvel had instructed Marie to buy specific herbs and "pharmacy remedies," and he used these substances in several ways. He prepared herbal concoctions for Jerline to drink and to bathe with; he occasionally crossed himself with a bottle of magical water ("Stand-back water"), and then sprinkled it on her head or held it up to her nose for her to inhale; he ground herbs and magical powders mixed with rum in a large mortar and spread the viscous solution over Jerline's body. As he administered these treatments, Nouvel would often mumble a prayer, in French or Creole, and insist that Jerline repeat it. However, Nouvel's words were often rushed and indistinct, and Jerline could usually say only a few fragments.

The effectiveness of Nouvel's treatments – the protective charms, the herbal preparations, and the "pharmacy remedies" – stems from the same symbolic principles underlying the healing rituals of other *houngan* (see chapter 6). I was told that the "Stand-back water" would force out whatever dead spirit was currently assailing Jerline. Jerline herself explained that by wearing a corpse's tooth, no dead spirit would try to enter her, for it would see that she already had a death upon her. Both treatments exemplify how an *houngan* symbolically transfers the potency inherent in a particular object to the person who wears or inhales it. Even the abstract designs traced in charcoal above the doors and windows to the Liron home were meant to trap a spirit trying to gain entrance and thereby protect the inhabitants.

At the same time Jerline received treatments from the *divinò* Morin, her mother also arranged for a group of lay Catholics, with about fifteen to twenty members, to hold services of prayer, worship, and exorcism at her home. Like Morin, they also carried out their first service only a few days after Jerline's illness began. Although unaccompanied by a priest, this group still had formal links to one of the outlying Catholic chapels in

Torbec. This was a *Laica* group, one of the lay organizations sponsored by most parishes in Haiti, whose members are mostly women who help conduct Mass and who sponsor their own prayer meetings in members' homes. The *Laica* group visited the Liron household two more times during that first week, and approximately once a week for the following month, each visit lasting several hours. The first few times they crowded into the two small rooms of Jerline's home, but her family later built a large thatch-and-bamboo arbor next to the house for their meetings.

In their performative logic, the *Laica* services were worlds apart from Jerline's consultations with an *houngan*. Morin's treatments were private affairs, often carried out in his own cramped, dirty consultation room, which strung together a shifting and amorphous series of prayers, spirit songs, and the actual application of remedies. By contrast, the visits of the *Laica* group to the Liron home were semi-public events. The composition of the group changed slightly each visit, and many of the women brought their children or younger siblings. *Laica* members freely moved about the house and often chatted with the onlookers who gathered during their services. Moreover, most of them dressed in the clean, somewhat formal dresses with white kerchiefs typically worn to Sunday Mass, and this enhanced the atmosphere of Catholic piety pervading their activities. Finally, their services followed an explicit two-part structure: the first section consisted of prayers, Bible passages, and individual meditations, while the second featured the actual exorcism.

On their first visit to Jerline's home, members of the *Laica* group arrived in the late afternoon, and several women immediately went into the bedroom to greet her and find out her condition. Sitting next to her fiancé, Jerline appeared calm although utterly exhausted. Her clothes were dirty and tattered and her hair disheveled, but she slowly spoke to one of the *Laica* women in her normal tone of voice: "I saw you yesterday. I wasn't here when I saw you, I was on top of the coconut tree . . . I heard what you were saying." The woman nodded and replied, "I talked to you, but you didn't answer," before launching into a five-minute religious exhortation about keeping faith in God, "whose power will help you find an answer to your illness." This woman then returned to the *Laica* members waiting outside and reported her conversation. They listened intently before discussing the course of Jerline's illness. "It was her good soul (*bon nanm*) which had left her body, and was perching on the tree," one woman said.

The meeting for worship began soon afterwards as members of the *Laica* group entered the outer room of the Liron house and sat on the floor. The first section of their service was structured around several different types of prayers. The leader of the group (the same woman who had earlier spoken with Jerline) began with a series of Bible readings in Creole. She would announce the number of a psalm or scripture passage, and then read alternate lines along with another member. Occasionally, she also delivered a short homily, stressing the general theme of God's power and benevolence. She often ended these by instructing the other women to offer their own individual messages to God. All of the *Laica* members would then kneel with their head in their hands and recite different extemporaneous prayers, which created a low hypnotic drone of indistinct voices, sometimes punctuated with cries of *O, Jezi* and *Mesi, senyè* (Oh, Jesus; Thank-you, Lord), and lasting for ten or fifteen minutes. As the buzz of different voices died down, the leader typically said the first few words of the Lord's Prayer or the Hail Mary, and all joined to recite these well-known prayers in unison.

The fading light of evening combined with the earnest themes of these prayers and Bible readings created a subdued and even somber mood. When the group began to sing hymns, however, the atmosphere "heated up" considerably, to use the Creole phrase. In fact, the enthusiasm and excitement generated by these songs was soon carried over into the actual exorcism rituals. The *Laica* women knew a huge number of hymns; usually one person belted out the first line of each verse before the rest of the women joined in. Keeping rhythm by clapping to the beat of a large upright drum (a *tanbou*, similar in shape and timbre to the African-style drums used in ceremonies for the *lwa*), the women poured tremendous energy and emotion into their singing. The hymns are the same ones sung in Mass and at other *Laica* meetings, and many of them repeat standard Christian themes of salvation and repentance. On occasion, the women continued to hum the melody after the song ended, while one person recited an extemporaneous prayer, usually filled with references to Jerline's condition and appeals to God to cure her. However, a few of the hymns aim specifically at repelling Satan, invoking the healing power of Jesus, or exhorting people to abandon the service of the spirits, and these were the ones most often sung at Jerline's house.

For example, they sang "It is You, Mary" (*Ou-menm Mari*) which has the following chorus (see Ligondé 1985:636):

> It is You, Mary, O Mother of our God,
> Wherever you appear, Satan disappears,
> We are going to fight, come before us, Mother,
> Raise your claws, crush the head of the devil.

People punctuated the last line by stamping their feet on the word "devil." The group also sang the hymn "You Cannot" (*Ou pa kapab*) which ingeniously pairs elements from both Catholicism and popular

Haitian religion. The chorus and the first verse lay out the opposition in unmistakable terms:

> You cannot be serving two masters at one time!
> No, you cannot, you cannot adore both God and the *lwa*.
> You are cursing before the one God.
> Never! Do not curse before the Eternal Father.
>
> You say: here's part for God, here's part for the *divinò*
>   Never! Do not curse before the Eternal Father.
> You say: Here's Jesus' part, here's part for Papa Legba.
>   Never! Do not curse before the Eternal Father.
> You say: The Holy Spirit instructs me, the *lwa* instruct me.
> You say: God is good, you say: The *lwa* are good too.
>   (Ligondé 1985:226)

This hymn continues for three more verses, which pair the Christian cross with the central pole of an *houngan*'s shrine room, the Virgin Mary with the *lwa* Erzili, communion with food offerings for the *lwa*, and the holy sacraments with *wanga*, a common name for protective charms. Ironically, this song condemns popular Haitian religion while demonstrating an intimate knowledge of most of its beliefs and practices.

This first section of the *Laica* service lasted for approximately two hours. As the evening wore on, however, Jerline's condition worsened steadily. She gradually lost the clear mental awareness she had earlier in the day, and began again to suffer the violent convulsions characteristic of her *foli*. The *Laica* women sitting in the adjacent room could hear her screaming and thrashing, as well as the urgent commands of the men and women who were restraining her from hurting herself or punching and biting others. After a particularly violent spasm, Marie's voice could be heard shouting instructions to tie Jerline's hands and feet and to check that the rope is not too tight. Sensing that the right moment had come, the leader of the *Laica* group then inaugurated the second section of the service: the actual exorcism of the satan assailing Jerline.

Throughout the preliminary cycles of prayers and songs, the *Laica* members had not explicitly directed their attention to Jerline, although they had mentioned her name several times and could certainly hear her screams. However, in the next stage of the service, the women quickly moved into Jerline's bedroom and surrounded the chair where she sat, while a small crowd of onlookers clustered outside the room's single window. As the group continued to sing hymns, one woman took out a handful of buds and placed them on a metal tray of smoldering coals. The leader of the group picked up the tray and spread the sweet incense in the air, in all the corners of the room, and under the bed. She then directly addressed the satan upon Jerline. "Leave Jerline!" she commanded. "It's time for you to go!" She held the plate by her side while another woman blew the incense directly into Jerline's face. As she breathed in the thick smoke, Jerline writhed and screamed even more intensely. She began to cough uncontrollably and violently struggled to free herself.

The *Laica* group sometimes adopted even more extreme bodily techniques to drive out Satan. For example, another exorcism session began with a *Laica* member whipping Jerline's back with a bunch of thorny twigs. Soon afterwards, a piece of tire rubber was added to the mixture of hot coals and incense, and one of the women again blew these acrid, noxious fumes directly into Jerline's face. She began to hack violently, then gag and vainly gasp for air. As the smoke filled the small room, everyone else began to cough, and I became genuinely concerned for Jerline's health. In fact, I was on the verge of physically disrupting the service to let her breathe, when the *Laica* members themselves threw water on the plate of incense and burning rubber and quickly opened the doors to air out the room.

Things did not go quite so far in this first *Laica* service. The women soon withdrew the tray of incense and again commanded Satan to leave. However, they addressed Satan in angry and suspicious tones which matched their aggressive exorcism techniques. For example, as one *Laica* member stirred the burning embers, Jerline began to stare at her movements with a half-smile on her lips. The woman snapped at her, "Why are you looking at me?" As Jerline was forced to inhale the incense for a second time, she managed to say between coughs that Satan was gone. Taking away the tray of coals, the leader of the *Laica* group cross-examined her: "You're not in Jerline any more? Where did you go?" Jerline muttered a confused response, which apparently was not enough to convince the *Laica* members. "Liar!" people shouted back, "Satan is playing tricks with us!"

This *Laica* service, like all of the others, did not end with the unambiguous expulsion of Satan from Jerline's body. After about half an hour, the women finished with their painful exorcism practices, even though Satan had not left Jerline and her illness remained unresolved. During the final stage of the *Laica* service, they continued their efforts at expelling Satan in less dramatic ways. This stage began when the leader instructed everyone present – *Laica* members and onlookers alike – to raise one arm and point towards Jerline. Almost the entire group of people standing in the bedroom, in the outer room, and in front of the house proceeded to recite a prayer in unison. The leader then moved next to Jerline (who, though no longer bound with ropes, was still physically restrained by three men) and began to sing the first line of a slow hymn. The rest of the women soon joined in, and with this hymn as background, the leader grabbed a handful of Jerline's hair and pressed down on her head while intoning a highly stylized prayer for Satan to stop afflicting "our sister."

Soon afterwards, the *Laica* service disbanded as each woman came up to Jerline, shook her hand, and said a few words of encouragement or prayer before leaving. Although these closing rituals employed the same verbal formulae as the earlier exorcism, the actual physical gestures produced a different overall effect. Instead of arraying the *Laica* group in opposition to Satan and attempting to force him to leave, these rituals incorporated Jerline into the group, and physically transmitted to her the benevolent power of Christian faith.

The religious and therapeutic work of the *Laica* group differs dramatically from the healing practice of Morin, the *houngan* consulted by Jerline's family. Their treatments use two different bodily techniques, which in turn reflect two competing conceptions of the spiritual entity causing Jerline's sickness. Morin constructs the satan inhabiting her as an essentially amoral entity: the lifeless vehicle of a human enemy's murderous designs. Therefore his healing techniques are externally directed: the goal of treatment is to guard Jerline against the enemy located somewhere in her social world.[6] The powders and oils he applies to the surface of Jerline's skin protect her from further spiritual attacks. These magical substances require Jerline's physical presence, but not her full participation or comprehension. This is why she does not have to repeat all of Nouvel's accompanying prayers, much less understand them, in order for the "pharmacy remedies" to be effective.

For the *Laica* women, however, Satan himself is the enemy, quite apart from the malicious intentions of other human beings. The lay Catholic group constructs Satan as an evil spiritual being who craftily dominates Jerline, its innocent victim, and temporarily dislodges her own "good soul." Jerline's body thus becomes the chief site for spiritual, even cosmological warfare between the benevolent forces of Christ and the evil Satan afflicting Jerline. Her body serves as a battleground where the stark oppositions of the Catholic moral perspective are rendered visible and then acted upon. The *Laica* group's exorcism techniques, therefore, are directed internally. Unlike Morin, the Catholic women do not apply substances to the surface of Jerline's skin. They rather fill the interior space of her body with acrid smoke in order to expel Satan once and for all, by making it physically unpleasant for it to continue dwelling in Jerline's body.

The lay Catholic women and the *houngan* thus have different readings of Jerline's sickness, and each proposes different conceptions of Satan and different bodily techniques to drive him out. Nonetheless, Marie Liron sees no contradiction in drawing on healing practices of both groups:

> Prayer chases away the spirits, and the person making the remedies [the *houngan*] also chases away the spirits. So, they are the same. They aren't divided, there aren't two of them . . . The two work as one.

Marie asserts here that Catholic prayer and the *houngan*'s "pharmacy remedies" are equally effective in ridding Jerline of the dead spirit (the *mò*) afflicting her, and that there is no essential difference between them. Her even-handed acceptance of the healing power of both groups was shared by the entire therapy management group. When I asked which type of treatment was stronger, Marie immediately responded that the *divinò* was stronger, but then Jean (Jerline's fiancé) broke in to correct her, "No, both have the same strength. There are two treatments, but they are the same."

The Protestant critique

Such fluency with both religious codes and the easy acceptance of both sorts of healing power is embedded in the overall cosmology of popular Haitian religion. Jean and Marie understand God as the somewhat distant architect and overseer of the universe, while they regard the *lwa* as more directly concerned with humankind and our ordinary afflictions (see Desmangles 1992). The only objection to this widespread accommodation between Catholicism and popular Haitian religion came from a handful of Protestant onlookers gathered outside Jerline's home. In fact, these members of a local Pentecostalist church actually issued their challenge in the middle of one of the exorcism ceremonies conducted by the *Laica* women. The leader of the *Laica* group was standing in Jerline's bedroom and reading the Gospel story of Jesus casting out demons. She followed this with a short homily relating the Biblical message to their present situation. "Today we come to our sister's house," she began, "our sister who is plagued with troubles. Come, find Jesus. Come, find God." The other *Laica* members in the room nodded their heads and murmured in agreement.

This *Laica* leader spoke while standing at the foot of the bed where Jerline lay restrained by three other people. At the same time, however, several onlookers peered in through the opposite window, and at the very moment when the leader said, "Come, pray for us, pray for my sister," one of these women interjected in a sharp tone of voice, "I can't pray for her! And even if we prayed for her, prayer cannot enter this house, because it has Satan upon it . . . You cannot serve two masters at the same time." The *Laica* leader, unsure how to respond, first addressed the Protestants in conciliatory tones. "You don't need to get angry," she said, trying to defuse the confrontation. "We all know that the power of God is stronger than the power of Satan. That is why we came here today." But the Protestant woman who began the attack was not mollified, and she continued to announce vociferously that she refused to pray for Jerline. After several more harsh words, she withdrew from the window and regrouped with several of her friends.

By this time, Marie had become visibly upset. Sitting in the room with Jerline, she had at first observed the confrontation without saying a word, but I now saw her in intense discussion with several *Laica* members. Because of her constant vigil over Jerline, Marie had barely gotten any sleep for the previous forty-eight hours, and the worry and sheer physical fatigue showed in her face. Nevertheless, she reacted to the Protestant challenge with immense energy and almost palpable anger. She strode out of her house and confronted the woman who had just made these accusations. "I didn't invite you here," Marie told her, her mouth trembling. She demanded that she leave, and then purposefully turned her back to return to Jerline. The Protestant woman, however, adopted an aggressive, combative posture and continued to talk to Marie, almost taunting her, saying that there were already two or three satans on her house. Marie had reached her limit; she turned around and responded with virtually a threat of death.[7]

This particular confrontation ended with the Protestant onlookers gathering up their belongings, hurling a few more accusations at the Liron household, and then walking away into the night. However, the topic surfaced several more times in the discussions among the onlookers at Jerline's home, Jerline's family, and the *Laica* members. A few Protestants continued to visit the home, although they did not issue any more direct challenges. I later asked one young man – a member of the Ebenezer Bethel congregation in Jeanty – to explain the Protestant position. He told me that he could pray for Jerline in the privacy of his own room, but until she asks for God herself, his prayers will be useless. He made the same point by analogy to a broad-brimmed hat he was wearing for protection from the sun. "I can give it to you," he said, "but not until you ask for it. And you won't ask for it until you think it would be useful for you."

Jerline's violent and dramatic convulsions became less frequent after approximately two weeks, and then disappeared entirely. For the following few months, Jerline had very little energy, and she was unable to resume her teaching duties at the church school. However, she helped with basic household activities and her mother's marketing, she fully participated in the *Laica* ceremonies, and her personality seemed unchanged by the illness.

Jerline's overall weakness was the symptom which led to her first (and only) visit to a biomedical setting approximately six weeks after the illness began. I offered to pay the expenses, so I accompanied Marie, Jerline, and my research assistant to the private office of a pediatrician in Les Cayes. (Marie had chosen the physician; he was the only physician with whom she had previous contact.) The young male doctor gave Jerline a quick but thorough physical examination, and then explained to me that he provisionally considered her "convulsive seizures" as symptoms of epilepsy, perhaps the result of an early head trauma. He said there were no positive neurological findings. The doctor ended the brief interaction by writing out a prescription for phenobarbital and handing it to Marie. Marie then spoke to the doctor for the first time (besides answering the basic questions about her daughter). She asked him to prescribe multivitamins for Jerline's weakness. The doctor smiled and began to say that she did not need them, but then changed his mind and added it to the list of medications to buy. We then walked to one of the main pharmacies in town, and spent 12 dollars to fill the prescription. Overall, Marie was pleased with the results of the visit to the doctor. The illness had clearly left Jerline in a weakened and fragile state, and surely the vitamins would help.

The contest for healing power

Catholic practitioners and the *houngan* offered different readings of Jerline's suffering, which depend on alternate definitions of the invisible entity which actually causes *maladi Satan*. For Morin, the specialist in popular Haitian religion, the afflicting spirit is simply "a satan," the lifeless vehicle of someone else's malice. For the *Laica* group, Jerline embodies Satan, the inverse image of Christ: an evil spiritual actor drawn from French Catholic cosmology. Each of these readings, in turn, implies different bodily practices to heal the person afflicted with an illness of Satan. In the first case, Jerline is given surface protections to repel any further attacks. The *Laica* members focus rather on the internal spaces of her body, which they make noxious in order to force Satan to leave.

The Protestants' critique, however, denounces both of the treatment choices made by Jerline's family. What accounts for the emotional force of their challenge as well as Marie's vehement reaction? Members of this fundamentalist Pentecostal church threaten the family's moral status as upright Christians who can legitimately expect God to heed their prayers for Jerline's health. The critique takes aim at two related targets: the Liron family's use of the "satanic" services of an *houngan* and its unwillingness to have Jerline convert to Protestantism. The Protestant reaction reproduces and exaggerates the conventional Catholic moral divide (cf. Conway 1978 and Romain 1986). They condemn as satanic the central activities of popular Haitian religion such as consulting an *houngan*, making offerings to the *lwa* at one's personal shrine, or paying for the large quasi-public ceremonies featuring dancing, possession, and animal sacrifice. However, they go one step further and condemn Catholicism itself for having struck a fatal compromise with the realm of the *lwa*. Indeed, in the standard fundamentalist rhetoric, not converting to a Protestant sect is tantamount to embracing Satan.

This is a harsh, exclusivist rhetoric of condemnation (and damnation). But it is convincing precisely because of the overlapping and syncretic relationship between formal Catholicism and service to the spirits. Marie's unproblematic resort to both the *Laica* group and the *divinò* is an obvious example of the widespread mixture of religious practices in Jeanty. Most of the people who consult with *houngan* or attend the ceremonies for the *lwa* also identify themselves as Catholics. Even those who claim not to worship the *lwa* do not always demonize them, and some Catholics will openly recommend consulting an *houngan* for cases of *maladi Satan* (see chapter 4).

Moreover, the *houngan* themselves incorporate a rich assortment of Catholic prayers and icons in their divination practice and ceremonies for the *lwa*.[8] In Haiti, as in other former plantation societies of the Afro-Caribbean, the imagery and ideology of European Catholicism reappears in new syncretic amalgams alongside West African deities and religious practices (see Bastide 1971 and Simpson 1970 for classic analyses of Afro-Caribbean syncretism, and Barnes 1989 and Mintz and Price 1992 for recent theoretical statements). Therefore, the cosmology of popular Haitian religion encompasses both the *lwa* and the Christian figures of God and Satan (as well as other Catholic spiritual beings such as guardian angels). Indeed, the *lwa* are ultimately subordinate to the Christian God (*Bondye*), although each has its own necessary place in the structure of the world.[9]

The rhetoric of fundamentalist Protestants capitalizes on this paramount feature of Haitian religious pluralism. It condemns the nominal Catholic faith of most Haitians as the virtual equivalent of serving the spirits. Ironically, Protestants in Jeanty incorporate the Catholics' own set of moral oppositions into their condemnation. They exploit the conventional divide (pitting Christ, angels, and good souls against Satan, the *houngan*, and the *lwa*) for the same purpose as Catholic midwives and herbalists: to secure their moral status by publicly distancing themselves from the realm of the *lwa*. However, the Protestants radicalize these oppositions. They conceive of an absolute difference between the moral world they inhabit and the one inhabited by those villagers who have not yet converted. Protestants claim that they alone are the true servants of Christ; in their idiom, they alone have "left the world," while the Catholics remain "in the world," entangled with the dirty, satanic spirits.

Protestants and Catholics thus use different means to claim the moral high ground in this plural religious landscape. The difference appears most clearly in their responses to sent sickness and their reasons for rejecting the realm of the *lwa*. The Catholic approach, focussing more on prevention than cure, consists of general admonitions to conduct your-self according to a few basic ethical rules: don't do anything evil, don't hurt anyone, and don't resort to illicit means to get ahead in the world (such as buying points from an *houngan* in exchange for wealth). From the Catholic perspective, following these rules ensures your personal innocence, and thus provides the strongest protection against sent sickness.

Catholic villagers denigrate the *lwa*, therefore, to demonstrate their allegiance to a general ethical code governing human relations. They associate the *houngan* with Satan, the inverse image of the benevolent Christ, because these sorts of immoral activities require the *houngan*'s expertise. After all, you must consult the *houngan* to send a sickness or to deliver the souls of your victims. The Catholic disdain for these religious specialists then easily generalizes to the *lwa* for a single reason: the *houngan* must call up the spirits in order to exercise their malevolent power and sow the seeds of social disharmony and bodily illness. Loudly devaluing the *houngan* and the *lwa* effectively communicates that you have no need for their services; hence, that you are leading a morally upright life.[10]

The Protestants, however, engage in a more thoroughgoing demon-ization of the realm of the spirits. They denigrate the *lwa* (and their servitors, the *houngan*) because of their intrinsically evil qualities, rather than their role as accomplices in the criminal designs of other human beings. The Protestants' reaction to sent sickness thus advances a different conception of personal innocence and guilt. From their perspective, the suspicion of guilt accompanying sent sickness grows more from the victim's likely recourse to an *houngan* for treatment, and less from the malicious activity which originally led to the illness. In the moral world of the Protestants in Jeanty, innocence or guilt is thus entirely the product of the position you adopt towards the ideology and practices of popular Haitian religion. Your actual conduct (and the hatred, jealousy, or malice it reveals) plays a much smaller role.[11]

Given the overlap and accommodation between formal Catholicism and worship of the spirits, Protestants conclude that it is impossible for any Catholic to avoid contact with the dangerous *lwa*. According to the Protestant position, most villagers inhabit a world that is tainted from the start. Conversion, therefore, provides the only available escape. By abandoning Catholicism, the convert makes the strongest possible claim that he has rejected the worship of the spirits once and for all. So decisive is this change that Protestants describe it with their own "Manichean" vocabulary: they are "outside the world" while all of the unconverted remain "in the world."

This theological background clarifies the challenge issued by the fundamentalist onlookers at Jerline Liron's front door. The Protestants claim that conversion is the only effective cure for Jerline's illness. From their perspective, Jerline's *maladi Satan* is due ultimately to her continued engagement in "this world," that is, in the moral universe of most Catholic Haitian villagers. As one Protestant woman told me, "only by leaving this world will her suffering end." The multiple layers of meaning in this statement alert us that conversion is a combined religious and therapeutic act. Leaving "this world" through Protestant conversion is the strongest antidote to both physical and spiritual suffering. Indeed, some anthropologists have claimed that conversion in response to sickness is the fundamental basis for the growth of the Pentecostal movement in Haiti (see Conway 1978:253). Members of Protestant churches in Jeanty often recite a long history of physical or mental afflictions which led to their decision to convert. In most of these stories, the speaker recounts spending many years visiting one *houngan* after another in search of an answer to her suffering. The decision to convert appears as the last step, after the more likely treatments for a *maladi Satan* have failed.

The Protestants standing outside the *Laica* meeting expressed their critique through a series of evocative metaphors. One young man used the following parables to show me why Jerline must abandon the dual recourse to the *Laica* group and the *houngan* in order to drive out the sickness:

Now they're eating the food which they like . . . If you like a certain food, even if it makes you sick, you'll still eat it. Isn't that right? If you have confidence in it, even if it makes you sick, you'll go back to eating it. You won't look for another food.

You go to the doctor, and he gives you a remedy. You drink it, because it makes you feel better. But *that* remedy, if you continue to drink it, will kill you.

From the Protestant position, the treatment choices made by Jerline's family are like food which does not nourish, food which is actually poison, a remedy which is worse than the original illness. Not only do these treatments offer only false comfort and essentially no protection from the deadly Satanic attack causing Jerline's illness, they also strengthen that attack. In this critique, the Protestants do not differentiate between Catholic prayer and service to the spirits, since each partakes of the symbolism and ritual practices of the other.

However, even when conversion does not banish physical suffering, it radically changes its meaning. One women in Jeanty explained that she decided to join the Baptists after a series of Satanic illnesses. Raised a Catholic, she initially prayed to God for an answer and also sought treatments from an *houngan*. But she hastened to add that

The other stuff wasn't serious. Before I entered the Protestant church, I was always sick. Now I have a lot of pain, but it is the pain that all people have.

After conversion, her bodily ills persisted, but they no longer signified her engagement with the disreputable realm of the *lwa*. Since she had already left the entanglements of "this world," the spiritual sickness was gone. The meaning of her physical illnesses had thereby changed: they were no longer a marker of her inferior moral status, but instead became the ordinary pain that all flesh is heir to.

The illness of Jerline Liron exposes the unstable, overlapping, and competitive relations between the three religions of Jeanty: formal Catholicism, fundamentalist Protestantism, and the worship of the spirits. (It also exposes the micropolitics of envy and the ongoing fragmentation of rural life; these topics are taken up in the next chapter.) People claiming allegiance to each of these three groups offered different therapies for *maladi Satan*: the most serious and disruptive category of illness in rural Haiti. It is tempting to ask what are the fundamental terms of debate by which people take up a position in this plural religious landscape, authorize a particular source of healing power as morally correct and therapeutically effective, and challenge the legitimacy of other options. However, it is impossible to give an exhaustive, all-encompassing answer. The best – indeed, the only possible – representation of moral dimensions of medical pluralism is a positioned one: a series of highly interested and strenuously defended points of view. There is, finally, no single map of all possible routes to locate definitively either the practice of healers or the strategies which villagers devise to negotiate between them (cf. Bourdieu 1977).

For example, the moral response of Catholicism towards sent sickness appears radically different when compared to popular Haitian religion vs.

Protestant fundamentalism:

(1) Compared to Jerline's treatment from Morin and his *lwa*, the prayers and exorcism of the Catholic *Laica* group enact the conventional Manichean world-view with its irreducible opposition between Satan and Christ. This reading of Jerline's illness contrasts with that of the *houngan*, who takes a pragmatic and this-worldly approach to protecting Jerline against attacks from her human enemy.

(2) Compared to the Protestants, however, the Catholics are the ones more interested in Jerline's actual personal relations and social conduct. Behind their public denunciations of the *lwa*, the Catholics attempt to enforce an essentially secular, this-worldly moral code. By contrast, the Protestant devotees interpret Jerline's sent sickness according to an exclusivist otherworldly cosmological scheme. The Protestant moral universe – a heightened version of the conventional Manichean divide – gauges personal innocence or guilt not by one's actual conduct but by the decision to serve the *lwa* or reject them through conversion.

In the first instance, the Catholic position seems "otherworldly," that is, concerned chiefly with general ethical and cosmological principles. In the second instance, it seems "this-worldly," that is, concerned with a particular individual's well-being and personal moral conduct. What accounts for the doubleness in the Catholic response to sent sickness?

It actually is not a contradiction, but rather a characteristic feature of the ways people construct the entire field of medical and religious pluralism. The Catholic oppositional scheme sets into motion the confusing welter of claims and counter-claims about therapeutic power and moral virtue. It animates the competing moral worlds that villagers inhabit.

Tables 1 and 2 illustrate the chief terms of the debates around religious affiliation, moral status, and the treatment for sent sickness. Table 1 begins at the top with the conventional Catholic opposition between God and Satan as expressed by people who claim not to serve the spirits. The next levels trace how the terms of this moral divide reappear in the discourse of midwives/herbalists and finally the *houngan* themselves.

Each level of this diagram exposes a different moral distinction which people use in presenting themselves as upstanding persons and healers. The first level directly corresponds to the most exclusivist version of the Catholic world-view. It underlies people's strident public denunciations of the *lwa* and their angry denials of any experience with *houngan*. Those people who claim to have no contact whatsoever with the *lwa* invoke the opposition between Christ and Satan in order to demonize all those who do.

Table 1. *The Catholic perspective*

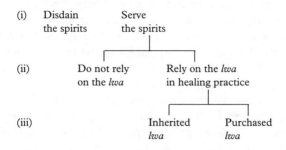

On this first level, the crucial moral question is simply whether or not one serves the spirits. However, the midwives and herbalists profiled in Chapter 5 make use of a finer distinction (level ii). Mme. Beaumont, for example, demonstrates her moral virtue not by demonizing the entire realm of the *lwa*, but rather by refusing to depend upon them as the source of healing power. She resists the importuning of the *lwa*, and while this annoys the spirit, it also ensures Mme. Beaumont's own moral status. By claiming that she does not "serve two masters at once," she reproduces the authority of the Catholic moral discourse even though she freely calls up her *lwa*.

The *houngan* make use of yet a third way to secure their moral virtue. All the *houngan* I spoke with claimed they inherited their own *lwa* from their family, in contrast to the purchased *lwa* invoked by other *divinò* (level iii). Inheritance is the only morally legitimate way to acquire a *lwa*. One purchases a *lwa* for a single reason: to make money by sending a sickness upon a client's enemy or helping the client illicitly gain enormous wealth. Thus Olivia claims that she relies on her *lwa* to carry out God's work of healing, unlike the other mercenary *houngan* who use their purchased *lwa* for malevolent, even murderous ends.

The Catholic-inflected distinction between good and evil is replicated at each level in Table 1. The most exclusivist reading of this moral divide (level i) subsumes many midwives and all *houngan* under the same category: non-Christian servitors of the *lwa*. Nevertheless, members of these two groups of healers follow their own discursive strategies to authorize themselves as morally worthy. Either they have a *lwa* but claim not to draw on it in their healing practice (level ii), or they describe serving an inherited *lwa* for benevolent ends instead of a purchased *lwa* for immoral ends (level iii).

The moral claims made by each succeeding group become less totalizing: that is, less dependent on abstract ethical principles and more

Table 2. *The Protestant critique*

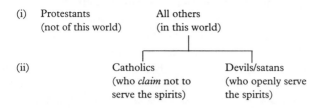

(i)   Protestants   All others
      (not of this world)   (in this world)

(ii)   Catholics   Devils/satans
                          (who *claim* not to   (who openly serve
                          serve the spirits)   the spirits)

closely tied to human conduct in this world. The "Manichean" opposition between Christ and Satan established on the first level is replaced
by the freely made choice to receive or resist the spirits on the second
level. As Mme. Beaumont makes clear, this decision is motivated by the
ordinary human dynamics of attraction and rejection, simple likes and
dislikes, instead of the grand moral questions of level one. Finally, on the
third level, the moral claims made by *houngan* refer exclusively to their
commitment to cure an individual's affliction. For *houngan* and
their clients, the *lwa* routinely appear in this world during consultations
for divination and healing. They are concerned not with personal virtue,
but rather with the virtuous use of the *lwa*'s power: protecting one's
client against human malice. The *houngan* and *mambo* thus occupy an
ambiguous position in this array. They have so attenuated the dominant
moral opposition that they offer essentially an alternative discourse to it.
Nonetheless, they do not consider themselves opposed to the Catholic
moral universe. They draw upon wholly other sources of healing power,
which the victims of sent sickness can use to assert their innocence and
protect against further attacks.

This entire array of moral claims now exists in opposition to the
Protestant condemnation of both Catholicism and the worship of the
spirits, summarized in Table 2.

At first glance, this diagram simply extends upwards by one level the
series of nested oppositions presented in Table 1. It subsumes both
Catholics and worshippers of the spirits under the same category, viz.,
those who remain "in this world." However, by pushing the Catholic
moral divide to the logical endpoint, the Protestants subvert it entirely.
Protestants discursively establish their moral virtue not only by rejecting
Satan in favor of Christ, but by claiming to exit this world. Since
"this world" refers to the moral universe of Haitian Catholicism, the
Protestant rejection of it implicitly denies the Catholics' own claim to be
good Christians and to have nothing to do with the *lwa*.

In the case of Jerline Liron, the Protestant onlookers used this
exclusionary rhetoric in their challenge to Marie Liron's treatment of her

daughter, and they target specifically Marie's more accommodating approach. A devout Catholic, she considers both the *Laica* group's prayers and the *houngan*'s treatments as equally effective; from her standpoint, recourse to both these healers does not threaten her moral status. This cardinal difference between the Catholic and Protestant approaches also appears in Tables 1 and 2. As Table 1 demonstrates, someone who rejects Satan as the cosmological principle of evil could still legitimately consult an *houngan*, as long as that *houngan* relies on inherited *lwa* for the benevolent purpose of healing. A midwife who has *lwa* or even an *houngan* can point to aspects of her practice which attest to her moral worth.

Table 2 summarizes the exclusionary approach of most fundamentalist churches: it really contains only a single all-encompassing opposition. For a Protestant, the only difference between people who claim to be good Catholics and those who worship the *lwa* is the hypocrisy of the Catholics. Indeed, the extensive overlap between formal Catholicism and popular Haitian religion grants a certain persuasive power to the fundamentalist position. Therefore, the opposition described in the second level of Table 2 – between Catholics and worshippers of the spirits – is a distinction without a difference. The ideology of Protestantism allows no way of securing one's moral status except by "leaving this world" through conversion.

Tables 1 and 2 do not provide fixed and stable coordinates for all the possible positions within these competing moral worlds. They only show what a given position looks like from yet another vantage point. For example, from the perspective of the *houngan*, the *Laica* group pays precious little attention to the worldly context of Jerline's suffering: the human enemy who originally sent the satan and the ways to protect her from future attacks. But from the perspective of the Protestant onlookers standing outside her house, the main problem is that Jerline has not converted, and that the prayers of the Laica group are ineffective because of the morally bankrupt overlap between Catholicism and the satanic realm of the *lwa*.

The shifting quality of moral and therapeutic claims in Jeanty endows each group with its own set of contradictions. A Catholic family like Jerline's responds to sent sickness by both demonizing the *lwa* and doing whatever is necessary, including consulting an *houngan*, to protect the victim from further attacks. The *houngan* claim to uphold the Catholic moral order, but they also leave it entirely by relying on the ambivalent power of the *lwa* to both harm and heal. The Protestants embrace the Manichean moral divide of village Catholicism but collapse many of its major distinctions.

The ethnographic description of a particular religious form of healing power will inevitably involve a contradiction, because the same choice, when viewed from another position, has radically different moral implications. Moreover, the very way people experience these moves towards healing power does not fit the neutral and utilitarian language of medical "choice" or "option." One can only enter these discourses by taking up a determinate position within them. When I said, "I'm not afraid of Satan, because I don't believe in him" (chapter 6), I quickly learned that to disbelieve in the existence of Satan is not a comprehensible position in this plural religious system (cf. Good 1994:15). To remain neutral about the power of Satan or the moral worth of the victim – to refuse to stake a claim to personal virtue and innocence somewhere among these religious options – is not allowable or even conceivable to the people I spoke with in Jeanty.[12]

Conversion, gender, and resistance

People's responses to sent sickness thus reproduce (and destabilize) the plural healing arrangements and sources of moral authority in Jeanty. The case-studies of Jerline Liron and Dieusauveur Martin (see chapter 4) have privileged mainly the competing religious discourses and the subtleties of body/self experience that converge in this illness. However, villagers' negotiations around *maladi Satan* also speak to the larger social and historical processes which are currently transforming their lives. Activities which, on the surface, seem strictly therapeutic or religious are also ways that villagers engage with the powerful global forces that are impoverishing them and redrawing their political, cultural, and national horizons. Through their struggles to understand and control sent sickness, people creatively respond to the contradictions in rural Haitian society and the fragmentation of its traditional order of signs and practices.

Jerline's vulnerability to sent sickness is linked to the micropolitics of her family and the range of gendered roles open to her as worker, breadwinner, mother, and wife. In each of these arenas, Jerline took advantage of the local opportunities for advancement, personal accomplishment, and security. However, this local world is threatened with delegitimation by political and economic forces originating in Port-au-Prince and the United States (cf. Kleinman and Kleinman 1991). The interpretation and treatment of sent sickness thus signify the intrusion of outside forces into the local calculus of moral authority and healing power. The negotiations around Jerline's condition represent one way to respond to this threat, but there are other possibilities which lead in radically different directions. Case-studies of other women suffering from sent sickness, but who actually converted to Protestantism, suggest how conversion is a new source of resistance to the contradictions in the lives of rural women.

In the months following Jerline's sickness, I spoke with two other women from Jeanty who suffered from *maladi mò*, caused by a dead spirit sent upon them. Both women sought treatment at the same Pentecostalist cult of healing which had sent its members to Jerline's doorstep. They chose precisely the same reading of their disorder which Jerline's mother so vehemently resisted. Officially named the Church of Faithful Israel (*Legliz d'Israel par la Foi*), most people refer to it simply as Pastor Gabriel's church. It carries out its activities in a string of buildings clustered on the outskirts of Milot, a village about 6 miles north of Jeanty. Prayer meetings and other services for worship take place in a large thatch arbor (*tonèl*) or the adjacent nearby private home. A number of ill individuals receiving treatment reside in yet another building in this *lakou* as well as the nearby home of Pastor Gabriel.

During one of the day-long prayer meetings at this church, Noelle Plaisimond, 20 years old, was lying on her back in the lap of Genor, another man currently under treatment by Pastor Gabriel. Noelle was conscious and aware of her surroundings, but could not focus her attention. Although she recognized me (I had visited her family several times in Jeanty), she said nothing. Her body was resting at an odd angle, and her head dangled off Genor's knee. Genor said to me that she was sick, and that "they sent a dead spirit upon her to kill her." Noelle was not suffering from the sort of violent seizures or convulsions which afflicted Jerline, and she did not need to be physically restrained. For perhaps an hour she said and moved very little. However, when the singing of hymns began in the nearby *tonèl*, she began to moan, and had a clearly pained expression on her face.

Her older sister explained that Noelle had seven dead spirits upon her, a mixture of children and adults. As with Jerline, the inability to speak was evidence of the spirit of a dead child. These multiple spirits had been removed over the course of three prayer services led by Pastor Gabriel, and Noelle continues to live at the Pastor's church. Although her sister says that Noelle is much better now, she adds that this church is "just like a hospital; they interned her, and they haven't yet let her leave." This was not the only time people described Pastor Gabriel's congregation in explicitly medical terms. One middle-aged man, formerly a patient of Gabriel, also described rooms where people with sent sickness were housed as the *salle d'opération* and the *dispensaire*.

Noelle was raised in Jeanty, but until a few months before her illness she had been working in Port-au-Prince at a "factory," (the English word

13 Women carry out most domestic chores in their households: purchasing food, preparing meals, and washing dishes and clothes.

is now used in Creole) located in the industrial zone near the airport. Such "factories" employed 60,000 people in 1980, and less by the middle of the decade (Grunwald *et al.* 1984), and they are mostly foreign-owned offshore assembly plants which pay their workers no more than the legal minimum wage (about 3 dollars per day in the late 1980s). Nonetheless, these are highly coveted positions, given the universal underemployment among most residents of Port-au-Prince. In fact, people often mention wage-labor in a factory as one of the appeals of life in the capital city, and one of the reasons for migrating out of the countryside (see Prince 1985; Fass 1988).

Against this background of rural emigration and the competitive urban wage-labor market, Noelle's sister had no trouble explaining who sent the seven dead spirits sent upon her: "Noelle was working in a factory in Port-au-Prince. Someone else wanted her job. That other person sent a dead spirit upon her to kill her, in order to take her job. It's a matter of ambition." I asked whether she knew who sent them. "I don't really care who sent them," she replied, "since the sickness has been cured. I am not going to seek revenge."

Marie Jussome was also a "patient" with *maladi mò* at Pastor Gabriel's church. In many respects, Marie resembles Jerline and Noelle Plaisimond. All three are young unmarried women, around 20 years old, and most economically ambitious and successful of their families. Jerline held a steady job as a schoolteacher. Noelle had a highly coveted job in a factory, work which is held by less than 7% of the city's population (Dupuy 1990:14–15). Marie was the only one of seven children to attend secondary school. At the time someone sent these dead spirits upon her, she had almost received the certificate for completing tenth grade.

Marie's appearance when the dead spirits actively afflict her is also familiar. Her father gave the following account: "When she has this sickness, she raises her body up and then throws it on the ground. She swears at you, she grabs on to you and tries to punch you. She calls out, 'Father, what am I doing here, where am I?' I hold her, but she tries to push me away." During calmer periods, Marie and her father speculate about who actually sent these spirits upon her. They mentioned two possibilities: fellow students who had harassed her and stolen her books and school supplies, and a man who offered money to sleep with her, and whom she refused. Marie's sent sickness differs only slightly from the ones described above. She is not possessed by the mute spirit of a dead child; the satan that is upon her, to use the Creole expression, can speak, although Marie cannot remember what it said after the episode of possession is over.

Each of these women was victimized by a sent sickness at the same crisis point in her economic and reproductive careers. To begin with, they were trying to move beyond the conventional roles for rural women – marketing the produce of the family gardens and engaging in petty commerce – and establish their identity and social position outside the local agricultural economy. Noelle accomplished this in the most dramatic way, by leaving the countryside entirely and entering the disciplined work force of multinational capitalism (a strategy that has parallels among young women elsewhere in the developing world, see Ong 1987). The others were steadily advancing through local institutions which nonetheless directly depended on, and provided a pathway to, supralocal powers – Jerline's job at Ebenezer Bethel church school, supported by a North American Protestant mission, and Marie's Catholic secondary school.

In the context of widespread rural poverty, Jerline and Noelle could advance only by removing themselves from the local moral economy and forms of production. However, this strategy also created profound contradictions in their lives. On the one hand, Jerline and Noelle were probably proud of their skills, and their families assuredly benefited from their salaries. On the other hand, their success made it hard for them to find a suitable husband or *menaj* (long-term partner). Women in similar positions complained that most village men would expect them both to bear several children *and* continue to bring in their dependable salaries. This would have been a nearly impossible feat for both Noelle and Jerline. For Noelle, the competition for factory jobs makes "maternity leave" an unheard-of luxury, and she did not have nearby kin in Port-au-Prince to care for newborns. Jerline's Protestant employers, I was told, would rather install a Protestant couple as teachers than a pregnant Catholic woman.

These women gained economic success by propelling themselves out of the dominant rural economy and into wage-labor at the periphery of global institutions. In doing so, however, they also spurned the typical reproductive career expected of rural women. In Jeanty, children are actively desired as a valuable social resource (to forge new kin ties with godparents and in-laws) and economic resource (to help with domestic, productive, and commercial activities, and to provide for one's old age) (see Lowenthal 1987). "Children are wealth" (*timoun se richès*) announces a Creole proverb, and this sentiment can catch successful but young and marriageable woman in a bind. The contradiction was especially acute for Jerline Liron: her family depended entirely on her salary, but her mother also needed to develop a wider kinship network in the region they had moved to, and Jerline was the only child of marriageable age.

To be assailed by the spirit of a dead child – indeed, a baby, who can neither speak nor control his/her body – was a powerfully expressive symptom of these contradictions in Jerline's life. In the months leading up to the illness, at least two men had actively courted her (a pattern which includes both social visiting and sexual contact). Less than a year later, Jerline had left her job at the Protestant school, had gotten married to Jean (one of the main caretakers for her during the illness), and was pregnant with their first child. Four years after that, Jerline had given birth to a second child and the family was planning to build a house next to Marie Liron's home. In light of this outcome, the spirit of a dead baby mediated people's expectations for Jerline's reproductive career; the illness effectively returned her to the typical domestic and sexual roles and economic routines for rural women.

Jerline was thus victimized by the *maladi mò ti moun* in several ways. The illness was an attack on her psychological integrity, for it temporarily displaced her "good self" (*bon nanm*). It threatened her moral status as an innocent and upright Catholic. It was a malicious social attack launched by someone jealous of her job and status. Finally, in its specific form as the spirit of a dead baby, it powerfully deflected her economic and social ambitions. In this sense, the *mò* sent upon her is a collective representation of the child she refused to bear, the child she could not bear and still advance through one of the few routes of upward mobility available in Jeanty. Her illness – originally caused by the spirit of a dead baby – was resolved by bearing a live infant, building a family in the traditional rural pattern, and stepping off the trajectory which led inexorably away from Jeanty, its local economy, and its narrow repertoire of women's roles and identities.

In another sense, however, Jerline's illness is a cultural performance which at once validates and victimizes her (cf. Frankenberg 1986). The political possibilities of resistance created by her illness arose from the very act of naming the invading entity. In general, there are several ways that individuals can respond to spirits, from the violent disorder and terror experienced by Jerline, through the ambivalent accommodation practiced by Mme. Beaumont (chapter 5), to the *houngan*'s fluent ease with possession by the *lwa* (chapter 6). Indeed, people have some choice about what they will call the spirit (Satan, dead spirit, or *lwa*) and the relationship they will establish with it. Of course, people do not always make these decisions explicitly or even consciously. They express them through the aesthetics of performance, which influences how others interpret the spirit possession as a whole (see Boddy 1989:348ff).

Jerline's obvious bodily distress and mental anguish demanded an immediate response. Her family decided with hardly any debate that she was afflicted by the spirit of a dead child. Nonetheless, Jerline may well have performed her affliction to favor this particular conclusion over the chief alternative: that she was being called to serve an ancestral *lwa*.[13] Given her mother's familiarity with local *houngan*, Jerline likely knew enough about the symbolic and gestural vocabulary of spirit possession to push the interpretations of her performance in one direction or another.

Did she modulate the visible signs of her experience in order to enact a violent protest against people's expectations? This is an oblique, but provocative reading of her muteness and bodily disorder. Jerline's performance did not suggest a *lwa* beckoning her to serve it or practice as a *mambo*. Jerline instead portrayed herself as invaded by a dead baby which drove her mad and which threatened her well-paying job, her moral virtue, and even her life. Through her illness performance, she rhetorically inverted people's expectations for her productive and reproductive career. The baby she embodied was malevolent and pathogenic; it disrupted the norms and routines of rural life, instead of embedding her more deeply within them.

Jerline's *maladi mò ti moun* thus embodies both people's social expectations and her forceful refusal of them. Her illness contains a public transcript – a record of words, gestures, and other signs (or symptoms) that reproduce the power of dominant categories and coercive roles. But it also contains a hidden transcript that contradicts the public, and publicly accepted, framework of gender relations (see Scott 1990). Her illness performance mediates in both directions; perhaps this is why the condition recurs among other women caught in the same double bind. Nonetheless, Jerline's refusal was short-lived. It was *only* performative, in the sense of a temporary expressive disruption of the normative flow of social life. As the illness lifted, Jerline accepted a more localized and restrictive future. She also acquiesced to the reading of her affliction from the Catholic prayer group and the *houngan*, and along with her family, refused to convert to the Pentecostal church.

Conversion, bodily control, and social critique

Ironically, this second, more explicit refusal to enter the Pentecostal church closed off another, more pervasive form of resistance to the contradictions of rural society. On one level, the dispute between Marie Liron and members of Pastor Gabriel's church concerned the power of conversion to heal Jerline and ensure her innocence. On another level, however, it revealed two divergent strategies for advancement within the limited opportunities of rural Haiti. Marie Liron, like most Catholics, quickly dismisses the Protestants' claim to moral authority. However, such dismissals often contain an honest evaluation of the pragmatic and material motives for conversion. As one young Catholic women told me directly, people often convert because they need money:

[Is it mostly the wealthy or the poor who become Protestants?] It's mostly people who can't do anything to better themselves. Because they're poor, they're looking for God to help them. Rich people almost never become Protestants. Because they're well off, they don't need God to give them anything.

Her stark answer that poverty motivates conversion shows how Catholic villagers locate converts in the political economy of rural Haiti: they are usually the poorest of the poor. Several people explained the indirect economic strategies which are embedded in the decision to convert. Their comments mixed moral disapproval with an honest appraisal of the few forms of upward mobility open to the poorer residents of Jeanty. One man discussed the typical motives for becoming Protestant pastors:

There are Haitians who, because of pride, will leave the Catholic church, and build their own church. Then they try to sell it to a congregation headed by an American, or some other *blan*. There are a lot of religions like that: it's the *blan* who directs them, and they install a Haitian who works on the ground. But the church itself is owned by the *blan*.

Apart from the accusation about ambitious pastors, this statement exposes the direct political and economic dependence of rural Protestant churches upon North American missionary organizations. This man went on to say that each of the five Protestant churches in the center of Jeanty was controlled by Americans at the highest levels. The only churches not affiliated with *blan* were, in his words, the "little churches that have just been built, like that church up in the hills," that is, Pastor Gabriel's Pentecostal congregation.

Many villagers can recount the step-by-step growth of local Protestant groups, from their founding, to the first visits from Americans, to the types of food aid and scholarships provided by the missionary groups which now support them. Moreover, people acknowledge how much the village of Jeanty as a whole depends on the services and opportunities provided by foreign-based religious organizations. Of all the local religious leaders, the French Catholic priest and the Haitian Baptist pastor have directed the most foreign resources into Jeanty (the pastor divides his time between Jeanty and his church in Cambridge, MA). "If the priest left," a young man once told me, only half in jest, "everyone in Jeanty would become Baptist." If both left, "There would be no one here to run our schools, and no one left to pull some strings (*fe kèk demach*) for Jeanty."

These comments accurately point out the consequences of dependency upon supralocal institutions for the residents of Jeanty. Not only do resources flow into the village from the outside, but the path of upward mobility usually leads out of the village, and Protestant pastors and their flocks have cast their lot with this option. Pastors often seek out ways to rise in the church hierarchy by ministering to congregations in Port-au-Prince or the USA. While ordinary church members cannot expect this career, joining the church nonetheless corrodes their ties to the local social world. Although the material gains available from the world beyond Jeanty may lie in the far future, the ideological removal begins at the moment of conversion. Becoming a Protestant removes people from the moral economy of Jeanty and reorients them away from its constricted life opportunities.

Protestantism not only subverts the traditional Catholic moral order (see above), it also undercuts the civic hegemony of village Catholicism. The rhetoric of "leaving this world" usually applied to conversion also describes the specific displacements experienced by converts as they loosen their sentimental and social attachments to Jeanty. For example, Protestants do not celebrate the patron saint festival in July (Notre Dame de Jeanty) with the rest of the town. They gather instead every year at a convention, always held in a different part of the country. These patron saint festivals celebrate villagers' ties to local space; they allow people publicly to affirm their identity as *moun Jeanty* and to welcome back long-absent kin now living abroad. By abandoning this festival, Protestants take an initial symbolic step into a supralocal space, and they affirm their membership in a social and moral community extending throughout the nation and financially supported by foreign missionary organizations.

Renunciation of the spirits extends this radical displacement into genealogical space. By vehemently denouncing the entire realm of *lwa* as Satanic and irremediably sinful, converts abandon the obligations to care for, memorialize, or embody their ancestral spirits. They thereby remove themselves from their lineage and the specific places associated with it (the family *lakou*, the spring, tree, or rock where offerings to one's family *lwa* are made). Converts forge fictive kinship ties with other church members to take the place of the extended coresidential lineage: members of Pastor Gabriel's church address each other as "Brother Paul" and "Sister Rose." Even certain forms of direct dependency on North American missionary groups are rhetorically recast as kinship relations. Many children receive monthly checks for tuition and meals at the Baptist school from Baptist parishioners throughout North America. Residents of Jeanty usually do not know their names, but will refer to them as the children's godparents.

Protestant conversion thus erodes people's ideological and sentimental attachments to the village of Jeanty as well as the sedimented memories of their extended family. It reorients people to new tropes of identity, new social ties, and new sources of material aid located in national and even transnational spaces. This removal from the dominant local order of signs and practices enacts a refusal to accept the constrictive life choices faced by the poorest residents of Jeanty. But what makes their refusal so convincing is a set of bodily practices that establish, in the most palpable and immediate terms, their ideological transformation and their separation from the normal routines of village life.

Specific techniques of bodily management are enjoined on converts to Pastor Gabriel's Pentecostal church. Some of these apply to ritual settings, others pervade daily life. During the singing and dancing preceding healing, several church members besides the pastor may feel another entity taking over their bodies. If they fall on the ground, the community will interpret it as possession by Satan, but if they remain standing, the experience is accepted as possession by the Holy Ghost. This bodily grammar of possession marks the difference between Pentecostalists and the world they have escaped. The spirits from "the world" or "outside" (representing, by synecdoche, the intermixture of Catholicism and service to the spirits, outside the new moral community converts have constructed) reveal themselves through bodily signs. Converts can detect their presence and properly defend themselves.

Bodily control also becomes important in much more mundane settings. Pastor Gabriel warns his congregation not to drink liquor or smoke. Women should not wear perfume or bodily adornments; both men and women should dress in a modest and even austere way. Both sexes should avoid dancing. These forms of bodily discipline represent another way to escape the dangers of "the world outside." Pentecostalists avoid the temptation to re-enter "the world" by controlling what the body consumes and the signs that it gives off. They remove themselves from the myriad social and bodily exchanges of daily rural life: the informal drinking around a men's game of cards or dominoes, the flirting during the dances held on patron saints' festivals. In theory (if not always in practice), these bodily signs mark the enduring disposition and social location of converts. They both publicly proclaim and enforce the division between the unavailing world converts have left and the more promising moral order they now inhabit.

Rituals of healing within the Pentecostalist church are perhaps the most potent of its bodily techniques. Conversion is almost always in response to illness, thus healing is the first type of bodily reform that converts encounter. The patients interned at Pastor Gabriel's church usually converted only after the "help-seeking process" was well under-way, and after the illness was defined as a *maladi Satan*. In his sermons, the pastor broadened the response to illness into a critical commentary on the entire social order. He actually led the new convert to reinterpret all illness, after the model of sent sickness, as one of the routine dangers of engagements in an immoral world. He defined this world both theologically – as the domain of Satan – and sociologically – as the sum of social relations governed by greed, jealousy, and competition over the meager local resources and opportunities for advancement.

Physical disorder thus becomes the emblem of the disordered social world, and members of Pastor Gabriel's church often referred to conversion as "leaving the world" or "escaping the world." Healing through conversion represents the escape into a bounded religious community whose moral and medical authority has a visible and palpable source entirely outside the historically dominant Catholic church. The pastor's healing power depends on his embodiment of the Holy Spirit: a state prepared for by donning special white robes, and facilitated by vigorous singing and rhythmic body movements. Actual possession by the Holy Ghost is marked by stereotypical bodily gestures: jerky movements of the arms and physical "tics," such as sudden neck craning or the rapid, explosive utterance of nonsensical syllables. Healing takes place through the physical laying on of hands, or rubbing holy oil on the convert's face or head.

This unmediated, embodied openness to God's healing power, and its physical transfer to the body of the ill individual, carried out in people's homes, implicitly criticizes the sedate, rule-bound, and spatially segregated Catholic liturgy. It ritually incorporates the convert into a poor, informal, locally based organization oriented towards Protestant North American sources of power and prestige. It removes converts, as a corporate group, from the Catholic church, sponsored by the Haitian state and, at least in Jeanty, financially dependent upon France. Healing through conversion is thus an embodied practice which effects a profound removal on two registers at once: away from the immoral intermixture of Christianity and worship of the *lwa*, and away from the hegemony of the Catholic church and the local world it legitimates. This local world is dependent on national and metropolitan powers which offer precious few opportunities to the poorest stratum of Jeanty. Protestants essentially switch their allegiance to another structure of dependency, and set their (this-worldly) sights on a transnational future.

The Pentecostal church of Pastor Gabriel is thus a cult of affliction, and like all such cults, it links the personal and social bodies in two ways: through the discourse and practice of healing and the reconstruction of everyday bodily experience. In both ritual healing and daily life, the body is manipulated in an attempt to reform the immediate social world, to reconstruct fragmented experience, and to deal with conflicts not addressed by dominant ideologies and institutions (Comaroff 1985). Anthropologists of the Caribbean continue to debate the long-term political possibilities opened and foreclosed by such fundamentalist Protestant groups.[14] But whatever their ultimate effect, groups like Pastor Gabriel's church offer an immediate refusal and creative response to contradictions of village Catholicism. Conversion represents a much more radical alternative to this dominant moral universe than service to the *lwa*. The Protestants' interpretation of *maladi Satan*, and their over-lapping rituals of healing and conversion, enunciate this alternative in symbolic and embodied forms. Fundamentalist conversion – the very route rejected by Jerline Liron's family – represents, in some ways, the most potent new source of moral authority and healing power in rural Haiti.

8   Conclusion

In the past twenty-five years, medical anthropology has moved beyond its original applied orientation and engaged with the central theoretical debates of the discipline (and in the human sciences generally) (see Good 1994). Because the interest in certain questions rises and falls over time, we must occasionally revisit older concerns and shake loose the conventional wisdom grown up around them. In this spirit, this book recuperates an early theme of medical anthropology – health-seeking and medical pluralism – and connects it to current debates about practice, agency, and the epistemological claims of anthropological research.

Medical pluralism and practice

The ethnography of illness and healing in Jeanty departs from the twin assumptions in many classic studies of medical pluralism: (1) individuals are rational and voluntaristic actors, and (2) the "health care sectors" of a community form a stable set of discourses and treatments which exist distinct from the subject (cf. Young 1981; Good 1986). This book has argued, first of all, for a more fluid and historicized account of plural healing arrangements. Different therapies do not make up a permanent background structure for people's observable "health-seeking behaviors" (defining symptoms, consulting healers, undergoing treatments, etc.; see Chrisman 1977). To the contrary, such behaviors themselves constitute, reproduce, and destabilize the local array of therapies.

Health-seeking is a form of practice in which people's diverse motivations for seeking out a healer are orchestrated by pre-existing (and in this sense, objective) medical discourses (see Bourdieu 1977:80ff). Over long periods of time, individual acts of consultation, diagnosis, divination, treatment, etc. become routinized and take on recognizable and stable forms. In this way, health-seeking practices reproduce a certain array of healing powers. For example, people in Jeanty predictably seek out a biomedical cure in hopes to avoid the diagnosis of *maladi Satan*. This can appear as a rule-bound piece of medical

190

behavior, and it also stabilizes the ideology and power of both bio-medicine and the *houngan*'s healing practice. But as the objective conditions change, and as this change is felt in subjective experience and local life-worlds, health-seeking practices transform the local forms of healing, in subtle or occasionally dramatic ways. The growing appeal of healing through fundamentalist conversion exemplifies this process. Profound changes in the objective conditions of life (in this instance, increasing rural poverty and a new openness to North American material and ideological influences) have transformed local accounts of affliction and altered the seemingly objective range of available therapies.

This approach does not oppose health-seeking to the range of available therapies as an "action" to its "context." It does not isolate health-seeking as a set of rule-bound, observable behaviors which maximize physical well-being or restore coherence and meaning to lives disrupted by illness. Health seeking, like all practices, grows out of the dialectic relation between objective social structures and the subjectivity of social actors; more precisely, the relations between the social arrangements of healing power and ways people engage with this power. Health-seeking involves subjective, but widely shared ways of interpreting illness and taking practical therapeutic action. These ways are calibrated to, but can also subvert, the local forms of healing. Plural healing arrangements, therefore, are both the objective constraints upon *and* the sedimented outcome of health-seeking practices. This dialectical, practice-oriented approach challenges several prevailing notions of medical pluralism.

Making a categorical distinction between biomedicine and other forms of healing is one step in the conventional study of medical pluralism. But it is nearly impossible to do this in the case of Haiti. Over the past few hundred years, Euro-American technologies of medical treatment and surveillance have been deflected and reappropriated by their intended subjects. The ethnography of biomedicine in Jeanty shows the long-term result of this process. On both the conceptual and the clinical level, the clear distinction between biomedicine and other forms of healing has broken down. Elements of biomedicine have diffused into all the other ways of representing and intervening in bodily disorder. People certainly invoke biomedicine as a distinctive set of signs and practices, but not in order to compare different medical options. They use it rather to make etiologic decisions: a *maladi satan* is, almost by definition, one which the doctors cannot cure.

There are two other steps in the conventional anthropology of medical pluralism: parsing the range of non-biomedical healers into stable categories, and examining how patients and their kin negotiate between them. This book has tried to show that the relevant distinctions among non-biomedical healers are not a matter of diagnostic styles, secular vs. sacred legitimating ideologies, or the use of psychosocial vs. techno-empirical treatments (e.g., herbalism) (cf. Harrell 1991). Moreover, the movement of patients and their kin between healers is not governed by a utilitarian logic to maximize health or a cultural logic symbolic linking certain symptoms to their appropriate therapies.

This book collapses into a single analytic framework both the range of healing specialists ("medical pluralism") and the strategies by which people negotiate between them ("health-seeking strategies"). Midwives, herbalists, and religious specialists, along with their clients, are all engaged in the move towards healing power. In this sense, healing power is an inclusive term with several flexible, interlocking meanings. It connotes clinical effectiveness, moral authority, political coercion and opportunity, and a resource for collective identity. However, in rural Haiti the contest for healing power is primarily an arena for assertions of personal innocence as well as creative responses to the deepening contradictions of rural social life. In Jeanty, a moral calculus informs the rhetoric and ritual practice of healers as well as illness narratives and short-term decisions of the people who consult them. As they struggle to make the correct choice among competing moral worlds, both patients and healers take up various positions on the same symbolic field, structured according to the same religious and therapeutic ideologies.

Body/self and body politic in medical anthropology

On the one hand, the plural healing arrangements in Jeanty make up a stable set of options facing the individual seeking care. On the other hand, they are a shifting, continuously negotiated set of positions generated by people's short-term moves towards moral authority (and other forms of symbolic capital). The problematic of medical pluralism is that it appears both as an objective structure and as a forever shifting set of compromises. It appears the first way chiefly to people seeking treatment, and it appears the second way to the outsider/anthropologist who tries to represent it. Examining this problematic more closely will expose some of the tensions in the current anthropology of the body and the social sources of sickness.

For residents of Jeanty faced with the emergent crisis of illness, the healing power and moral meanings of the *lwa* appear as fundamentally different from biomedicine, herbalism, Protestant conversion, etc. But for the anthropologist (historian, cultural critic, etc.), these healing discourses actually depend on each other. The persuasiveness of funda-mentalism depends on the way it revalues and subverts the signs of

Catholicism. Both Catholicism and Protestantism consolidate themselves by constructing the realm of the *lwa* as their demonic inverse
image. This disjuncture between insider and outsider perceptions
appears in still another form. People seeking out treatment are concerned
only with the current array of healing powers; they thus routinely insert
body/self disorders into seemingly stable medical discourses. But for
the outsider, such discourses contain traces of multiple ideologies and
institutions which have competed for dominance over long historical
periods. And certain of them (such as fundamentalist Protestantism) are
the leading edge of newer political forces that are transforming rural
society.

It is a truism that a single medical system looks quite different to a
patient (or specialist) actively engaged in the contest for healing power
and an outsider whose own health and moral status are never at issue.
But these two readings are different not only because one is practical and
the other is theoretical and speculative. The disjunctive readings actually
represent two different points of entry into the same general recursive
model linking body/self experience – via several mediations – to large-
scale social forces (see Kleinman 1986; Kleinman and Kleinman 1991;
Scheper-Hughes 1992a, 1992b; Scheper-Hughes and Lock 1987). This
general model is a continuum which begins at one end with embodied
experience: the bloating, headache, or dizziness described by Janine
Dutoit (chapter 4) or the dissociation, loss of control, and mental
anguish, experienced by Jerline Liron (chapter 7). In the next moment,
people undertake the work of cultural interpretation and define these
body/self experiences as symptoms with recognizable causes and treatments. This work inaugurates yet more strategies to inscribe the sufferer
as innocent and morally upstanding within competing religious frameworks. By documenting these interlocking moments, we imagine ourselves as insiders to the plural medical and religious discourses of Jeanty.

However, these discourses have a "momentous" history of their own.
They are the historical residue (or the avant-garde) of powerful supra-
local groups and ideologies. In Jeanty, discourses of religious healing
reveal traces of the foreign ideologies which have created local tropes of
identity and strategies for advance. For example, the Catholics' vehement denunciations of the *lwa* echoes the French colonists' fear of
African religious practices during the historical construction of Haitian
society in the seventeenth and eighteenth centuries (see Thornton 1992).
The popularity of Protestant conversion indexes the current transnational displacement of Haitians into North America and the ideological colonization of Haiti by North American missionaries.

How should we represent all of these entailments between body/self experience and the relations of Jeanty to global forces? If we array them in a single synthetic theoretical model, it would constitute the outsider's perspective *par excellence*. Such a systematic account might well be "theoretically powerful," but it is situated outside the system altogether. It privileges all terms equally and does not explore the practical mastery of people who recognize or deploy the links between them in daily life. This brand of objectivism is problematic in the wake of not only practice theory, but also the general critique of static ethnographic representations which deny the emergent, contested qualities of culture (e.g., Clifford 1986). The goal should rather be to negotiate between the insider and outsider perspectives and thereby document how residents of Jeanty use bodily experience and moral claims to make sense of their social world, establish their position in it, and articulate its contradictions.

However, even this recursive, dialectical framework does not do away with the disjuncture between insider and outsider perspectives. It merely restates it in the form of a question. How much of the continuum stretching from bodily disorder to global forces is actually represented in people's awareness, in their talk about sickness, and their therapeutic actions? This is, in fact, a core epistemological question in much current medical anthropology. The outsider-anthropologist usually strives for a totalizing view of the continuum between body/self experience and macrosocial forces. Does this view guarantee a more accurate and politically potent understanding? Or does the very inclusiveness of the outsider's perspective seriously misrepresent how people understand and maneuver within their local social world?

This dilemma is rooted, of course, in the recurring tension in anthropology between empirical social description and the phenomenology of experience, and between local and global units of analysis. With the entry of medical anthropology into the main theoretical debates of the discipline, the dilemma has reappeared in several different forms. For example, Iranian townspeople associate explicitly from certain self/body experience (exemplified by the local disorder "heart distress") to oppressive or unavailing social conditions. People thus connect their pounding, trembling, or squeezed hearts to poverty, cramped living conditions, and oppressive gender hierarchies. They articulate their experience of social conflict through local medical discourses, and hence open up more room to maneuver in their constricted worlds. But they do so primarily through the "unspoken meanings" of heart distress (or other medical idioms) (see B. Good 1977; M. Good 1980; B. Good and M. Good 1980). The question remains, if the meanings are unspoken, how should we represent them? Are the micropolitical meanings of heart distress primarily tools which people use for short-term advantage (which is how most Iranians probably view them)? Or are they instead a fleeting, perpetually possible, but usually aborted synthetic vision leading from bodily suffering to the distressed and contradictory social order? Must we privilege one representation over the other in our anthropological accounts?

Taussig (1992) directly addresses this question in terms of the power of biomedical discourse to mystify the social origins of bodily suffering. Taussig describes a woman with polymyositis who occasionally manages to draw powerful connections between her muscle degeneration and her life experiences of oppression. Nonetheless, most of the time she accepts the alienated, asocial, and reductionist account of her condition supplied by medical specialists. Her partial and ephemeral insights are subverted by the dominant biomedical discourse. Although her loss of autonomy is never complete – she continues, tentatively, to assert her own judgment about her pain and disability – Taussig doubts that she will deploy the imagery of her disorder to construct a serious critique of social institutions (1992:91). At the end, it is Taussig who must speak for her about the connections between her own bodily suffering and social oppression.

By contrast, Martin (1987) is much more sanguine about the ability of women to overcome the reified biomedical definition of particular bodily conditions (pre-menstrual syndrome and menopause). But despite the celebratory tenor of her book (cf. Price 1994), she too draws an equivocal portrait of people who both make the critical connections between physical experience and the social order while remaining mystified, to some extent, by our culture's dominant reductionist accounts. Her Gramscian interpretation of pre-menstrual rage is one of many examples. This rage is a shared and embodied form of consciousness that potentially unites all disempowered women into a single, hence stronger group. But its political meaning is "implicit in activity" – mood swings, emotional outbursts, etc. – not in people's words. Indeed, it is directly contradicted by women's explicit consciousness which individualizes rage, blocks the awareness of its social roots, and deflects its political possibilities (Martin 1987:135).

Good, Taussig, and Martin all ask how to represent the hidden, fleeting, or implicit connections between body/self disorder and local structures of oppression. But Martin also asks how to render these connections explicit, and thereby to chip away the hegemonic power of medical discourses which disguise the palpable effects of domination. She thus pushes the debate to include the liberatory potential for anthropological research. As a partial response, Scheper-Hughes (1992a and b) advocates open dialogue between anthropologists and their "others" which would criticize the taken-for-granted discourse of bodily affliction (cf. Freire 1970). In her study of poverty, hunger, and loss in northeast Brazil Scheper-Hughes tries to lead shanty-town dwellers to deconstruct popular idioms which medicalize hunger into "nerves." In these dialogues, she explicitly aims at a comprehensive critique linking the lived experience of hunger to specific forms of political and economic violence. This critique finds its epistemological roots in both the immediate practical knowledge of local residents and the theoretical, synthetic knowledge of outsiders.

Scheper-Hughes poses the same central question: is the continuum stretching from bodily disorder to national and global forces actually represented in people's talk about illness and healing? Her first answer is familiar: people are aware of these connections, but in an oblique and coded way. Although shanty-town residents consciously accept the individualizing disease categories of biomedicine, their coded idiom of "nerves" implicitly connects bodily experience to social oppression. But Scheper-Hughes is not content with this portrait in contradictory consciousness. She asserts that acquiescence to biomedicine – the system of practical knowledge used by most shanty dwellers in dealing with illness – is an example of bad faith: the active consent of subordinate groups to their own oppressed condition. The goal Scheper-Hughes upholds for anthropological analysis is to counteract this alienation. She thus claims that members of subordinate groups could reclaim this embodied knowledge and transform its implicit social meanings into explicit critique and political action. To expose the "hidden" metaphors for bodily disorder thus becomes, for the anthropologist, the first step in liberatory social criticism: e.g., a man with paralysis in his legs is shown to be "paralyzed within a stagnant semi-feudal economy"; a man whose says his legs collapsed under him is "sinking, yielding" to these overwhelming social conditions (1992b:236). At the end, the task is somehow to get the shanty-town residents to draw the same connections themselves.

Let us restate this central epistemological question in terms of medical pluralism in Haiti. What do residents of Jeanty actually accomplish as they negotiate between different forms of healing power? Are they primarily making short-term moves towards personal moral worth and social advancement (the insider's perspective)? Are they also enunciating – in more or less oblique ways – the connections between personal affliction, contradictions in the local social world, and the global forces which are fragmenting rural Haitian society? We must somehow include both perspectives in anthropological texts, not seize on one or the other alternative. On the one hand, we should resist the temptation of fetishized closure in our depictions of local idioms of healing and morality. On the other hand, it is risky to emphasize only the social awareness that sufferers can develop, or the forces that currently block it. "Critical" medical anthropologists tend to see all experiences of body/self disorder as a potential register for social critique and resistance. This produces a heroic representation of people usually marginalized in global politics, but it also threatens to delegitimize people's literal (and often more circumscribed) accounts of body/self experience (see Abu-Lughod 1990).

Subjectivity, pluralism, and practical knowledge

One way to negotiate between the insider and outsider perspectives is to connect the analysis of medical pluralism in Jeanty to the unstable and hybrid identities circulating in Haiti, much of the Caribbean region, and the "Black Atlantic" world in general (cf. Gilroy 1993). This means overcoming the myth of Haitian exceptionalism and inserting the study of morality and religious identity in Jeanty into a broad comparative framework (cf. Trouillot 1990b). The goal is a picture of medical pluralism which neither fetishizes the insider's perspective nor lionizes the few organic intellectuals in the village who agree with us about the mediations between body/self disorder and global forces.

The fragmentation and reconstruction of identity is an emerging theme in both anthropology and critical social theory. It informs debates over the marginalization of difference in contemporary Euro-America (e.g. West 1993), as well as the ways people self-consciously contest and construct their social roles (feminist anthropologists in particular have led the way here; see Ginsburg and Tsing 1990). The Caribbean region has much to contribute to this intellectual project. Social and cultural heterogeneity has long been the master trope for the study of Caribbean societies, and it also figures in the forms of consciousness among Caribbean peoples themselves. Most of this literature explores the forms of legitimacy, political power, and ideological domination in poly-cultural Caribbean societies (e.g., Williams 1991; Austin 1984). However, the study of the subjective dimension of pluralism is more directly relevant to the confluence of moral, medical, and religious idioms in Jeanty.

Throughout Haiti (and the Caribbean region), people do not remain encapsulated within a single social or cultural enclave (see Drummond 1980). Therefore, a single Caribbean community carries the sedimented traces of the many ideologies and institutions which have competed for people's allegiance over long historical periods. Even residents of an ethnically homogeneous village like Jeanty routinely speak more than one language, participate in several structurally distinct economies, and mix practices from diverse religions.

How are these competing cultural ideas perceived, and how do they affect people's idiosyncratic feelings, especially their moves towards healing power and their strategies to ensure moral worth? For most of their history, Afro-Caribbean societies have operated with a bicultural system where elite and popular forms undercut each other. Articulated through a pervasive ideology of naturalized racial characteristics, this system shapes language use, religious participation, kinship and conjugal patterns, and even conceptions of illness and therapy (see Fisher 1985 [for Barbados]; Wilson 1973 [Providencia]; Philippe 1985 [Haiti]). However, these two cultural registers are not equally legitimate. The elite system originated in metropolitan centers of power, and it became consolidated on the islands during the long period of colonial rule. The bicultural system thus gives the highest value to that which is affectively the most foreign, while it explicitly devalues people's closest identifications (see Fanon 1967). But although the elite and subordinate codes undercut each other, people jointly employ them in the presentation of self and the interpretation of personal experience, and this is the source of unstable, fragmented, and hybridized identities.

Seemingly up-to-date with the latest Euro-American postmodern theory, residents of Caribbean communities thus constitute and experience the self as a site of contradictions (Ginsburg and Tsing 1990:9). In Jeanty, these contradictions emerge in the arena of competing religious affiliations, and the search for healing power is the arena for people to negotiate between them. However, residents of Jeanty do not experience these contradictions through a simple bicultural system. They negotiate among three overlapping religious discourses, each indexing a different historically formed social identity: the Catholicism of the French colonial and Haitian neocolonial elite, reinvented West African religious forms rooted to kin and land, and the fundamentalist ideologies of North American Protestant missionaries. Moreover, people experience the contradictions between these religious forms not as a general psychological strain, but as specific challenges to their moral worth.

Medical pluralism in Jeanty exposes the subjective dimensions of the Haitian variant of Caribbean cultural pluralism. The tropes of identity and morality used in everyday life, and especially in people's negotiation of their religious affiliation,[1] pervade local understandings of illness, healing power, and the body. Body/self disorders give rise to pressing moral questions which residents of Jeanty try to answer through competing religious discourses. The situation in Jeanty thus confirms one of the central anthropological insights about the body, first stated by Marcel Mauss (1979): physical disorders are inevitably related to emotional and moral worlds, therefore notions about disease and healing emerge out of an organizing realm of moral concerns (see also Douglas 1966, 1973; Kirmayer 1992; Taussig 1992). These moral discourses are fundamentally and explicitly used to organize diagnoses, consultations with healers, narratives of illness, and healing rituals.

At the same time, however, such discourses index supralocal powers and ideologies (typical for the Caribbean), and these associations also enter people's awareness and health-seeking strategies. In their moral contests for healing power, residents of Jeanty develop both local and global perspectives on affliction: precisely the perspectives that are separated as insider vs. outsider knowledge in much of medical anthropology. People's moral response to sickness is thus the best vantage point for us to analyze the mediation between body/self disorder and global forces.

To state this another way: the search for healing power between Catholicism, worship of the *lwa*, and fundamentalist Protantism operates on several registers at once. It is the local face of macrosocial powers which have created and are now fragmenting rural Haitian society. It is the idiom for profound changes in personal identity and one's position in competing moral worlds. Finally, the search for healing engages people's bodies and emotions: their palpable experience and their feelings of innocence and guilt. Taken as a whole, therefore, the contest for healing power mediates between body and society, private suffering and public cultural codes, the local village and metropolitan centers, and the present social arrangements in rural Haiti and the contradictory historical trends which are transforming them.

Are people in Jeanty aware of these multiple mediations? Yes, and their practical awareness, emerging in local struggles over moral authority and healing power, entails a more critical knowledge of the dominant and alternative sources of social value. People must constantly choose which gods to worship, and which forms of healing power and moral legitimation to accept, and they know the practical consequences of embracing one over another. People know that disdaining the *lwa* allies them with the centralized Catholic church: a traditional source of legitimation and advance. They know that fundamentalist conversion leads away from local allegiances and would propel them into a transnational space, politically centered in North America. The very structure of Haitian religious pluralism therefore animates people's knowledge –

both practical and historically engaged – about the links between body/self experience, the local social world, and supralocal powers.

This book argues against the conventional opposition between the enclaved or "mystified" understanding of most local residents and the synthetic vision held only by a few indigenous organic intellectuals and critical outsiders. When faced by an unexplained or suspicious sickness, most people in Jeanty enter a complicated search for healing power, and they become aware of the mediations between their bodily experience and the national and global forces which are fragmenting rural Haitian society. They become aware, often via an unwelcome accusation, of the shifting and competing moral discourses in Haiti, and hence are forced to choose among the traditional legitimating ideology of village Catholicism, the subordinated and disdained realm of the *lwa*, and Protestant conversion, which criticizes both religions and opens up new routes of transnational advance. By entering these discourses, as they must, people reproduce them. By remapping their position within them, people resist the various types of ideological domination and exclusion which have long characterized rural Haitian society (cf. Giroux 1992:209).

In conclusion, this ethnography offers a novel definition of healing power and a general processual method to study medical pluralism. One time-honored method involves ferreting out stable medical discourses and recurrent patterns of health-seeking, and then using them to interpret particular healing encounters. However, discourses exist only as they are spoken or enacted in ongoing practice (Giddens 1984). Isolating them as background structures, as opposed to the foregrounded action of health-seeking, imposes a false stability on the ever-evolving flow of healing encounters. In Haiti, moreover, particular healing encounters do not necessarily speak with one voice, because religious practices in Haiti are irreducibly plural. Consulting an *houngan* or converting to Pentecostalism shows the voice of competing cultural claims. Therefore, people's moves towards healing power do not necessarily exemplify a stable symbolic or social order: they "may equally be evidence of the on-going dismantling of structure or attempts to create new ones" (Moore 1987). Health-seeking within a plural medical system refers both to how people choose among an objective array of therapies, as well as to how they reproduce and transform this array. Health-seeking can both ratify and subvert a society's forms of common sense, especially concerning the body, morality, and religious identity.

Healing power denotes moral authority, clinical effectiveness, and a source of group identity and social memory. In choosing between competing forms of healing power, people in rural Haiti accomplish several things at once. They insert immediate and inchoate forms of body/self experience into local discourses and therapeutic practices. They authorize themselves as upright, ethical persons who have made the right choice among competing moral worlds. They defend themselves against others' accusations of guilt and immorality. They align themselves with traditional or novel sources of legitimacy, and choose among local and supralocal routes of social advance. Finally, they engage with some of the historically ancient contradictions in Haitian society, as well as the emerging ones which are currently fragmenting rural life.

This book has developed a processual and practice-based approach to medical pluralism. It interprets the stable array of therapeutic options as the objectified product of countless struggles over healing power. These struggles take place on several registers simultaneously: clinical, moral, religious, and political. By focussing on religious healing, the book has tried to counter the impression of an objective structure of either medical or religious pluralism. The dominant moral and religious discourses in this society can change, as people oppose each other about the true or appropriate use of religious healing (cf. Bourdieu 1988:158). Therefore, a comprehensive account of healing power cannot escape the tensions and contradictions in the way this power circulates in society. At best, such an account can shed light on the discourses and therapies which carry healing power, the ways people approach it, and its dialectic effect on body/self experience and the social order.

Notes

1 INTRODUCTION

1 Some of the landmark studies of therapeutic pluralism in Asian societies include Kleinman 1980; Kleinman *et al.* 1978; Leslie 1976; Amarasingham 1980; Lock 1980; Kakar 1982; Nichter 1980; Unschuld 1985; Zimmerman 1978. For reports from African settings, see Janzen 1978a and 1987; Janzen and Feierman 1979; Feierman and Janzen 1992; Young 1976; Comaroff 1980; Mullings 1984; from the Middle East, see Crapanzano 1973; Good 1976; Early 1988; and from the Latin American and Caribbean region, see Laguerre 1987; Foster 1978; Fabrega and Silver 1973; Cosminsky and Scrimshaw 1980; Staiano 1986, Sobo 1993; Littlewood 1993.

2 Most previous ethnographers of the remarkably diverse healing traditions in rural Haiti begin with precisely these assumptions (e.g., Coreil 1979, 1983, 1988; Clerismé 1979). They conceive of the individual patient or family member as an autonomous actor who chooses from the range of therapeutic options according to a certain rationale. Most often, this rationale is some kind of "adaptive strategy" to maximize health or survival in the face of biological or economic constraints, and it finds its philosophical roots in the utilitarian model of human behavior (Coreil 1979). When applied to the organization of healing practices, this approach yields a functionalist model of "health care sectors" which ranks particular healers according to their degree of specialization, their affiliation with other institutions, or the empirical efficacy of their healing techniques (e.g., Coreil 1983).

3 Even the term "Vodoun" has taken on a life of its own in the representations of Haitian culture. Despite its African origin (from the Dahomean Fon language), the word is rarely heard in village Haiti (cf. Smucker 1984). In this book, Vodoun will refer not only to the ways individuals serve the spirits (e.g., through becoming possessed themselves, making offerings at a cult shrine, or honoring their family ancestors) but also to the ideology and social context of such practices.

4 A sampling of recent studies would include Brown 1976, 1991; De Heusch 1989; Desmangles 1992; Hurbon 1987a and b, 1993; Larose 1977; Lowenthal 1978; and Dayan 1995 among many others. See the bibliographies by Laguerre (1979, 1982).

2 METROPOLITAN MEDICINE AND STRATEGIES OF RULE

1 My phrase "metropolitan medicine" partially overlaps with Dunn's definition of cosmopolitan medicine as "worldwide rather than limited or provincial in scope or bearing" (1976). He prefers the terms "cosmopolitan," "scientific," or "Western" medicine, since scientific elements are present in many local or regional systems. I introduce the term "metropolitan medicine" here not only to avoid a false picture of other forms of healing as unscientific, but also to emphasize the links between this form of medicine and either direct foreign control or domination by national elites whose rule depends on foreign power and prestige.

2 The medical corps in eighteenth-century France included four groups: physicians, surgeons, apothecaries, and other "empirics," such as midwives, oculists, and bonesetters. Physicians were members of a liberal profession, conversant with medical theory, who claimed to practice primarily "internal" medicine, while denigrating the lower-status surgeons who practiced the mechanical "external" operations of bleeding, purging, lancing, etc. (Ramsey 1988:19). In fact, surgeons often practiced the same Galenic medicine as physicians, and both groups were internally ranked by education and expertise (1988:20ff)

3 Before the Haitian wars of independence, no other European nation seriously challenged French control of this area. Moreover, the military did not play a significant role in the discipline of slaves, which took place mostly on self-contained plantations.

4 There were no sugar plantations in the colony in 1690; 100 were established between 1700 and 1704, and there were nearly 800 by the 1780s (Fick 1990:22). The pan-Caribbean trend towards larger sugar estates was especially marked on St. Domingue; by the 1740s, the average estate was over 200 acres and employed nearly 100 slaves (Klein 1986:53). In the late seventeenth century, the colonial population stood at approximately 8,000: 55% free white, 42% African slave, and 3% affranchi (freed people of color). By 1789, the population had increased to over half a million: 8% white, 5% affranchi, and 87% enslaved (Leyburn 1966 [1941]:18).

5 The hôpitaux at Cap François and Léogane did intern two groups of whites not affiliated with the military: sailors from commercial ships (whose stay in the colony was brief) and indigent new arrivals from France. These new arrivals did, in fact, pose a potential threat of disorder, since they seemed unlikely to join any of the established sectors of white society (Girod 1972:91).

6 The financial accounts from Boucassin reveal a substantial investment in the hôpital. It cost 2000 livres to build, compared to 6000 livres for the planter's house, the most substantial building on the estate (Debien 1945:28).

7 In several cases, colonists of means attempted to open hôpitaux généraux for members of this poor white class. Depending entirely on the generosity of their founder and his heirs, these institutions rarely operated for very long and probably did not serve a large population (see accounts in Moreau de St.-Méry 1958:1317ff and 1334).

8 Records from the *habitation* Bellevue list the following contemporary pharmaceuticals in the slave *hôpital*: mercury and "antisyphilitic syrup" (for venereal disease), quinquna, nitrate salt, cream of tartar, wine balm, Castillon anti-scurvy powder, Pacquet pills, Sidenham drops, spermaceti, Egyptian unguent, theriacal, and aloe (Cauna 1988:219). Joubert introduced smallpox inoculation to St. Domingue in 1768, although it was widely used during epidemics only after 1780 (Cauna 1988:217, n. 27).

9 The medical attention paid to slaves differed between plantations. The contact slaves had with European medicine depended on the size of the plantation, its owner's wealth, and the owner's response to shifting political conditions in the colony and France. For example, Fleuriau's preoccupation with his slaves' health may have served another motive: to counter abolitionist sentiment in Paris with evidence of the benevolent paternalism of slavery (Cauna 1988:221).

10 I have found no evidence that these terms were used in describing French colonists' illnesses.

11 The original French notation in Arnaudeau's telegraphic style runs as follows:

Nota: Indépendamment de ces quatres enfants, il en est né cinq dont trois garçons et deux filles qui ont péri par le mal dit mâchoire, ce mal moins réel que né de la malice et du libertinage des mères m'a toujours singulièrement affecté. Il n'est pas d'efforts que je n'ai fais pour l'empêcher, vous le verrez par la copie que je vous envoie du règlement que j'ai fait à ce suject en 1781 et ma façon de penser sur la cause de ce mal est consignée dans la lettre que j'eus l'honneur de vous écrire le 22 février de la même année. Il n'y a qu'une roideur inébranlable qui soit capable de le réprimer; quelques châtiments que j'aie faits, je n'ai pas eu assez de fermeté pour les pousser à l'extrême.

12 Foucault's claim that "in the 'excesses' of torture, a whole economy of power is invested" is thus as relevant to St. Domingue sugar plantations as to Colombian rubber plantations one hundred years later (Taussig 1987:27).

13 Malenfant adapted the French orthography of his day in order to record the slaves' spoken Creole response: "Procureur là li mentor trop, lorsque li voir négresse grosse li juré tant comme diable, quand petit veni au monde, tout de suite li vlé que maman allé dans travail, li jamais vlé baillé ren à nourrice. Quand maman là cité Gouraud, il dit que procureur là li gâte nègres." Cauna translates this into modern French as follows: "Ce procureur est trop menteur: lorsqu'il voit une négresse grosse, il jure comme un diable, quand le petit vient au monde, tout de suite il veut que la mère aille travailler, il ne veut jamais rien donner à la nourrice. Quand la mère cite les enfants de l'habitation Gouraud, il dit que ce procureur-là gâte les nègres."

14 In the Creole recorded by Malenfant, "ca pas coquin blan ci la la?" In current Creole orthography, "se pa koken, blan sila la?"

15 Malenfant's Gallicized Creole reads as follows: "Nous té connai que métier procureur là fait le maître nous. Li gagné habitation dans morne; c'est nègres Fleuriau planté café, qui fait tout travail là. Li gagné 15 à 20 nègres à li. Toutes les semaines li envoyé en habitation li 30 à 40 nègres Fleuriau: ça pas coquin blac ci la là? Nous connais, nous doit pas travail sur habitation procureur nous." Cauna again provides a French translation: "Nous ne

savions pas que le métier de procureur faisait de lui notre maître. Il a une habitation dans les mornes; ce sont les nègres de Fleuriau qui plantent le café, qui font tout le travail. Il a 15 à 20 nègres à lui. Toutes les semaines il envoie sur son habitation 30 à 40 nègres de Fleuriau. Est-ce que ce n'est pas un coquin que ce blanc-là? Nous savons bien que nous ne devons pas travailler sur l'habitation de notre procureur."

16 Around the time of Arnaudeau's letters mentioning *mal de mâchoire*, several colonial neighbors were monitoring the plantation for Fleuriau, and their reports often blamed disappointing sugar yields on Arnaudeau's ignorance and inept administration (Cauna 1987:76–77). The manager may have wanted to portray himself as a loyal and effective worker, whose best efforts were frustrated by resistant slaves, in order to counter these critics. Perhaps he knew that the incompetence and unduly harsh discipline of managers was a common theme in this correspondence (see Debien 1973: 130).

17 The two most famous chroniclers of the French West Indies, R. du Tertre and Père Labat, reviled the ignorance of colonial doctors and surgeons and their impotence in the face of tropical disease (Bougerol 1985:126). Based on documents from Jamaica, Bush adds that the slave's remembered treatments from Africa were probably more effective for tropical diseases of the West Indies than contemporary British therapies. Moreover, she suggests that the slaves' herbal-based, African-derived medical system had fewer iatrogenic effects than the heroic medicine of contemporary Europe, which relied heavily on bleeding, purging, and the use of mercury- and arsenic-based preparations (Bush 1990:154–55).

18 The beginnings of this medical system may have resembled the hypothetical "original moment" of Afro-Caribbean religion outlined by Mintz and Price (1992:45–46). Suppose a recently arrived slave on a new plantation gives birth to twins, an event that required special ritual assistance in most central or West African societies. If the mother had no ritual expertise herself, she would seek out someone familiar with the twin cult of a different African ethnic group. "Once such people had 'exchanged' ritual assistance in this fashion," the authors conclude, "there would already exist a micro-community with a nascent religion [and a nascent medical system] that was, in a real sense, its own."

19 The many Amerindian terms in the pharmacopeia of current-day domestic medicine in Haiti strongly suggests an early flow of medical knowledge from Indians to slaves (see Weniger 1985; Weniger et al. 1986).

20 Other scenarios about slaves' motives for poisoning whites included vengeance against a master who had separated a couple, ambitious mothers who assassinate the mistress of a plantation in order to put their daughters at the head of the household, and slaves working in the military *hôpital* who poison soldiers interned there (Bougerol 1985).

21 Medical discourse usually kept these two images separate; for example, Galbaud du Fort's dry litany of slave deaths contains none of the paranoid fears of revenge expressed by would-be victims of poison. It sometimes conflated them in one person, as in the scenarios of slaves poisoning themselves, which depict the same individual as both the master's property and rebelliously destroying that property.

22 J. B. Dehoux, a prominent Port-au-Prince physician, mentions several therapies still in use in the 1870s which recalled practices of seventeenth- and eighteenth-century French medicine (Dehoux 1891). Writing in 1860, Hunt describes a similar persistence of eighteenth-century humoral beliefs among the more educated classes (Hunt 1860, cited in Leyburn 1966 [1941]). According to these contemporary reports, certain French medical practices that were introduced to colonial St. Domingue in the eighteenth century continued to flourish among the peasantry several generations later. S. Allman makes a similar argument based on ethnographic research conducted in the 1970s and 1980s. She shows that several health care practices followed by Haitian mothers with their newborn children are remarkably similar to eighteenth-century therapies and models of disease (Allman 1983, 1985, and 1986). Bougerol also examines the structural similarities in representations of the body and medical discourse between eighteenth-century France and contemporary Guadeloupe (1983).

23 Formal medical instruction began in Haiti under Pétion, who established two *écoles de santé* connected to the *hôpitaux* at Port-au-Prince and Les Cayes in 1808, but they offered a low level of instruction and basically ceased operation after twenty years (Bordes 1979; see also Parsons 1930:66). In 1838, the school in Port-au-Prince was reorganized as the National School of Medicine, and President Geffrard improved it further during his reformist reign from 1859 to 1867. The Paris-trained Dr. Dehoux was notable for introducing contemporary French medical practices to the school during his deanship from 1870 to 1879 (Parsons 1930:66ff).

24 The invasion of Haiti in July 1915 was only one of a longer series of conquests and acquisitions which advanced American domination of the Caribbean. Although expansionist policy-makers and adventurists in the United States had long urged annexation of Caribbean territories, the strategic and military importance of Haiti sharply increased in the early 1900s for several reasons: to ensure safe shipping routes to the Panama Canal (opened in 1914), to protect recent American capital investments, and to limit Haiti's growing dependence upon foreign (i.e, German and French) financiers. (For the Haitian and American background to the occupation, see Schmidt 1971; Plummer 1988; Trouillot 1990.)

25 Smedley Butler, a Marine major and head of the *Gendarmerie d'Haiti*, testified to a Senate subcommittee that "we were imbued with the fact that we were trustees of a huge estate that belonged to minors. That was my viewpoint" (in Plummer 1992:95).

26 For example, American medical officers oversaw several mass inoculation programs for yaws and smallpox in the 1920s. One even operated a traveling clinic to provide vaccines against yaws (Parsons 1930). Only in the 1970s did the government again attempt large-scale immunization campaigns. The *Service d'Hygiène* also had ambitious plans for a network of rural clinics (Parsons 1930). Actual construction probably fell far short of this goal, and similar plans did not appear again until the 1970s (cf. Segal 1984:324). The network of rural clinics fell into disuse and disrepair (see, e.g., Bordes and Couture 1978:52).

3 BIOMEDICINE IN JEANTY

1 Although it is most closely associated with the Agency for International Development, the RHDS project also depended on the financial support and technical expertise from multilateral organizations such as PAHO, the Inter-American Development Bank (IADB), the United Nations Fund for Population Activities (UNFPA) as well as several other private organizations.

2 The specialized clinics are always crowded, with barely enough benches in the waiting room for the women and their children. Two of the general walk-in clinics are held on the market days in Jeanty, which bring into town many residents from the entire surrounding region. Under the RHDS plan, rural dispensaries treat whoever walks in, and part of the dispersed population that converges on Jeanty during its market days also crowds into the dispensary for general consultations.

3 This analysis of daily life in the dispensary does not implicitly contrast it to the egalitarian, contractual norm of patient/provider relations now popular in Euro-American medicine. The goal is not to criticize the deferential relations between patients and staff on the basis of this (relatively recent) norm. It is rather to show how this deference is a local phenomenon which reproduces (in the details of individual behavior) some of the ways that national institutions structure village life.

4 In a systematic sample of charts for adult patient contacts at the Jeanty dispensary clinic over three years (N = 294 charts), virtually every entry noted at least one drug prescribed by the nurse or physician.

5 These are two of the many brands of widely marketed inexpensive pain-killers (other popular brands are Saridon and the cleverly named Dolostop). These small white pills are usually composed of a mixture of caffeine and aspirin.

6 During one interview, he produced the following eleven drugs from his valise: tetracycline, ampicillin, aspirin, Dolostop, Saridon, Valadon, Cafenol, Magnopirol (a tablet of permanganate), Pommade St. Yves (a lineament), Multivaforte (a Haitian brand of multivitamin), Appetivit (another vitamin supplement, widely advertised as an appetite stimulant), and Vicks cough drops.

7 Most of the medications stored in the "community pharmacy" room of the dispensary carry labels from one of four sources: the AGAPCO pharmacy, Pharmacie DuCoin and Pharmacie Thomas (two large pharmacies in Port-au-Prince) and 4C: Canadian Caribbean Chemical Company. Michelle, the pharmacy director, has long since abandoned the original RHDS plan of purchasing stock exclusively at the AGAPCO warehouse in Les Cayes. She presumably finds better prices by buying the same medications from other wholesale sources.

8 Medicines in the community thus include items obtainable elsewhere (aspirin, Valenol, tetracycline, ampicillin, etc.) as well as vitamin C tablets, vitamin A and B solutions, ear drops, special aspirin for children, cold medicines, cough syrup, and sedatives.

4 MEDICALIZATION AND ILLNESS EXPERIENCE: TWO CASE-STUDIES

1 The translation of anatomical terms from Haitian Creole presents several difficulties. The original expression – *M te santi anba vant-mwen ap fe mal, bò senti-m* – features two words with obvious French roots: *vant*, from "ventre" (= stomach, abdomen, womb) and *senti*, from "ceinture" (= waist, middle). I have translated *vant* as stomach, although Janine may not mean exactly the same organ denoted by that English (or French) word. I translate *senti* as lower back, since villagers invariably point to their lower back when using the term *doulè senti* (*senti* pain).

2 I leave this term untranslated for two reasons. The meaning of the English word "indisposed" is too weak for the loss of consciousness and mental confusion which the Creole term implies. Moreover, most published references to this disorder also preserve the untranslated *indisposition* (Philippe and Romain 1979; Charles 1979; Weidman 1979).

3 There are only three vehicles reliably found in Jeanty: the ancient Landrover owned by the Catholic priest and two large trucks, converted for passenger transport, used for regularly scheduled trips to Les Cayes and Port-au-Prince. On market days, several more trucks arrive with market-women and their wares and then leave by the mid-afternoon.

4 Bastien described a similar situation in the Marbial valley (also in the south, near the city of Jacmel): "The placement of the houses is not fixed . . . a number of people have constructed their houses in such a way that they are able, during their moments of leisure, to keep an eye on the movement of people from their veranda, to observe their business and their gestures . . . in a similar group of buildings, you can see at times the façades, at times the backs of houses, oriented in the direction of the dominant winds" (1985:48; my translation).

5 In Jeanty, the *lakou* pattern is found most often in the small hamlets located throughout the hills and in the neighboring Cayes plain. In the village center, near the marketplace and Catholic church, kin may occupy adjacent dwellings, but in only a few instances do the homes of a single family group form an identifiable compound. The few times this does occur, the family is invariably relatively wealthy. Even in these cases, I rarely heard people use the word *lakou* (the term itself is probably derived from the French "la cour"). The most common expression used is *kay*. For example, the cluster of buildings within Gilbert Pierre-Louis' compound is known as *kay Gilbert*. However, the kin makeup of these *kay* strongly resembles that of the traditional *lakou*.

6 Further details of family organization in rural Haiti appear in Bastien 1961; Comhaire-Sylvain 1961; Murray 1977; Smith 1963.

7 However, reckoning kinship through the male line is the most persuasive, since the *lakou* as a residential unit is usually composed of consanguineous male relatives (women ideally leave to live in the *lakou* of their husbands, cf. Comhaire-Sylvain 1961). Indeed, this is the strategy Janine adopted for each of the intermediate relatives except her mother (who, in any case, remained closely involved with the Dutoit family after the death of Janine's father and lived between two direct descendants of the original seven brothers).

8 The present wave of Haitian migration to the United States began in the early years of François Duvalier's rule, when political opponents and members of the newly disempowered mulatto elite escaped the country (Laguerre 1984; Diederich and Burt 1969). However, since the beginning of Jean-Claude's rule in 1971, conditions in the countryside have worsened considerably: a combination of governmental corruption, drought, and global economic dislocations caused severe food shortages and other forms of deprivation. Massive outmigration from the countryside is the continuing result (cf. Buchanan 1980; Locher 1984; Stepick 1984).

9 Villagers increasingly point to remittances from North America as the source for the wealth of such families as the Dutoits. The common Creole expression is *yo plenn moun lòt bò*: they've got plenty of relatives abroad.

10 Mme. Beaumont may well have learned the term during her three-month period of training at the state hospital (l'Hôpital d'Immaculée Conception) in Les Cayes. This seminar was designed to incorporate traditional birth attendants into the system of rural dispensaries, and was funded and administered as part of the Rural Health Delivery System project (see chapter 2). A standard American medical textbook defines eclampsia as

> a severe degree of toxemia that occurs in one out of several hundred pregnancies . . . toxemia of pregnancy is characterized by inflammation and spasm of the arterioles in many parts of the body . . . Eclampsia is characterized by extreme vascular spasticity throughout the body, clonic convulsions followed by coma, greatly decreased kidney output, malfunction of the liver, hypertension, and a generalized toxic condition of the body. Usually, it occurs shortly before, or sometimes within a day or so, after parturition. Even with the best treatment, including delivery of the baby, some 5 per cent of eclamptic mothers still die. (Guyton 1977:876)

11 The translation of *malkadi* as epilepsy is also made in the Creole–French dictionary compiled by linguists and educators from l'Université René Descartes and l'Institut Pédagogique National Haïtien (Nougayrol *et al.* 1976).

12 Anthropologists who have documented such blood syndromes in Haiti include Murray 1976; Philippe and Romain 1979; Charles 1979; Weidman 1979; Laguerre 1987; Singer *et al.* 1988; Farmer 1988. The importance of blood in popular medical systems of other New World African communities is examined by Bougerol (1983) in Guadeloupe, by Dressler (1982) in St. Lucia, Snow (1980, 1993) for North American blacks, Sobo (1993) in Jamaica, and Littlewood (1993) in Trinidad.

13 A partial list includes *fibròm* in Haiti (Singer *et al.* 1988), *infección* in Guatemala (Cosminsky and Scrimshaw 1980), neurasthenia/*shenjing shuairuo* in China (Kleinman 1986) and even hypertension and hypoglycemia in North America (Blumhagen 1980; Hunt *et al.* 1990). As this list suggests, these transformations in meaning have been studied in diverse settings: peasant communities within Latin America; civilizational societies with several sophisticated, but non-biomedical, categories of health professionals; and "non-expert" communities in North America.

14 Not all perturbations of the blood are linked to emotional upset; they also have several dietary and physiological causes. Blood that is "too poor" may result from pregnancy, and this scenario may have influenced people's

insertion of Janine's *eklampsi* into the domain of blood-related disorders. Eating pineapple can prevent the onset of menses in adolescent girls (Wiese 1976). However, emotional and other etiologies of blood disorders may overlap, as in the practice of adding salt to beverages (such as coffee) in order to "purify" blood that has been excited by strong emotions (Hess 1983:93).

15 The Creole terms for these overwhelming emotions are linguistically marked to differentiate them from similar emotional states which are less potent and cannot endanger one's health. Comparing the sentences *Li vin fache* and *li t ap fe youn kòlè* captures this distinction. The first one can be translated as "he became angry." In the second, anger is nominalized, and is best translated as "he was having a fit of anger"; this is the sort of anger that starts the blood climbing. Similarly, *li sezi* differs from *l'ap fe youn sezisman*. The first indicates surprise and sometimes dismay, as when she is "shocked" at someone's unusual or inappropriate behavior. The second is more grave: she is "in a state of shock" which can lead, again through the medium of blood, to convulsions and even death.

16 This particular expression refers to the upward flow of blood towards the head as well as the itchy rash which "rises up" on the surface of the skin. Such a rash is one of the most commonly cited symptoms of bad blood (*move san*) (see Farmer 1988).

17 Indeed, in the standard explanation, a state of shock (*youn sezisman*) due to witnessing someone's death can cause a wide range of medical problems: diarrhoea, fever, paralysis, or muteness. Furthermore, such a shock heats the blood and makes one's body extremely vulnerable to contact with "cold" environmental agents. For example, dipping your foot in cool water or eating such categorically "cold" foods as bananas or pineapples after witnessing a great tragedy can result in instantaneous death.

18 These terms (*kriz*, *kriz de ner*, and *indisposition*) have a number of usages which anthropologists have analyzed. City dwellers in Port-au-Prince claim that a *kriz* connotes extreme bodily agitation, in contrast to the general collapse and loss of consciousness characteristic of *indisposition* (Phillipe and Romain 1979). Other investigators report that a *kriz de ner* can occur along with the fainting spells of *indisposition*, and afflicts chiefly middle-class adolescent girls (Charles 1979:136).

19 Domestic violence afflicted several households in Jeanty, although I do not know its exact prevalence. Children typically receive corporal punishment from either parent, and I knew of at least three cases of wife-beating, which people often blamed on the husband's alcoholism.

20 The Catholic school in Jeanty enrolls a number of students who belong to Protestant sects, and this is one of many arenas of daily life where Protestant affiliation makes little practical difference. Indeed, one's religious identity as a Protestant, and the separation it implies from the majority of Catholic villagers, becomes important only in specific contexts (see chapter 5).

21 Several expatriate development workers I interviewed also regard Bonne Fin as the most sophisticated in-patient hospital in the south.

22 Coreil (1979) also reports the common expectation that families spend up to the limit of their resources for treatments of a sick relative, even when the illness's prognosis is poor.

23 This lay biomedical practitioner fits the profile of the injectionists described by Clerismé (1979) and Coreil (1979) for other communities on the southern peninsula.

24 This prayer meeting took place at the time of the army-controlled elections of January 17, 1988, in which Leslie Manigat was elected as president. Recalling the horrific violence of the aborted presidential elections of November 29, 1987 (when at least thirty-four voters were massacred in streets and at polling stations by army troops and Tontons Macoutes), many residents of Port-au-Prince fled the city to stay with their families in rural areas. In the late 1980s the countryside was usually not the focus of the army's crackdown on political opposition movements for democratic reforms.

25 This second phrase is my rendering of *mezanmi* into idiomatic English. The Creole word means literally "my friends," but it is most often used to connote surprise, shock, or disbelief.

26 For example, the bodily practices applied to Arnaud are virtually identical to those used to control Jerline Liron when she was possessed by the spirit of a dead child (chapter 6). The mourners' seeming loss of personal volition, bodily control, and self-awareness parallels the behavior of women possessed by the Holy Spirit in the course of a Pentecostalist healing service (chapter 5).

27 François here used the Creole expression *blese*, which refers to external injuries or wounds. He ascribed Dieusauveur's pain and lower body paralysis to a blockage in his lower back (*santi li bloke*).

28 This Creole term is related to the French word *expedition*, and it draws on its meanings of a "dispatch" or a "thing sent."

29 Wiese (1971) describes the factors of "heat" and "cold" which are implicated in the construction of numerous disorders in rural Haiti. She claims that the equilibrium between hot and cold constitutes the essential framework of understanding for all sicknesses without supernatural causation (1971:87).

30 The etymology of this Creole word is from the French *simples*, or medicinal plants. In Jeanty, *senps* are used to protect the body against further depredations after death from a *maladi mò*. Examples of such *senps* include placing thread with an eyeless needle in the coffin, so when people come to claim the body, they will become preoccupied with the fruitless task of threading the needle and eventually leave without taking the victim. However, other *senps* can cure a *maladi Satan* before someone's death, and these are usually made from certain leaves or the page of a bible or other "magical book."

5 THE CATHOLIC PRACTICE OF HEALING

1 In the Creole phrase he uses – *se youn vye nanm, youn vye nanm rebèl* – the word "old" (*vye*) has a strong pejorative connotation. People often use this word when discussing the *lwa* or the activities of *houngan*, and they invariably say it with the same air of disgust: e.g., "I'm Catholic, and I don't believe in it. I don't want anything to do with those dirty old things" (*Se katolik mwen ye, m pa kwe ladan. M pa okipe m ak vye bagay sal sa yo*); "When he sings those

spirit songs, it's a bunch of old words he's saying" (*lè l chante chante lwa sa yo, se youn pakèt vye pawòl l ap di*).

2 Ogoun is the name of one of the most common and most powerful *lwa*, cf. Barnes 1989.

3 In this context, "Satan" symbolizes much more than the evil spiritual actor from French Catholicism. In a process typical of Latin American societies, residents of Jeanty have appropriated Catholic icons and concepts, and then inserted them in a recombined and synthetic religious framework, without ceasing to consider themselves as Catholic (cf. Taussig 1980; Warren 1978:38, 47; Watanabe 1990).

4 To describe the spirit as "entering" Mme. Beaumont is the most common English rendering of several Creole expressions: the spirit mounts her horse (*lwa-a monte chwal li*), the spirit dances in her head (*lwa-a konn danse nan tèt li*), the spirit takes her (*lwa a pran ni*), or, most simply, she has spirits (*li gen lwa*).

5 *Mambo* refers to the female equivalent of an *houngan*. The terms I heard most often in Jeanty for these religious specialists were *houngan* (or a close variant, *ganga*), *mambo*, and the French-derived labels *divinò* (male) and *divinèz* (female). I encountered the designation *bokò* much less frequently, although it is commonly cited in the literature on Vodoun (cf. Courlander 1960; Hurbon 1987; Laguerre 1979; Maximilien 1945; Simpson 1970).

6 While God (*Bondye*), understood largely in Christian terms, rules the entire universe and endows humans with the *bon nanm* which makes possible moral action, the *lwa* are concerned only with humankind and their ordinary afflictions and desires. Villagers have a relatively distant relationship with the exalted Christian god. Communication with this god is mediated by the Catholic priest and the rituals of the Mass. Communication with the *lwa* is much more direct, since the *lwa* more closely resemble their human worshippers. Human beings can appeal directly to the spirits/ancestors and even influence their actions.

7 *Lwa-yo existe, men m pa rekonèt yo.* The verb *rekonèt* comes from the French "reconnaître," and retains the meaning of recognizing the relatedness of children and one's obligations towards them.

8 Dripping water on the ground constituted an offering to the spirit. Erzili is a *lwa* from Mme. Beaumont's family line, so she therefore has the status of a quasi-ancestor (although she is not identified as any particular forbear); offerings are thus made to the earth, where one's ancestors are buried. Many *houngan* included the same ritual before calling up their *lwa*. The distinctive cross-wise hand-shaking is also used by many of the *lwa* when they first enter their human servitor.

9 People such as Mme. Beaumont, who admit to some engagement with the realm of the *lwa*, commonly represent the spirits in a Catholic framework which lacks the damnatory quality of the conventional moral divide described above. The most well-known example is the analogy between spirits and saints established through visual icons and people's talk (see Begot 1983; Leiris 1953; Métraux 1972:325). People may also refer to the spirits as "mysteries" or even "angels," as in one of the expressions denoting possession: the angels mount him (*zanj-yo konn monte l*).

6 *HOUNGAN* AND THE LIMITS TO CATHOLIC MORALITY

1 Given the discipline's Romanticist legacy, many anthropologists would share this delight in seeking out the superficially irrational aspects of the ethnographic encounter: those aspects which challenge the Western-trained sense of what is proper and possible (see Crapanzano 1980). The danger of this feeling in the Haitian case is that the attraction to the exotica of *Vodoun* indexes many other racial and imperial constructions of Haiti in the popular American imagination. This dangerous delight which suffuses Euro-American writing about Haiti deserves more scholarly attention along the lines of Hurbon 1987b, 1993; Plummer 1992:121–38; and Woodson 1993.

2 One of the most common explanations for *maladi Satan* involves a pact which someone makes with an *houngan*, in which he provides a certain number of human souls in exchange for the *houngan*'s help in acquiring fantastic wealth. The individual who "buys points" (or "buys a condition") from the *houngan* is therefore responsible for the death of the people he has secretly "sold." These deaths, of course, are attributed to *maladi Satan*. The most popular examples focus on the wanton greed of the person who buys points, rather than his enmity for the ultimate victims. Such individuals can sell their own children and spouse, or sacrifice many innocent people. For example, people's talk about a tragic bus accident made references to the bus owner "buying a condition" to ensure the success of his business; the loss of his passengers' lives was a debt that he owed to the *houngan*.

3 After visits to two different *houngan*, Louis concluded that his troubles were caused by an ancestral spirit, angry that Louis had forgotten it. He eventually decided to prepare a small shrine in his home and leave offerings of cola, cookies, and other foodstuffs in propitiation to this *lwa*.

4 Many *houngan* had similar volumes with titles like *Le Petit Albert* or *Le Chat Noir*. As Sally Price has noted (personal communication), these are reprinted European *grimoires* (occult books with instructions about angels, demonology, exorcism, etc.) which contributed to the early formation of non-biomedical healing practices and beliefs in the French-colonized Caribbean islands.

5 This spirit name is probably not derived from a West African language, like those of more well-known *lwa* such as Erzili, Ogoun, or Damballah. It is rather a Creole compound name meaning "Good-and-evil," related to the French "Bien ou mal."

6 Although André was the only *houngan* I interviewed who employed automatic writing, other *houngan* used essentially the same technique of reading the cards, differing only in the details (such as while holding the cards in their hands instead of laying them down). "Reading the cards" is my idiomatic English translation of the Creole expressions for this divination practice: *bat kat*, to hit the cards, and *bay youn kou d kat*, to give a hit of the cards.

7 Brown describes the use of card-readings by *houngan* and *mambo* as a way to induce clients to tell their life stories and render themselves psychologically receptive to healing (1991:338). Among the consultations which I witnessed,

however, card-reading was not used to engage the subjectivity of the client, but rather to establish the healer's divinatory authority.

8 There is an important caveat here. The *lwa* do not always conclude that a given client suffers from *maladi Satan*. Several *houngan* reported that some people who arrive for a consultation are already too sick for them to treat. The *lwa* apparently can detect this; they therefore conclude, through divination, that the client has a *maladi doktè*, that is, one which requires a doctor's care. In these cases, *houngan* may refer their clients to biomedical settings.

9 These two motives often converge in the same stratagem of magically aided economic advancement. The prime route to a coveted job involves sending a sickness upon its current holder. He/she then becomes sick or dies, thus clearing a way for the *houngan*'s client to take the job. The case-studies presented in the next chapter exemplify this widespread formula for the etiology of *maladi Satan*.

10 They mention both those *fèy* found in the general pharmacopoeia of Catholic herbalists (and ordinary villagers) and certain species considered effective only for *maladi Satan*. Crosschecking information about herbal remedies from interviews with both *houngan* and *doktè fèy* revealed several plants which were judged appropriate only for cases of sent *maladi Satan*. Weniger (1985) reports the same finding for the Plateau Central.

11 The client present in the consultation room, however, is not necessarily the victim of the sent sickness. Often a relative of the sick individual will visit an *houngan*, and then report the results of the divination to patient and other family members. The sick individual will then receive treatment from the *houngan* during subsequent consultations.

12 Price (1966) describes a similar set of non-biomedical substances in Martinique which are sold in pharmacies but destined for ritual purposes such as the protection of fishermen and their canoes.

13 I personally witnessed *houngan* employing all of these modes of application. In general, the waters are rarely drunk: they are usually either inhaled or utilized for massages. The powders are either added to concoctions which people drink or applied directly to their skin.

14 The Creole verb *kase* has the literal meaning of "to break" (parallel to the French *casser*), and the figurative meanings of "to disband, to revoke, or to dismiss from office" (Nougayrol *et al.* 1976). *Kan* is a local variant of the more common *chan*, or field (from the French *champ*).

15 I never attended a consultation in which the client arranged to send a spirit of a dead person or a malevolent *limyè* or *poud*. Indeed, no one in the village ever admitted to attending one. I therefore do not have any information about how the *houngan* actually uses these substances to ensorcel the client's enemy, and whether this process involves a similar metonymic transfer of attributes. However, while excoriating those *houngan* with purchased spirits, people often referred to them "mixing up some things" or "putting their own satanic leaves" into concoctions somehow connected with sending sickness.

16 Until the reforms of the Second Vatican Council in the early 1960s, Catholic priests sang Mass in Latin and/or French: languages which 85–90% of Haitians cannot understand.

7 RELIGIOUS HEALING AND THE FRAGMENTATION OF RURAL LIFE

1 The settlements of Torbec, laid out along the handful of unpaved roads which crisscross the Cayes plain, are visibly impoverished relative to Jeanty, because the parish has no centralized market to draw traders and commercial activity to the region. Moreover, neither the Protestant pastors nor the Catholic priest vigorously pursue outside sources of aid. Therefore, unlike families living in the village center of Jeanty, almost all households in Torbec lack electricity and have no easy access to potable water.

2 Two other cases of *maladi Satan* in Jeanty required the same sort of physical restraints. For example, a few weeks earlier the teenage son of a local herbalist began to exhibit several odd behaviors: speaking in fragmentary, circuitous phrases, appearing constantly distracted, and wandering aimlessly in the hills. His father sequestered him indoors and placed his legs between two planks of wood, forming stocks from which escape was impossible. At the start of his illness, his hands were also tied together by a short rope. His father explained that he did this in order to keep his son from simply running away from home or unintentionally injuring himself during the course of his herbal treatments.

In another more celebrated case, the victim of a *maladi foli* has remained in stocks long after his illness began. Gilles Leger is a middle-aged man who became sick several years ago. Because he belongs to one of the wealthiest families in the village, most people know something about his condition. They say he was the victim of a sickness sent by a man angry at him for sleeping with his wife. In fact, this sent sickness was so powerful that it almost killed him. Although Gilles was strong enough eventually to escape with his life, he was rendered *fou*. During the early phase of his madness, he would violently threaten people and destroy property, including his own substantial home overlooking the *savann Liron*. Ever since, he sits under the wreckage of his house with his feet bound in two wooden stocks. Gilles' family pays a woman living nearby to bring a daily meal to him, and this constitutes his only regular human contact. Dirty and wild-looking, he sits in a small rattan chair where he can reach his Bible and a few other odd objects, talking or ranting to himself, and occasionally teased by passing children.

3 At the start of her illness, the core of Jerline's therapy managing group consisted of her mother, sister, stepfather, and fiancé. Jerline was never left alone at any time in the first few days. When the risk of violence or self-injury was the greatest, Jerline was constantly held by her sister and/or fiancé, occasionally assisted by other friends. Her convulsions initially gripped her quite frequently, separated by only twenty minutes of relative calm. This group of people would therefore hold and restrain Jerline for many hours at a time, without eating or sleeping.

4 My friends in Jeanty were also inclined to reject St. Denis' reading of Jerline's illness as a *kou d poud*. They said that the illness came on her like a *kriz*, and that it did not at all resemble the conditions (usually physical syndromes such as unremitting abdominal pain or inflammation) caused by a "powder hit" or a "light hit" (*kou d poud* or *kou d limyè*). Indeed, I never heard anyone else use

these expressions to describe this sort of dissociation and violent, uncontrolled behavior.

5 This visual motif is found in the *veve* (semi-abstract geometric designs symbolizing the *lwa*) for the spirits Ayizan (see Deren 1970 [1953]:147, 224) and Simbi-yandezo (Métraux 1972:106). Marie Liron, however, did not consider it a representation of particular *lwa* (see below).

6 Morin never identified the person responsible for sending the sickness upon Jerline. In general, people who consult an *houngan* in cases of *maladi Satan* maintain that this knowledge is not necessary for successful treatment. What advantage do you gain from knowing who sent the sickness, they ask, unless you are going to take revenge on him? To take revenge, i.e., to send a sickness in return, is not only immoral, but also prohibitively expensive, since an *houngan* charges even more to send a sickness than to repel one.

7 The Creole phrase she used was *m-ap regle ou, m-ap regle zafè ou*. The direct English translation, "I am going to take care of you, I'm going to take care of your business" does not capture the seriousness and anger of this phrase.

8 Most anthropologists of religion in rural Haiti have described the Catholic images, concepts, and ritual practices which appear in both services for the spirits and the world-view of the servitor. For example, Lowenthal notes that

> [e]ach *seremoni* opens with a fixed number of prayers from the Catholic litany, recited responsively from memory in French . . . These prayers are followed by the chanting of a number of *katik* (canticles), learned in church, again in French. The prayer and songs are not actually directed to the lwa, but stand as an opening invocation to the Holy Trinity and the saints to bless the proceedings and the participants. (1978:403)

A generation earlier, Leyburn made the same point:

> The Vodun service regularly begins with a long ritual which the observer who knows both the Creole language and the Catholic liturgy recognizes as being almost entirely Roman. While the Vodun houngan sits quietly by, a special officiant known as the *pret' savanne* (bush priest) reads or pretends to read from the Catholic prayer book. For the Pater Noster, the creed, the Ave Maria, the Salve Regina, and the prayers, the worshippers kneel or stand as they would in church. Candles burn, water is sprinkled, the sign of the cross is made, the chants are sung. (1941:168)

9 Ethnographic analyses of the links between formal Catholicism and popular Haitian religion can be found in Herskovits 1937:267–92; Métraux 1972:323–59; Conway (1978). Hurbon (1987a) offers the most sophisticated theological reading. Desmangles (1992) provides a valuable review of the evidence for syncretism, although he ultimately dismisses its effects on the neo-African core of popular Haitian religion (see Brodwin 1994).

10 This dominant concern with a person's conduct in the world and interior moral status explains a common reaction of Catholic villagers to the victim of a sent sickness. When the person is poor, church-going, and without a reputation for malicious or immoral behavior, others often express surprise at her condition: But she is innocent! She has never hurt anyone! Why would anyone want to do her in? (See also Farmer 1992.)

11 Although admonitions against immoral behavior pepper the sermons of many local pastors and the talk of Protestant villagers, these usually warn

against specific personal habits (e.g., drinking alcohol, going to dances, and women wearing too much make-up) rather than the types of unethical interpersonal conduct mentioned most often by Catholics.

12 Favret-Saada discovered the same thing in the discourse about illness and witchcraft which she entered in rural western France:

> In short, there is no neutral position with spoken words . . . there is no room for uninvolved observers . . . The same is true about asking questions. Before the ethnographer has uttered a single word, he is involved in the same power relationship as anyone else talking about it. Let him open his mouth, and his interlocutor immediately tries to identify his strategy, estimate his force, guess if he is a friend or foe . . . (1980:10–11)

13 In the context of the quasi-public ceremonies of popular Haitian religion, the *lwa* first possesses its devotee in a wild and uncontrolled manner. These are the *lwa bosal* (the "untamed" spirits) which overpower their horse with their unrestrained, unpredictable behavior (see Herskovits 1937:143ff). Before they are "tamed" through ceremonial baptism, they dominate the devotee with symptoms resembling Jerline's condition at its worst moments: spasmodic convulsions, bodily stiffness or loss of muscular control, and dissociation (see Métraux 1972:121).

14 Three major questions have guided recent research into fundamentalist churches in Latin America which stress inner-worldly discipline. Do they prepare the disinherited in rural areas to succeed as proletarians in urban wage-labor? Do such sects serve as a vehicle for the cultural protest of the poor? Or do they rather diffuse conflict and obliterate dissenting cultural forms? (Stoll 1990; Austin-Broos 1991–92).

8 CONCLUSION

1 The term moral logic may be misleading. Although rooted in certain propositions about the self, God, Jesus, angels, spirits, etc., it is not a rigorous and internally consistent philosophical system. Nor is it wholly an ethnopsychology, although it provides subtle accounts of the self and its fragmentation in cases of possession and satanic sickness. This informal moral logic is instead animated by the force of emotions – the immediate need to safeguard one's self-image of morally upstanding person. It is equally animated by direct body/self experiences: the palpable flow of blood which functions as a socio-moral barometer (Farmer 1988) and the changes in consciousness which index morally repugnant pathogenic attacks or the acquisition of ethically and/or effective healing power.

Bibliography

Abu-Lughod, Lila 1990 The Romance of Resistance: Tracing Transformations of Power through Bedouin Women. *American Ethnologist* 17:41–55.

Alleyne, Mervyn 1988 *Roots of Jamaican Culture*. London: Pluto Press.

Allman, Suzanne 1983 Etude ethnolinguistique du lexique de la fécondité et de la maternité en Créole haitien. Ph.D. dissertation, Université de Provence, France.

1985 Santé et soins du nouveau-né en Haiti. Unpublished manuscript.

1986 Childbearing and the Training of Traditional Birth Attendants in Rural Haiti. *Medical Anthropology Quarterly* 17(2):40–43

Amarasingham, Lorna Rhodes 1980 Movement among Healers in Sri Lanka: A Case Study of a Sinhalese Patient. *Culture, Medicine, and Psychiatry* 4:71–92.

Anderson, Warwick 1992 "Where every prospect pleases, and only man is vile": Laboratory Medicine as Colonial Discourse. *Critical Inquiry* 18(3):506–29.

Antoine, Paul 1980 La Place de Palma Christi dans la culture populaire (mémoire de folklore). In *Cahier de folklore et des traditions orales d'Haiti*. Max Benoit, ed. Pp. 151–71. Port-au-Prince: l'Imprimerie des Antilles.

Apter, Andrew 1991 Herskovits's Heritage: Rethinking Syncretism in the African Diaspora. *Diaspora* 1(3):235–60.

1992 Black Critics and Kings: *The Hermeneutics of Power in Yoruba Society*. Chicago: University of Chicago Press.

Austin, Diane J. 1984 *Urban Life in Kingston, Jamaica: The Culture and Class Ideology of Two Neighborhoods*. New York: Gordon and Breach Science Publishers.

Austin-Broos, Diane J. 1991–92 Religion and the Politics of Moral Order in Jamaica. *Anthropological Forum* 6(3):293–319.

Bakhtin, Mikhail 1981 Discourse in the Novel. In *The Dialogic Imagination*. Michael Holquist, ed. Pp. 259–442. Austin: University of Texas Press.

Balch, Emily Greene 1972 *Occupied Haiti*. New York: Garland Publishing, Inc.

Barnes, Sandra, ed. 1989 *Africa's Ogun: Old World and New*. Bloomington: Indiana University Press.

Barthes, Roland 1968 *The Elements of Semiology*. New York: Wang and Hill.

Bastide, Roger 1971 *African Civilisations in the New World*. New York: Harper and Row (Torchbook Library).

1978 *African Religions in Brazil*. Baltimore, MD: Johns Hopkins University Press.

Bastien, Remy 1961 Haitian Rural Family Organization. *Social and Economic Studies* 10 (4):478–510.

1985 *Le Paysan haitien et sa famille.* Paris: ACCT (Agence de Cooperation Culturelle et Technique) – Karthala.

Bates, J. A., Michel Descouens, Maggie Huff, and Jon Rohde 1985 Doing Business in Primary Health Care: Selling Essential Drugs in Haiti. Prepared for Management Sciences for Health/Haiti. Unpublished manuscript.

Begot, Danielle 1983 La Peinture vaudou comme écriture. *Etudes Créoles* 6(2):9–28.

Bellegarde, Dantes 1953 *Histoire du peuple Haïtien (1492–1952): Collection du tricinquantenaire de l'Indépendence d'Haïti.* Lausanne, Switzerland: L'Imprimerie Held, S.A.

Bellegarde-Smith, Patrick 1990 Haiti: *The Breached Citadel.* Boulder, CO: Westview Press.

Bisaillon, S. M. A. 1988 Rapport presenté au Ministère de la Santé Publique et de la Population (Haitian Ministry of Public Health and Population). Unpublished manuscript.

Black, Jan Knippers 1991 *Development in Theory and Practice: Bridging the Gap.* Boulder, CO: Westview Press.

Blumhagen, Dan 1980 Hyper-tension: A Folk Illness with a Medical Name. *Culture, Medicine, and Psychiatry* 4:197–227.

Boddy, Janice 1989 *Wombs and Alien Spirits: Women, Men, and the Zar Cult in Northern Sudan.* Madison: University of Wisconsin Press.

Bordes, Ary 1979 *Evolution des sciences de la santé et de l'hygiène publique en Haiti. Tome I: Fin de la période coloniale – 1915.* Port-au-Prince: Publication du Centre d'Hygiène Familiale.

Bordes, Ary and Andrea Couture 1978 *For the People, for a Change: Bringing Health to the Families of Haiti.* Boston: Beacon Press.

Bougerol, Christine 1983 *La Médecine populaire à la Guadeloupe.* Paris: Editions Karthala.

1985 Medical Practices in the French West Indies: Master and Slave in the 17th and 18th Centuries. *History and Anthropology* 2:125–43.

Bourdieu, Pierre 1977 *Outline of a Theory of Practice.* Cambridge: Cambridge University Press.

1988 Program for a Sociology of Sport. *Sociology of Sport Journal* 5:153–61.

1990 *The Logic of Practice.* Stanford, CA: Stanford University Press.

Bourdieu, Pierre and Loic J. D. Wacquant 1992 *An Invitation to Reflexive Sociology.* Chicago, IL: University of Chicago Press.

Bourguignon, Erika 1976 *Possession.* San Francisco, CA: Chandler and Sharp Publishers, Inc.

Breathett, George, ed. 1983 *The Catholic Church in Haiti, 1704–1785: Selected Letters, Memoirs, and Documents.* Salisbury, NC: Documentary Publications.

Brodwin, Paul 1992a The Power of an "Absent Ethnicity": Social Value and Medical Commodities in Rural Haiti. *Museum Anthropology* 16(3):34–40.

1992b Guardian Angels and Dirty Spirits: The Moral Basis of Healing Power in Rural Haiti. In *Anthropological Approaches to the Study of Ethnomedicine.* M. Nichter, ed. Pp. 57–74. Philadelphia, PA: Gordon and Breach Science Publishers, S.A.

1994 Review of The Faces of the Gods: Vodou and Roman Catholicism in Haiti. *New West Indian Guide* 68(3/4):381–87.

Brown, E. Richard 1979 *Rockefeller Medicine Men: Medicine and Capitalism in America*. Berkeley: University of California Press.

Brown, Jonathan 1972 *The History and Present Condition of St. Domingo*. London: Frank Cass and Company, Limited. Reprint of the Philadelphia 1837 edition.

Brown, Karen McCarthy 1976 The Veve of Haitian Vodou. Ph.D. dissertation, Temple University, Philadelphia, PA.

1989 Systematic Remembering, Systematic Forgetting: Ogou in Haiti. In *Africa's Ogun: Old World and New*. Sandra Barnes, ed. Pp. 65–89. Bloomington: Indiana University Press.

1991 *Mama Lola: A Vodou Priestess in Brooklyn*. Berkeley: University of California Press.

Bryce-Laporte, R. S. 1967 M. G. Smith's Version of Pluralism – The Questions it Raises. *Contemporary Studies of Society and History* 10(1):114–20

Buchanan, S. 1980 Scattered Seeds: The Meaning of Migration for Haitians in New York City. Ph.D. dissertation, Anthropology Department, New York University.

Bush, Barbara 1990 *Slave Women in Caribbean Society: 1650–1838*. Bloomington: Indiana University Press.

Candler, John 1842 *Brief Notices of Hayti: With its Conditions, Resources, and Profits*. London: publisher unknown.

Casimir, Jean 1982 Two Classes and Two Cultures in Contemporary Haiti. In *Contemporary Caribbean: A Sociological Reader*. Susan Craig, editor. Pp. 181–210. Maracas, Trinidad and Tobago: The College Press.

Castor, Suzy 1988 *L'Occupation américaine d'Haïti*. Port-au-Prince: Imprimerie Henri Deschamps.

Cauna, Jacques 1987 *Au Temps des Isles à Sucre: Histoire d'une plantation de Saint-Domingue au XVIIIe siècle*. Paris: Editions Karthala.

1988 Etat sanitaire des esclaves et politique en matière de population sur une grande sucrerie de Saint-Domingue: l'Habitation Fleuriau de Bellevue, 1777–1788. In *De la Traite à l'esclavage du XVIIIème au XIXème siècle*. Serges Daget, ed. Pp. 205–21. Actes du Colloque International sur la Traite des Noirs. Nantes: Centre du Recherche sur l'Histoire du Monde Atlantique.

Charles, Claude 1979 Brief Comments on the Occurrence, Etiology, and Treatment of Indisposition. *Social Science and Medicine* 13B:135–36.

Chrisman, Noel J. 1977 The Health-Seeking Process: An Approach to the Natural History of Illness. *Culture, Medicine, and Psychiatry* 1:351–77

Clerismé, Calixte 1979 *Recherches sur la médecine traditionelle*. Port-au-Prince: Ateliers Fardin.

Clifford, James 1986 Introduction: Partial Truths. In *Writing Culture: The Poetics and Politics of Ethnography*. Pp. 1–26. Berkeley: University of California Press.

1988 *The Predicament of Culture: Twentieth-Century Ethnography, Literature, and Art*. Cambridge, MA: Harvard University Press.

Clifford, James and George Marcus, eds. 1986 *Writing Culture: The Poetics and Politics of Ethnography*. Berkeley: University of California Press

Comaroff, Jean 1980 Healing and the Cultural Order: The Case of the Baralong boo Ratshidi of Southern Africa. *American Ethnologist* 7:637–77.
1983 The Defectiveness of Symbols or the Symbols of Defectiveness? On the Cultural Analysis of Medical Systems. *Culture, Medicine, and Psychiatry* 7:3–20.
1985 *Body of Power, Spirit of Resistance: The Culture and History of a South African People.* Chicago: University of Chicago Press
1994 The Diseased Heart of Africa: Medicine, Colonialism, and the Black Body. In *Knowledge, Power, and Practice: The Anthropology of Medicine and Everyday Life.* Shirley Lindenbaum and Margaret Lock, eds. Pp. 305–29. Berkeley: University of California Press.
Comaroff, John L. 1982 Dialectical Systems, History and Anthropology: Units of Study and Questions of Theory. *Journal of Southern African Studies* 8(2):143–72.
Comhaire-Sylvain, S. 1961 The Household in Kenscoff, Haiti. *Social and Economic Studies* 10(2):192–211.
Conrad, Peter and Joseph W. Schneider 1992 Afterword: Deviance and Medicalization: A Decade Later. In *Deviance and Medicalization: From Badness to Sickness.* Pp. 277–92. Philadelphia, PA: Temple University Press, expanded edition.
Conway, Frederick 1978 Pentecostalism in the Context of Haitian Religion and Health Practice. Ph.D. Dissertation, Anthropology Department, American University, Washington, DC.
Coreil, Marie Jeannine 1979 Disease Prognosis and Resource Allocation in a Haitian Mountain Community. Ph.D. Dissertation, Anthropology Department, University of Kentucky.
1983 Parallel Structures in Professional and Folk Health Care: A Model Applied to Rural Haiti. *Culture, Medicine, and Psychiatry* 7:131–51.
1988 Innovation among Haitian Healers: The Adoption of Oral Rehydration Therapy. *Human Organization* 47(1):48–58.
Cosminsky, Sheila and Mary Scrimshaw 1980 Medical Pluralism on a Guatemalan Plantation. *Social Science and Medicine* 14B:267–78.
Courlander, Harold 1960 *The Drum and the Hoe: Life and Lore of the Haitian People.* Berkeley: University of California Press
Crandon-Malamud, Libbet 1991 *From the Fat of Our Souls: Social Change, Political Process, and Medical Pluralism in Bolivia.* Berkeley: University of California Press.
Crapanzano, Vincent 1973 *The Hamadsha: A Study in Moroccan Ethnopsychiatry.* Berkeley: University of California Press.
1980 *Tuhami: Portrait of a Moroccan.* Chicago: University of Chicago Press.
Csordas, Thomas 1985 Medical and Sacred Realities: Between Comparative Religion and Transcultural Psychiatry. *Culture, Medicine, and Psychiatry* 9:103–16.
1988 The Conceptual Status of Hegemony and Critique in Medical Anthropology. *Medical Anthropology Quarterly* (n.s.) 2(4):416–521.
1990 Embodiment as a Paradigm for Anthropology. *Ethos* 18(1):5–47.
1993 Somatic Modes of Attention. *Cultural Anthropology* 8(2):135–56.

Curtin, Philip D. 1990 *The Rise and Fall of the Plantation Complex: Essays in Atlantic History.* Cambridge: Cambridge University Press.

Dayan, Joan 1995 Haiti, History, and the Gods. In *After Colonialism: Imperial Histories and Postcolonial Displacements.* Gyan Prakash, ed. Pp. 66–97. Princeton, NJ: Princeton University Press.

Debbasch, Yvan 1973 Le Maniel: Further Notes. In *Maroon Societies.* Ricard Price, ed. Pp. 143–48. New York: Anchor Press/Doubleday.

Debien, Gabriel 1941 *Une Plantation de Saint Domingue: la sucrerie Galbaud du Fort (1690–1802).* Cairo: L'Institut Français d'Archéologie Orientale.

1945 *Comptes, profits, esclaves, et travaux de deux sucreries de Saint-Domingue (1774–1798).* Notre histoire coloniale VI. Port-au-Prince: Valcin.

1956 *Etudes antillaises (XVIIIe siècle).* Cahier des Annales. Paris: Librairie Armand Colin.

1959 *Un Colon sur sa plantation.* Publications de la Section d'Histoire 1. Dakar, Sénégal: Faculté des Lettres et Sciences Humaines.

1973 Marronage in the French Caribbean. In *Maroon Societies.* Ricard Price, ed. Pp. 107–42. New York: Anchor Press/Doubleday.

1974 *Les Esclaves aux Antilles françaises, 17e à 18e siècles.* Basse-Terre, Guadeloupe: Société d'Histoire de la Guadeloupe.

De Heusch, Luc 1989 Kongo in Haiti: a New Approach to Religious Syncretism. *Man* 24:290–302.

Dehoux, Jean-Baptiste 1891 *Rapport au Gouvernement sur les institutions hospitalières et médicales d'Haïti – leur passé depuis 1804, leur état actuel.* Jacmel, Haiti: Imprimerie Nationale.

Dejean, Yves 1980 *Comment écrire le Créole d'Haïti.* Outremont, Quebec: Collectif Paroles.

Département de la Santé Publique et Population (DSPP) n.d. *Toward Health for All in Haiti.* Port-au-Prince: Department of Public Health and Population.

Deren, Maya 1970 [1953] Divine Horsemen: The Living Gods of Haiti. New Paltz, NY: McPherson and Co. (Documentext).

Desmangles, Leslie G. 1992 *The Faces of the Gods: Vodoun and Roman Catholicism in Haiti.* Chapel Hill: University of North Carolina Press.

Diederich, Bernard and Al Burt 1969 *Papa Doc and the Tontons Macoutes.* New York: McGraw-Hill.

Dirks, Nicholas, ed. 1992 *Colonialism and Culture.* Ann Arbor: University of Michigan Press.

Division d'Hygiène Familiale (Division of Family Hygiene) 1982 Analyse du programme de santé communautaire à Arniquet. Communications présentées au seminaire, Les Cayes, Septembre, 1982. Unpublished manuscript.

Dorsainvil, J. C. n.d. *Histoire d'Haïti* (cours supérieur). Port-au-Prince: Imprimerie Henri Deschamps.

Douglas, Mary 1966 *Purity and Danger: An Analysis of Concepts of Pollution and Taboo.* London: Routledge and Kegan Paul.

1973 *Natural Symbols.* New York City: Vintage Press.

Dressler, William 1982 *Hypertension and Culture Change: Acculturation and Disease in the West Indies.* South Salem, NY: Redgrave Publishing Co.

Dreyfus, Herbert L. and Paul Rabinow 1982 *Michel Foucault: Beyond Structuralism and Hermeneutics* (2nd edition). Chicago: University of Chicago Press.

Drummond, Lee 1980 The Cultural Continuum: A Theory of Intersystems. *Man* 15(2):352–74.

Dunn, Frederick 1976 Traditional Asian Medicine and Cosmopolitan Medicine as Adaptive Systems. In *Asian Medical Systems: A Comparative Study*, C. Leslie, ed. Pp. 133–58. Berkeley: University of California Press.

Dunn, Frederick and Byron Good 1978 Priorities for Research to Advance the Comparative Study of Medical Systems: Summary of the Discussion at the Final Session of the Conference. *Social Science and Medicine* 12: 135–37.

Dupuy, Alex 1982 Class Formation and Underdevelopment in Nineteenth-Century Haiti. *Race and Class* 24(1):17–31.

1990 *Haiti in the World Economy: Class, Race, and Underdevelopment since 1700.* Boulder, CO: Westview Press.

Early, Evelyn A. 1982 The Logic of Well Being: Therapeutic Narratives in Cairo, Egypt. *Social Science and Medicine* 16:1491–497.

1988 The Baladi Curative System of Cairo, Egypt. *Culture, Medicine, and Psychiatry* 12:65–84.

Fabrega, Horacio, Jr. and Daniel B. Silver 1973 *Illness and Shamanistic Curing in Zinacantan: An Ethnomedical Analysis.* Stanford, CA: Stanford University Press.

Fanon, Frantz 1965 *A Dying Colonialism.* New York: Grove Press.

1966 *The Wretched of the Earth.* New York: Grove Press.

1967 *Black Skin, White Masks.* New York: Grove Press.

Farmer, Paul 1988 Bad Blood, Spoiled Milk: Bodily Fluids as Moral Barometers in Rural Haiti. *American Ethnologist* 15(1):62–83.

1990 Sending Sickness: Sorcery, Politics, and Changing Concepts of AIDS in Rural Haiti. *Medical Anthropology Quarterly* 4(1):6–27.

1992 *AIDS and Accusation: Haiti and the Geography of Blame.* Berkeley: University of California Press.

Fass, Simon 1988 *Political Economy in Haiti.* New Brunswick, NJ: Transaction Books.

Favret-Saada, Jeanne 1980 *Deadly Words: Witchcraft in the Bocage.* Cambridge: Cambridge University Press.

Feierman, Steven 1985 Struggles for Control: The Social Roots of Health and Healing in Modern Africa. *African Studies Review* 2/3:73–147.

Feierman, Steven, and John M. Janzen, eds. 1992 *The Social Basis of Health and Healing in Africa.* Berkeley: University of California Press.

Fick, Carolyn E. 1990 *The Making of Haiti: The Saint Domingue Revolution from Below.* Knoxville: University of Tennessee Press.

Fisher, Lawrence 1985 *Colonial Madness: Mental Health and the Barbadian Social Order.* New Brunswick, NJ: Rutgers University Press.

Fleurant, Gerdes 1973 Caste, Class Conflict, and Status Quo in Haiti. In *Ethnic Conflicts and Power: A Cross-National Perspective.* Donald Gelfand and Russell Lee, eds. Pp. 178–93. New York: John Wiley and Sons.

Foster, George 1976 Disease Etiologies in Non-Western Medical systems. *American Anthropologst* 78:772–82.

1978 Hippocrates' Latin American Legacy. In *Colloquia in Anthropology*, II. E. K. Wetherington, ed. Pp. 3–19. Dallas, Texas: Southern Methodist University, Fort Burgwin Research Center.

1982 Applied Anthropology and International Health: Retrospect and Prospect. *Human Organization* 41:189–97.

1994 *Hippocrates' Latin American Legacy: Humoral Medicine in the New World.* Langhorne, PA: Gordon and Breach.

Foucault, Michel 1973 *Madness and Civilization: A History of Insanity in the Age of Reason.* R. Howard, trans. New York: Vintage/Random House.

1975 *The Birth of the Clinic: An Archaeology of Medical Perception.* New York: Vintage/Random House.

1976 *The Archaeology of Knowledge.* New York: Harper and Row.

1980 *Power/Knowledge: Selected Interviews and Other Writings, 1972–1977.* New York: Pantheon.

Fouchard, Jean 1988 *Les Marrons de la Liberté.* Port-au-Prince: Editions Henri Deschamps.

Fox, Richard G. 1991 Introduction: Working in the Present. In *Recapturing Anthropology: Working in the Present.* Richard Fox, ed. Pp. 1–16. Santa Fe, NM: School of American Research Press.

Frankenberg, Ronald 1986 Sickness as Cultural Performance: Drama, Trajectory, and Pilgrimage Root Metaphors and the Making Social of Disease. *International Journal of Health Services* 16(4):603–26.

1988 Gramsci, Marxism, and Phenomenology: Essays for the Development of Critical Medical Anthropology. *Medical Anthropology Quarterly* (new series) 2(4):323–459.

Freire, Paolo 1970 *Pedagogy of the Oppressed.* New York: Seabury Press.

Friedson, Eliot 1970 *Profession of Medicine.* New York: Dodd, Mead, and Co.

Garro, Linda C. 1986 Intracultural Variation in Folk Medical Knowledge: A Comparison between Curers and Noncurers. *American Anthropologist* 88(2):351–70.

Giddens, Anthony 1984 *The Constitution of Society.* Berkeley: University of California Press.

Gilroy, Paul 1993 *The Black Atlantic: Modernity and Double Consciousness.* Cambridge, MA: Harvard University Press.

Ginsburg, Faye and Anna Lowenhaupt Tsing 1990 Introduction. In *Uncertain Terms: Negotiating Gender in American Culture.* Faye Ginsburg and Anna Lowenhaupt Tsing, eds. Pp. 1–18. Boston, MA: Beacon Press.

Girod, François 1972 *La Vie quotidienne de la société créole (Saint-Domingue au 18ème siècle).* Paris: Librairie Hachette.

Giroux, Henry A. 1992 Resisting Difference: Cultural Studies and the Discourse of Critical Pedagogy. In *Cultural Studies.* Lawrence Grossbert, Cary Nelson, and Paula Treichler, eds. Pp. 199–222. New York City: Routledge.

Glick-Schiller, Nina and Georges Fouron 1990 "Everywhere We Go, We Are in Danger": Ti Manno and the Emergence of a Haitian Transnational Identity. *American Ethnologist* 17(2):329–47.

Good, Byron 1976 The Professionalization of Medicine in a Provincial Iranian Town. In *Transcultural Health Care Issues and Conditions.* Madeleine Leininger, ed. Pp. 51–65. Philadelphia, PA: F. A. Davis Co.

1977 The Heart of What's the Matter: The Semantics of Illness in Iran. *Culture, Medicine, and Psychiatry* 1:25–58.

1986 Explanatory Models in Care-Seeking: A Critical Account. In *Illness Behavior: A Multi-Disciplinary Model*. Sean McHugh and T. Michael Vallis, eds. Pp. 161–71. New York: Plenum Press.

1990 *Medicine, Rationality, and Experience: An Anthropological Perspective.* 1990 Lewis Henry Morgan Lectures, delivered at the University of Rochester, Rochester, New York.

1994 *Medicine, Rationality, and Experience: An Anthropological Perspective.* Cambridge: Cambridge University Press.

Good, Byron J. and Mary-Jo Good 1980 The Meaning of Symptoms: A Cultural Hermeneutic Model for Clinical Practice. In *The Relevance of Social Science for Medicine*. Leon Eisenberg and Arthur Kleinman, eds. Pp. 165–96. Dordrecht, Holland: D. Reidel Publishing Co.

Good, Mary-Jo 1980 Of Blood and Babies: The Relationship of Popular Islamic Physiology to Fertility. *Social Science and Medicine* 14b:147–56.

Gordon, Deborah 1988 Tenacious Assumptions in Western Medicine. In *Biomedicine Examined*. Margaret Lock and Deborah Gordon, eds. Pp. 19–56. Dordrecht, Holland: Kluwer Academic Publishers.

Goubert, Jean-Pierre 1980 The Art of Healing: Learned Medicine and Popular Medicine in the France of 1790. In *Medicine and Society in France – Selections from the "Annales Economies, Sociétés, Civilisations,"* R. Foster and O. Ranum, ed. Pp. 1–23. Baltimore, MD: Johns Hopkins University Press.

Grunwald, Joseph, Leslie Delatour, and Karl Voltaire 1984 Offshore Assembly in Haiti. In *Haiti – Today and Tomorrow: An Interdisciplinary Study*. Charles Foster and Albert Valdman, eds. Pp. 231–52. Lanham, MD: University Press of America.

Guyton, Arthur C. 1977 *Basic Human Physiology: Normal Functions and Mechanisms of Disease*. Philadelphia, PA: W. B. Saunders Co.

Hall, Gwendolyn Midlo 1972 Saint Domingue. In *Neither Slave Nor Free: The Freedmen of African Descent in the Slave Societies of the New World*. David W. Cohen and Jack P. Greene, eds. Pp. 172–92. Baltimore, MD: Johns Hopkins University Press.

Halstead, Scott, Julia Walsh, and Kenneth Warren, eds.1985 *Good Health at Low Cost. Proceedings of a Rockefeller Foundation Conference, Bellagio, Italy, April 29–May 3, 1985*. New York: Rockefeller Foundation

Harrell, Steven 1991 Pluralism, Performance and Meaning in Taiwanese Healing: A Case Study. *Culture, Medicine, and Psychiatry* 15:45–68.

Hawkins, John 1984 *Inverse Images: The Meaning of Culture, Ethnicity and Family in Postcolonial Guatemala*. Albuquerque: University of New Mexico Press.

Hawley, John Stratton 1994 *Fundamentalism and Gender*. New York: Oxford University Press.

Hebdige, Dick 1979 *Subculture: The Meaning of Style*. London: Routledge.

Hefner, Robert W. 1993 *Conversion to Christianity: Historical and Anthropological Perspectives on a Great Transformation*. Berkeley: University of California Press.

Heinl, Robert D. Jr. and Nancy G. Heinl 1978 *Written in Blood: The Story of the Haitian People, 1492–1971*. Boston, MA: Houghton Mifflin Company.

226   Bibliography

Herskovits, Melville 1937 *Life in a Haitian Valley*. New York: Alfred A. Knopf.

Hess, Selina 1981 *The Semiotic in Medical Anthropology*. National Museum of Man Mercury Series, Canadian Ethnology Service 78:40–53.

1983 Domestic Medicine and Indigenous Medical Systems in Haiti: Culture and Political Economy of Health in a Disemic Society. Ph.D. dissertation, Anthropology Department, McGill University.

Hoffman, Léon-François 1990 *Haïti: couleurs, croyances, créole*. Port-au-Prince: Editions Henri Deschamps.

Hunt, Benjamin 1860 *Remarks on Hayti as a Place for Settlement of Afric-Americans*. Philadephia, PA: publisher unknown.

Hunt, Linda M., Carole H. Browner, and Brigitte Jordan 1990 Hypoglycemia: Portrait of an Illness Construct Everyday Use. *Medical Anthropology Quarterly* (new series) 4(2):191–210.

Hurbon, Laennec 1987a *Dieu dans le vaudou haitien*. Port-au-Prince: Editions Henri Deschamps.

1987b *Le Barbare imaginaire*. Port-au-Prince: Editions Henri Deschamps.

1987c *Comprendre Haïti: essai sur l'état, la nation, la culture*. Port-au-Prince: Editions Henri Deschamps.

1993 *Les Mystères du vaudou*. Paris: Gallimard.

Illich, Ivan 1976 *Medical Nemesis: The Expropriation of Health*. New York: Pantheon.

L'Institut Pédagogique National 1979 Ki Jan Pou Ekri Kreyòl. Bulletin No. 1 (December). Mimeographed copy.

James, C. L. R. 1963 *The Black Jacobins*. New York: Random House.

Janvier, Louis-Joseph 1979 *La République d'Haïti et ses visiteurs (1840–1882)* I. Port-au-Prince: Ateliers Fardin. Reprint of the Paris 1883 edition.

Janzen, John M. 1978a *The Quest for Therapy: Medical Pluralism in Lower Zaire*. Berkeley: University of California Press.

1978b The Comparative Study of Medical Systems as Changing Social Systems. *Social Science and Medicine* 12:121–29.

1987 Therapy Management: Concept, Reality, Process. *Medical Anthropology Quarterly* (new series) 1(1):68–84.

Janzen, John M. and Steven Feierman, eds. 1979 The Social History of Disease and Medicine in Africa. *Social Science and Medicine* (special issue) 13B:239–356.

Jayawardena, C. 1980 Culture and Ethnicity in Guyana and Fiji. *Man* 15(3):430–50.

Joerger, Muriel 1980 The Structure of the Hospital System in France of the Ancien Régime. *In Medicine and Society in France: Selections from the Annales – Economies, Sociétés, Civilisations* VI. Robert Forster and Orest Ranum, eds. Elborg Forster and Patricia M. Ranum, trans. Pp. 104–36. Baltimore, MD: Johns Hopkins University Press.

Johnson, Thomas A. and Carolyn F. Sargent, eds. 1990 *Medical Anthropology: Contemporary Theory and Method*. New York City: Praeger Publishers.

Justice, Judith 1986 *Policies, Plans, and People: Foreign Aid and Health Development*. Berkeley: University of California Press.

Kakar, Sudhir 1982 *Shamans, Mystics, and Doctors*. New York: Alfred A. Knopf.

Katz, Richard 1976 Education for Transcendence: !Kia-Healing with the Kalahari !Kung. In *Kalahari Hunter-Gatherers*. R. B. Lee and I. DeVore, eds. Pp. 281–301. Cambridge, MA: Harvard University Press.

Keen, Benjamin 1992 *A History of Latin America*, 4th edition. Boston, MA: Houghton-Mifflin Co.

Kiev, Ari 1986 The Psychotherapeutic Value of Spirit Possession in Haiti. In *Trance and Possession States*. Raymond Prince, ed. Pp. 143–48. Montreal: R. M. Bucke Memorial Society.

Kirmayer, Laurence 1992 The Body's Insistence on Meaning: Metaphor as Presentation and Representation in Illness Experience. *Medical Anthropology Quarterly* 6:323–46.

Klein, Herbert S. 1986 *African Slavery in Latin America and the Caribbean*. New York: Oxford University Press.

Kleinman, Arthur 1980 *Patients and Healers in the Context of Culture*. Berkeley: University of California Press.

   1986 *Social Origins of Distress and Disease: Depression, Neurasthenia, and Pain in Modern China*. New Haven, CT: Yale University Press.

   1988 The Experience of Suffering and its Professional Transformations: Somatization and Human Tragedy. Paper presented at the Hamburg Conference: "Anthropologies of Medicine: A Colloquium on West European and North American Perspectives," Hamburg, Germany.

Kleinman, Arthur and Joan Kleinman 1991 Suffering and its Professional Transformations: Toward an Ethnography of Interpersonal Experience. *Culture, Medicine, and Psychiatry* 15(3):275–301.

Kleinman, Arthur, Peter Kunstadter, E. Russell Alexander, and James L. Gale, eds. 1978 *Culture and Healing in Asian Societies: Anthropological, Psychiatric, and Public Health Studies*. Cambridge, MA: Schenkman Publishing Company.

Kopytoff, Igor 1986 The Cultural Biography of Things: Commoditization as Process. In *The Social Life of Things: Commodities in Cultural Perspective*, A. Appadurai, ed. Pp. 64–91. Cambridge: Cambridge University Press.

Kunstadter, Peter 1978 The Comparative Anthropological Study of Medical Systems in Society. In *Culture and Healing in Asian Societies: Anthropological, Psychiatric, and Public Health Services*, A. Kleinman, P. Kunstadter, E. R. Alexander, and J. L. Gale, ed. Pp. 393–406. Cambridge, MA: Schenkman Publishing Company.

Labelle, Micheline 1987 *Idéologie de Couleur et Classes Sociales en Haïti*. Montreal: Les Presses de l'Université de Montréal

Lacerte, Robert K. 1978 The Evolution of Land and Labor in the Haitian Revolution, 1791–1820. *Americas* 34: 449–59.

Laguerre, Michel 1979 *Etudes sur le vodou haïtien: bibliographie analytique*. Travaux du Centre de Recherches Caraïbes. Montreal: Les Presses de l'Université de Montreal.

   1980 *Voodoo Heritage*. Beverly Hills, CA: Sage Library of Social Research.

   1982 *The Complete Haitiana: A Bibliographic Guide to the Scholarly Literature, 1900–1980*. Millwood, NY: Kraus International Publications.

   1984 *American Odyssey: Haitians in New York City*. Ithaca, NY: Cornell University Press.

1987 *Afro-Caribbean Folk Medicine.* South Hadley, MA: Bergin and Garvey Publishers, Inc.

Lambek, Michael 1981 *Human Spirits: A Cultural Account of Trance in Mayotte.* Cambridge: Cambridge University Press.

Langley, Lester D. 1980 *The United States and the Caribbean in the Twentieth Century.* 4th edition. Athens: University of Georgia Press.

Larose, Serge 1977 The Meaning of Africa in Haitian Vodu. In *Symbols and Sentiments: Cross-Cultural Studies in Symbolism.* Ioan Lewis, ed. Pp. 85–116. London: Academic Press.

Leach, Edmund 1970 *Claude Lévi-Strauss.* Penguin Modern Masters. New York: Penguin Books Ltd.

Leiris, Michel 1953 Notes sur l'usage de chromolithographies par les vaudouisants. *Mémoires de l'Institut Français d'Afrique Noire* 27:201–07.

Leslie, Charles 1976 *Asian Medical Systems.* Berkeley: University of California Press.

1978 Theoretical Foundations for the Comparative Study of Medical System. *Social Science and Medicine* 12(2B):65–138.

1980 Medical Pluralism. *Social Science and Medicine* 14B(4):191–296.

Lévi-Strauss, Claude 1966 *The Savage Mind.* Chicago: University of Chicago Press.

Lewis, Gordon K. 1983 *Main Currents in Caribbean Thought: The Historical Evolution of Caribbean Society in its Ideological Aspects, 1492–1900.* Baltimore, MD: The Johns Hopkins University Press.

Lewis, I. M. 1971 *Ecstatic Religion: An Anthropological Study of Spirit Possession.* Baltimore: Pelican Books.

Leyburn, James G. 1966 [1941] *The Haitian People.* New Haven, CT: Yale University Press.

Ligondé, François W. 1985 *N'ap Réglé Tout Bagay an Chantan: Liv Sòm, Chanté, Lapriyé Kréyòl Kominoté Sint-Mari té rasanblé pou fè tout péyi Dayiti chanté gloua pou Bondié.* Miami, FL: Editions Idéal.

Lindenbaum, Shirley and Margaret Lock, eds. 1993 *Knowledge, Power, and Practice: The Anthropology of Medicine and Everyday Life.* Berkeley: University of California Press.

Littlewood, Roland 1993 *Pathology and Identity: The Work of Mother Earth in Trinidad.* Cambridge: Cambridge University Press.

Locher, Uli 1984 Migration in Haiti. In *Haiti – Today and Tomorrow: An Interdisciplinary Study.* Charles Foster and Albert Valdman, eds. Pp. 325–36. Lanham, MD: University Press of America.

Lock, Margaret 1980 *East Asian Medicine in Urban Japan.* Berkeley: University of California Press.

1986 Plea for Acceptance: School Refusal Syndrome in Japan. *Social Science and Medicine* 23(2):99–112.

1987 Introduction: Health and Medical Care as Cultural and Social Phenomena. In *Health, Illness, and Medical Care in Japan.* Edward Norbeck and Margaret Lock, eds. Pp. 1–23. Honolulu: University of Hawaii Press.

1988 New Japanese Mythologies: Faltering Discipline and the Ailing Housewife. *American Ethnologist* 15(1):43–61.

Lowenthal, Ira 1978 Ritual Performance and Religious Experience: A Service for the Gods in Southern Haiti. *Journal of Anthropological Research* 34(3):392–414.

1984 Labor, Sexuality, and the Conjugal Contract in Rural Haiti. In *Haiti – Today and Tomorrow: An Interdisciplinary Study*. Charles Foster and Albert Valdman, eds. Pp. 15–34. Lanham, MD: University Press of America.

1987 Marriage is 20, Children are 21: The Cultural Construction of Conjugality in Rural Haiti. Ph.D. dissertation, Anthropology Department, The Johns Hopkins University.

Lundahl, Mats 1979 *Peasants and Poverty: A Study of Haiti*. London: Croom Helm.

Lutz, Catherine 1985 Depression and the Translation of Emotional Worlds. In *Culture and Depression: Studies in the Anthropology and Cross-Cultural Psychiatry of Affect and Disorder*. Arthur Kleinman and Byron Good, eds. Pp. 63–100. Berkeley: University of California Press.

Macleod, Roy and Milton Lewis, eds. 1988 *Disease, Medicine, and Empire: Perspectives on Western Medicine and the Experience of European Expansion*. London: Routledge.

Madiou, Thomas 1988 *Histoire d'Haïti, Tome V, De 1811 à 1818*. Port-au-Prince: Edition Henri Deschamps.

Maguire, Robert 1984 Strategies for Rural Development in Haiti: Formation, Organization, Implementation. In *Haïti – Today and Tomorrow: An Interdisciplinary Study*. Charles Foster and Albert Valdman, eds. Pp. 161–72. Lanham, MD: University Press of America.

Malenfant (Colonel) 1814 *Des Colonies et particulièrement celle de St. Domingue*. Paris: publisher unknown.

Marcelin, Milo 1947 Les Grands Dieux du vodou haïtien. *Journal de la Société des Americanistes de Paris*, n.s. 36:51–135.

Marcus, George and Michael Fischer 1986 *Anthropology as Cultural Critique: An Experimental Moment in the Human Sciences*. Chicago: University of Chicago Press.

Martin, Emily 1987 *The Woman in the Body: A Cultural Analysis of Reproduction*. Boston, MA: Beacon Press.

Mathurin, Augustin 1972 *Assistance sociale en Haïti*. Port-au-Prince: Imprimerie des Antilles.

Mauss, Marcel 1979 Body Techniques. In *Sociology and Psychology*. Pp. 93–135. London: Routledge and Kegan Paul.

Maximilien, Louis 1945 *Le vodou haïtien: rite rada-canzo*. Port-au-Prince: Imprimerie de l'Etat.

Métraux, Alfred 1972 *Voodoo in Haiti*. New York: Schocken Books.

1978 *Itinéraire 1. Carnets de notes et journaux de voyage*. Payot: Paris.

Millspaugh, Arthur C. 1931 *Haiti Under American Control, 1915–1930*. Boston, MA: World Peace Foundation.

Mintz, Sidney 1966 The Caribbean as a Socio-Cultural Area. In *Peoples and Cultures of the Caribbean*. Michael M. Horowitz, ed. Pp. 17–46. Garden City, NY: The Natural History Press.

1974 *Caribbean Transformations*. Baltimore, MD: Johns Hopkins University Press.

1985 *Sweetness and Power: The Place of Sugar in Modern History*. New York: Penguin Books.

Mintz, Sidney and Richard Price 1992 *The Birth of African-American Culture: An Anthropological Perspective*. Boston, MA: Beacon Press.

Moll, Aristides A. 1944 *Aesculapius in Latin America*. Philadelphia, PA: W. B. Saunders Company.

Moore, Sally Falk 1987 Explaining the Present: Theoretical Dilemmas in Processual Ethnography. *American Ethnologist* 14(4):727–36.

Moreau de Saint-Méry, M.-L.-E. 1958 *Description topographique, physique, civile, politique, et historique de la partie française de l'Ile Saint-Domingue* (Nouvelle edition, prepared by Blanche Maurel and Etienne Taillemite). Paris: Société de l'Histoire des Colonies Françaises and Libraire Larose.

Morgan, Lynn 1989 The Importance of the State in Primary Health Care Initiatives. *Medical Anthropology Quarterly* (new series) 3(3):227–31.

1990 The Medicalization of Anthropology: A Critical Perspective on the Critical-Clinical Debate. *Social Science and Medicine* 30 (9):945–50.

Morsy, Soheir 1978 Sex Roles, Power, and Illness in an Egyptian Village. *American Ethnologist* 4:137–50.

1990 Political Economy in Medical Anthropology. In *Medical Anthropology: Contemporary Theory and Method*. Thomas M. Johnson and Carolyn F. Sargent, eds. Pp. 26–46. New York: Praeger Press.

Mullings, Leith 1984 *Therapy, Ideology, and Social Change: Mental Healing in Urban Ghana*. Berkeley: University of California Press.

Mulrain, George 1984 *Theology in Folk Culture: The Theological Significance of Haitian Folk Religion*. New York: Peter Lang.

Murray, Gerald 1976 Women in Perdition: Fertility Control in Haiti. In *Culture, Natality, and Family Planning*. John Marshall and Steven Polgar, eds. Pp. 59–78. Chapel Hill: North Carolina Population Center.

1977 The Evolution of Haitian Peasant Land Tenure: A Case Study in Agrarian Adaptation to Population Growth. Ph.D. dissertation, Anthropology Department, Columbia University.

1980 Population Pressure, Land Tenure, and Voodoo: The Economics of Haitian Peasant Ritual. In *Beyond the Myths of Culture*. Eric Ross, ed. Pp. 295–321. New York: Academic Press.

Murray, Gerald and Maria Alvarez 1973 Childbearing, Sickness, and Healing in a Haitian Village. Unpublished manuscript submitted to the Département de la Santé Publique et de la Population de la République d'Haïti. Port-au-Prince, Haiti.

de Nau, Le Baron Emile 1963 *Histoire des Caciques d'Haïti* I and II. Port-au-Prince: Editions Panorama.

Nettleford, Rex M. 1978 *Caribbean Cultural Identity: The Case of Jamaica*. Kingston: Institute of Jamaica.

Ngubane, Harriet 1992 Clinical Practice and Organization of Indigenous Healers in South Africa. In *The Social Basis of Health and Healing in Africa*. Steven Feierman and John M. Janzen, eds. Pp. 366–375. Berkeley: University of California Press.

Nicholls, David 1979 *From Dessalines to Duvalier: Race, Colour, and National Independence in Haiti*. Cambridge: Cambridge University Press.

1984 Past and Present in Haitian Politics. In *Haiti – Today and Tomorrow: An Interdisciplinary Study*. Charles Foster and Albert Valdman, eds. Pp. 253–64. Lanham, MD: University Press of America.

Nichter, Mark 1980 The Layperson's Perception of Medicine as Perspective into the Utilization of Multiple Therapy Systems in the Indian Context. *Social Science and Medicine* 14B:225–33.

Nougayrol, P., P. Vernet, C. Alexandre, and H. Tourneux 1976 *Ti Diksyonnè Kreyol-Franse*. Port-au-Prince: Editions Caraïbes.

Ong, Aihwa 1987 *Spirits of Resistance and Capitalist Discipline*. Albany, NY: State University of New York Press.

Ortner, Sherry 1984 Theory in Anthropology since the Sixties. *Comparative Studies in Society and History* 26(1):126–66.

Paquin, Lyonel 1983 *The Haitians: Class and Color Politics*. Brooklyn, NY: Multi-Type.

Parry, J. H. and P. M. Sherlock 1956 *A Short History of the West Indies*. New York: St. Martin's Press.

Parsons, Robert P. 1930 *History of Haitian Medicine*. New York: Paul B. Hoeber, Inc.

Patterson, Orlando 1967 *The Sociology of Slavery: An Analysis of the Origins, Development, and Structure of Negro Slave Society in Jamaica*. Rutherford, NJ: Fairleigh Dickinson University Press.

1975 Contest and Choice in Ethnic Alliance: A Theoretical Framework and Caribbean Case Study. In *Ethnicity*. Nathan Glazer and Patrick Moynihan, eds. Pp. 305–49. Cambridge, MA: Harvard University Press.

1982 *Slavery and Social Death*. Cambridge, MA: Harvard University Press.

Paul, Benjamin D., ed. 1955 *Health, Culture, and Community: Case Studies of Public Reactions to Health Programs*. New York: Russel Sage Foundation.

Philippe, Jeanne 1985 *Classes sociales et maladies mentales en Haïti*. Port-au-Prince: Les Ateliers Fardin.

Philippe, Jeanne and Jean B. Romain 1979 *Indisposition* in Haiti. *Social Science and Medicine* 13B:129–33.

Plummer, Brenda 1988 *Haiti and the Great Powers, 1902–1915*. Baton Rouge: Louisiana State University Press.

1992 *Haiti and the United States: The Psychological Moment*. Athens: University of Georgia Press.

Press, Irwin 1990 Levels of Explanation and Cautions for a Critical Clinical Anthropology. *Social Science and Medicine* 30(9):1001–09.

Pressoir, Catts 1927 *La Médecine en Haïti*. Port-au-Prince: Imprimerie Modèle.

Price, Richard 1966 Fishing Rites and Recipes in a Martiniquan Village. *Caribbean Studies* 6(1):3–24.

Price, Richard, ed. 1973 *Maroon Societies: Rebel Slave Communities in the Americas*. Garden City, NY: Anchor Press/Doubleday.

Price, Sally 1994 The Curse's Blessing: The False Sense of Harmony in Ethnography. *Frontiers* 14(2):123–43.

Prince, Raymond 1976 Psychotherapy as the Manipulation of Endogenous Healing Mechanisms: A Transcultural Survey. *Transcultural Psychiatry Research Review* 13 (October):115–33.

Prince, Rod 1985 *Haiti: Family Business*. London: Latin American Bureau.

232   Bibliography

Ramsey, Matthew 1988 *Professional and Popular Medicine in France, 1770–1830: The Social World of Medical Practice.* Cambridge: Cambridge University Press.

Ranger, Terence O. 1992 Godly Medicine: The Ambiguities of Medical Mission in Southeastern Tanzania. In *The Social Basis of Health and Healing in Africa.* Steven Feierman and John M. Janzen, eds. Pp. 256–82. Berkeley, CA: University of California Press.

Rhodes, Lorna A. 1991 *Emptying Beds: The Work of an Emergency Psychiatric Clinic.* Berkeley: University of California Press.

Rigaud, Milo 1953 *La Tradition voudoo et le voudoo haïtien.* Paris: Niclaus.

Robertson, A. F. 1984 *People and the State: An Anthropology of Planned Development.* Cambridge: Cambridge University Press.

Rohde, Jon 1986 The Rural Health Delivery System Project: Initiative and Inertia in the Ministry of Health. In *Politics, Projects, and People: Institutional Development in Haiti.* Derrick Brinkerhoff and Jean-Claude Garcia-Zamor, eds. Pp. 117–52. New York: Praeger Press.

Romain, Charles-Poisset 1986 *Le Protestantisme dans la société haïtienne: contribution à l'étude sociologique d'une religion.* Port-au-Prince: Imprimerie Henri Deschamps.

Rosaldo, Renato 1980 *Ilongot Headhunting: 1883–1974.* Stanford, CA: Stanford University Press.

Rubel, Arthur, ed. 1979 Parallel Medical Systems: Papers from a Workshop on "The Healing Process." *Social Science and Medicine* 13B(1):1–84.

Rubin, Vera, ed. 1960a Social and Cultural Pluralism in the Caribbean. *Annals of the New York Academy of Sciences* 83 (Article 5):761–916.

1960b *Caribbean Studies: A Symposium.* Seattle: University of Washington Press

Rulx, Léon 1928 *La Pratique médicale à St. Domingue.* Paris: Les Presses Modernes.

1978 *Notes bio-bibliographiques: médecins et naturalistes de l'ancienne colonie française de St.-Domingue.* Port-au-Prince: Imprimerie Panorama.

Scheper-Hughes, Nancy 1992a Hungry Bodies, Medicine, and the State: Toward a Critical Psychological Anthropology. In *New Directions in Psychological Anthropology.* Theodore Schwartz, Geoffrey M. White, and Catherine A. Lutz, eds. Pp. 221–47. Cambridge: Cambridge University Press.

1992b *Death Without Weeping: The Violence of Everyday Life in Brazil.* Berkeley: University of California Press.

Scheper-Hughes, Nancy and Margaret M. Lock 1986 Speaking "Truth" to Illness: Metaphors, Reification, and a Pedagogy for Patients. *Medical Anthropology Quarterly* 17:137–40.

1987 The Mindful Body: A Prolegomenon to Future Work in Medical Anthropology. *Medical Anthropology Quarterly* 1:6–41.

Schmidt, Hans 1971 *The United States Occupation of Haiti, 1915–1934.* New Brunswick, NJ: Rutgers University Press.

Schoelcher, Victor 1843 *Colonies étrangères et Haïti: résultats de l'émancipation anglaise.* Paris: Pagnerre.

Scott, James C. 1990 *Domination and the Arts of Resistance: Hidden Transcripts.* New Haven, CT: Yale University Press.

Scott, Joan W. 1988 Deconstructing Equality-Versus-Difference: Or, the Uses of Post-Structuralist Theory for Feminism. *Feminist Studies* 14(1):33–50.

Segal, Aaron 1984 Demographic factors in Haitian Development. In *Haiti – Today and Tomorrow: An Interdisciplinary Study*. Charles Foster and Albert Valdman, eds. Pp. 315–24. Lanham, MD: University Press of America.

Simpson, George 1970 *Religious Cults of the Caribbean: Trinidad, Jamaica, and Haiti*. Rio Pedras, Puerto Rico: Institute of Caribbean Studies.

Singer, Merrill 1989 The Limitations of Medical Ecology: The Concept of Adaptation in the Context of Social Stratification and Social Transformation. *Medical Anthropology* 10:223–34.

Singer, Merrill, Lani Davison, and Gina Gerdes 1988 Culture, Critical Theory, and Reproductive Illness Behavior in Haiti. *Medical Anthropology Quarterly* (new series) 2(4):370–85.

Smith, Raymond T. 1962 *British Guiana*. London: Oxford University Press (Royal Institute of International Affairs).

1963 Culture and Social Structure in the Caribbean: Some Recent Work on Family and Kinship Studies. *Contemporary Studies in Society and History* 6 (1):24–46.

1982 Race and Class in the Post-Emancipation Caribbean. In *Racism and Colonialism: Essays on Ideology and Social Structure*. Robert Ross, ed. Pp. 93–119. Comparative Studies in Overseas History, Publications of the Leiden Centre for the History of European Expansion. The Hague, Netherlands: Martinus Nijhoff.

Smucker, Glenn 1984 The Social Character of Religion in Rural Haiti. In *Haiti – Today and Tomorrow: An Interdisciplinary Study*. Charles Foster and Albert Valdman, eds. Pp. 35–56. Lanham, MD: University Press of America.

Snow, Loudell 1980 Ethnicity and Clinical Care: American Blacks. *Physician Assistant and Health Practitioner*, July: 50–54.

1993 *Walkin' Over Medicine*. Boulder, CO: Westview Press.

Sobo, Elisa Janine 1993 *One Blood: The Jamaican Body*. Albany: State University of New York Press.

Staiano, Kathryn Vance 1986 *Interpreting Signs of Illness: A Case Study in Medical Semiotics*. Hawthorne, NY: Aldine de Gruyter.

Starr, Paul 1982 *The Social Transformation of American Medicine*. New York: Basic Books.

Stepick, Alex 1984 The Roots of Haitian Migration. In *Haiti – Today and Tomorrow: An Interdisciplinary Study*. Charles Foster and Albert Valdman, eds. Pp. 337–50. Lanham, MD: University Press of America.

Stoll, David 1990 *Is Latin America Turning Protestant? The Politics of Evangelical Growth*. Berkeley: University of California Press.

Strauss, Anselm *et al.* 1985 *Social Organization of Medical Work*. Chicago: University of Chicago Press.

Street, John M. 1960 *Historical and Economic Geography of the Southwest Peninsula of Haiti*. Technical Report, Office of Naval Research, Contract 222 (11) NR388 067. Berkeley: Department of Geography, University of California-Berkeley.

Tambiah, Stanley 1985 *Culture, Thought, and Social Action: An Anthropological Perspective*. Cambridge, MA: Harvard University Press.

Taussig, Michael 1980 *The Devil and Commodity Fetishism in South America.* Chapel Hill: University of North Carolina Press.

1987 *Shamanism, Colonialism, and the Wild Man: A Study in Terror and Healing.* Chicago: University of Chicago Press.

1992 Reification and the Consciousness of the Patient. In *The Nervous System.* Pp. 83–109. New York: Routledge.

Taylor, Christopher C. 1992 *Milk, Honey, and Money: Changing Concepts in Rwandan Healing.* Washington, DC: Smithsonian Institution Press.

Thomas, Louis C. 1988 *Sections rurales ou section communale: subdivision géographique typiquement haïtienne.* Port-au-Prince: Imprimerie Henri Deschamps.

Thornton, John 1992 *Africa and Africans in the Making of the Atlantic World, 1400–1680.* Cambridge: Cambridge University Press.

Tomich, Dale W. 1990 *Slavery in the Circuit of Sugar: Martinique and the World Economy, 1830–1848.* Baltimore, MD: Johns Hopkins University Press.

Trouillot, Henock 1969 La Condition des travailleurs à Saint-Domingue. *Revue de la Société Haïtienne d'Histoire, de Géographie, et de Géologie* 34: 79–81.

Trouillot, Michel-Rolph 1986 *Les Racines historiques de l'état duvalierien.* Port-au-Prince: Editions Deschamps.

1990a *Haiti – State Against Nation: The Origins and Legacy of Duvalierism.* New York: Monthly Review Press.

1990b The Odd and the Ordinary: Haiti, the Caribbean and the World. *Cimarron* 2(3):3–12.

1992 The Caribbean Region: An Open Frontier in Anthropological Theory. *Annual Reviews of Anthropology* 21:19–42.

Unschuld, Paul 1985 *Medicine in China: A History of Ideas.* Berkeley: University of California Press.

van der Geest, Sjaak, and Susan Whyte 1988 *The Context of Medicines in Developing Countries: Studies in Pharmaceutical Anthropology.* Dordrecht, Holland: Kluwer Academic Publishers.

Vaughan, Megan 1991 *Curing Their Ills: Colonial Power and African Illness.* Stanford, CA: Stanford University Press.

Vernet, Pierre and Bryant Freeman 1988 *Diksyonè Otograf Kreyòl Ayisyen.* Port-au-Prince: Sant Lengwuistik Aplike, Inivèsite Leta Ayiti.

Vess, David M. 1975 *Medical Revolution in France, 1789–1796.* Gainesville: University of Florida Press.

Vilaire, Patrick, Michele Oriol, *et al.* 1981 *Images d'Espanola et de St. Domingue.* Port-au-Prince: Imprimerie Henri Deschamps.

Wagner, Roy 1980 *The Invention of Culture.* Chicago: University of Chicago Press.

Walsh, Julia A. and Kenneth S. Warren 1979 Selective Primary Health Care: An Interim Strategy for Disease Control in Developing Countries. *New England Journal of Medicine* 301(18): 967–74.

Warren, Kay B. 1978 *The Symbolism of Subordination: Indian Identity in a Guatemalan Town.* Austin: University of Texas Press.

Watanabe, John M. 1990 From Saints to Shibboleths: Image, Structure, and Identity in Maya Religious Syncretism. *American Ethnologist* 17(1):131–50.

Weatherly, Ulysses B. 1926 Haiti: An Experiment in Pragmatism. *American Journal of Sociology* 22(3):353–366.

Weidman, Hazel Hitson 1979 Falling-Out: A Diagnostic and Treatment Problem Viewed from a Transcultural Perspective. *Social Science and Medicine* 13B:95–112.

1982 Research Strategies, Structural Alterations, and Clinically Applied Anthropology. In *Clinically Applied Anthropology*. Noel J. Chrisman and Thomas W. Maretzki, eds. Pp. 201–41. Dordrecht, Holland: D. Reidel Publishing Co.

1983 Research, Service and Training Aspects of Clinical Anthropology: An Institutional Overview. In *Clinical Anthropology: A New Approach to American Health Problems?* Demitri B. Shimkin and Peggy Golde, eds. Pp. 119–53. New York: University Press of America.

Weidman, Hazel Hitson, et al. 1978 Miami Health Ecology Project Report. Departments of Psychiatry and Pediatrics, University of Miami School of Medicine. Unpublished manuscript.

Weniger, Bernard 1985 La Médecine populaire dans le plateau central d'Haïti. Ph.D. dissertation (thèse pour le Docteur de 3me Cycle), Université de Metz, France.

Weniger, B. et al. 1986 La Médecine populaire dans le plateau central d'Haïti. 1. Etude du système thérapeutique traditionnel dans un cadre socio-culturel rural. 2. Inventaire ethnopharmacologique. *Journal of Ethnopharmacology* 17:1–30.

West, Cornel 1993 The New Cultural Politics of Difference. In *Keeping Faith: Philosophy and Race in America*. Pp. 3–32. New York City: Routledge.

Whyte, Susan Reynolds and Sjaak Van der Geest 1988 Medicines in Context: An Introduction. In *The Context of Medicines in Developing Countries*. Sjaak van der Geest and Susan Reynolds Whyte, eds. Pp. 3–11. Dordrecht and Boston: Kluwer Academic Publishers.

Wiese, H. Jean C. 1971 The Interaction of Western and Indigenous Medicine in Haiti in Regard to Tuberculosis. Ph.D. dissertation, Anthropology Department, University of North Carolina, Chapel Hill.

1976 Maternal Nutrition and Traditional Food Behavior in Haiti. *Human Organization* 35(2):193–200.

Wilentz, Amy 1989 *The Rainy Season: Haiti Since Duvalier*. New York: Simon and Schuster (Touchstone).

Williams, Brackette F. 1991 *Stains on My Name, War in My Veins: Guyana and the Politics of Cultural Struggle*. Durham, NC: Duke University Press.

Williams, Eric 1944 *Capitalism and Slavery*. Chapel Hill: University of North Carolina Press.

1970 *From Columbus to Castro: The History of the Caribbean*. New York: Random House.

Willis, Paul 1977 *Learning to Labor: How Working Class Kids Get Working Class Jobs*. New York: Columbia University Press.

Wilson, Peter J. 1973 *Crab Antics: The Social Anthropology of English-Speaking Negro Societies of the Caribbean*. New Haven, CT: Yale University Press.

1974 *Oscar: An Inquiry in the Nature of Sanity*. New York: Random House.

Wilson, Samuel M. 1990 *Hispaniola: Caribbean Chiefdoms in the Age of Columbus*. Tuscaloosa: University of Alabama Press

Wimpffen, Francis Alexander Stanislaus, Baron de 1797 *A Voyage to Saint Domingo in the Years 1788, 1789, and 1790*. J. Wright, trans. London: T. Caddell Jr. and W. Davies.

Woodson, Drexel G. 1993 Which Beginning Should Be the Hindmost?: Surrealism in Appropriations of Facts about Haitian "Contact Culture." Bureau of Applied Research in Anthropology, University of Arizona. Unpublished manuscript.

World Health Organization (WHO) and United Nations International Children's Fund (UNICEF) 1978 International Conference on Primary Health Care. In *Health for All*, Series No. 1. Geneva, Switzerland: WHO.

Wright, Ann L. and Johnson, Thomas M. 1990 Critical Perspectives in Clinically Applied Medical Anthropology. *Social Science and Medicine* 30(9):945–1013.

Young, Allan 1976 Internalizing and Externalizing Medical Belief Systems: An Ethiopian Example. *Social Science and Medicine* 10:147–56.

    1980 The Discourse of Stress and the Reproduction of Conventional Knowledge. *Social Science and Medicine* 14B:133–46.

    1981 When Rational Men Fall Sick: An Inquiry into Some Assumptions Made by Medical Anthropologists. *Culture, Medicine, and Psychiatry* 5:317–55.

Young, J.C. 1981 *Medical Choice in a Mexican Village*. New Brunswick, NJ: Rutgers University Press.

Zimmerman, Francis 1978 From Classic Texts to Learned Practice: Methodological Remarks on the Study of Indian Medicine. *Social Science and Medicine* 12:97–103.

Zola, Irving 1978 Medicine as an Institution of Social Control. In *The Cultural Crisis of Modern Medicine*. John Ehrenreich, ed. Pp. 80–100. New York: Monthly Review Press.

Index